The Iambics of Newfoundland

ALSO BY ROBERT FINCH

Death of a Hornet and Other Cape Cod Essays

Common Ground: A Naturalist's Cape Cod

The Primal Place

Outlands: Journeys to the Outer Edges of Cape Cod

Special Places on Cape Cod and the Islands

The Norton Book of Nature Writing (co-editor with John Elder)

The Cape Itself (with photographs by Ralph MacKenzie)

A Place Apart: A Cape Cod Reader (editor)

The Smithsonian Guide to Natural America: Southern New England

The Iambics of
NEWFOUNDLAND

NOTES FROM AN UNKNOWN SHORE

Robert Finch

COUNTERPOINT

A Member of the Perseus Books Group

New York

Books published by Counterpoint books are available at special discounts for bulk purchases in the United States by corporations, institutions, and other organizations. For more information, please contact the Special Markets Department at the Perseus Books Group, 2300 Chestnut St., Philadelphia, PA 19103, or e-mail special.markets@perseusbooks.com.

Designed by Brent Wilcox

Set in 11 point Janson Text

A CIP catalog record for this book is available from the Library of Congress.

ISBN-13: 978-1-58243-154-3

ISBN-10: 1-58243-154-X

10 9 8 7 6 5 4 3 2 1

For Penny, who opened the door

CONTENTS

PREFACE

Most of the material in this book is based on my travels and sojourns in Newfoundland during the years 1987–1996. Since that time, of course, many changes have occurred in the people, places, and situations I describe herein (not the least of which is the change in the official name of the province from "Newfoundland" to "Newfoundland and Labrador"). Rather than trying to update these accounts, however, I have chosen to let them stand as they were then, for whatever value they may possess as reports written during a period of great transition in that province.

The other thing that needs to be said is that this is intended to be a book of impressions and observations by an outsider, rather than an attempt to create a definitive account or analysis of a very complex place. It is therefore no doubt subject to all the limitations, inaccuracies, misinterpretations, and distortions of such an approach. Nevertheless, as the writer John Daniel observed, the value of the outsider, or stranger, however limited or unreliable his account might be, is that "he might tell a story, a story no one in the family or local community is capable of telling, and children might hear that story and imagine their lives in a new way."

Early Visits:
St. John's and the
Avalon Peninsula

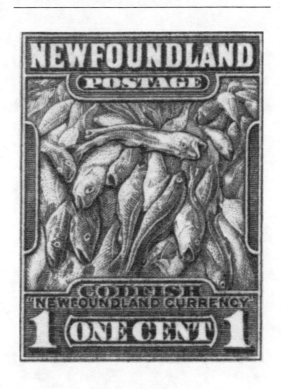

The Iambics of Newfoundland

I picked him up on the Trans-Canada Highway just outside Whitbourne Junction. He was standing in the middle of nowhere, his thumb out, a big, strapping Newfoundlander in his late thirties who talked nonstop to me for the five miles or so I could give him a ride before turning off to Cape St. Mary's. His name was George. He belonged to Lumsden, on Deadman's Bay, where he lived with his mother. He kept talking about how Newfoundland was a very enjoyable place, not like any other place in the world, "if you can get the iambics of it." He knew that was the wrong word but he kept laughing at himself, repeating and emphasizing the word, as if to turn it into the right one: "You got to get the *iambics* of the place."

He seemed to have made a career out of hitchhiking, usually down to the States. He told me how he'd been stopped by police out in Omaha, how they'd asked him who he was, and when he said he was a Canadian they said well you know you're not allowed to hitchhike on the interstates and he said well, sar, you see, I seem to be doing it. Well, they said, you have to wait here while we call your mother, so they called his mother, who must be in her seventies, and she said well now what would you be wanting me for and they said well your son George is here and she said well now you tell him to come home, so he started hitchhiking home and he was about to go through a tunnel at Detroit on his way into Canada when he saw this police flasher and thought he better stop or else they might machine-gun him down, didn't know whether they'd do that there, and they had to assure him that they probably wouldn't and asked him for his identification and so he

3

showed it to them and they said now you wouldn't be that fellow from Newfoundland that the FBI told us about in Omaha was heading this way back to Canada and he said well, sar, you see that's what I's trying to do. Well they said your mother's waiting for you so you best go on.

He's been through it all, he said, all over the continent, but there's no other place like Newfoundland, if you can get the iambics of it.

St. John's I: Time Warp

The first time I saw St. John's, the capital and major city of Newfoundland, I felt as if I had fallen into a time warp, a wormhole into my own past. Though it was 1987, there were things I had not seen since my childhood in northern New Jersey in the 1950s. The gas station signs still advertised "ESSO," not "EXXON" products. Gasoline itself, because it is sold in liters here, not gallons, was priced at a nostalgic fifty cents. A local downtown Woolworth's still had a functioning lunch counter, and washed-out color photographs in the windows offered midday specials for a dollar twenty-five. Most of the traffic lights were still mounted on wooden telephone poles, and, most startling of all, drivers actually stopped for pedestrians, even between corners.

Some signs bespoke an older, more genteel era. One, posted at several curbsides, offered the following instructions for pedestrians:

> HOW TO CROSS THE STREET:
> -LIFT ARM
> -PUT ONE FOOT DOWN ON STREET AND WAIT
>   FOR DRIVER TO STOP
> -CROSS STREET
> -THANK DRIVER

Other signs suggested I was in a place I had never experienced. The window of a butcher shop, for instance, at the corner of Pilot Hill and Duckworth Streets, sported handwritten placards taped to the inside of the glass:

LAWLOR's MEATS LTD.

"0" LOOK "0"

YOUNG SEAL CARCAS

3 LB PIECES (APPROX.)

49C LB.

SALT JOWL

SALT HOCKS

SALT PORK

SALT TONGUES

SPECIAL: PICKLED SALMON PICKLED CHAR

I went inside the shop, its wooden floor covered with sawdust. The butcher, a squat, balding man with a mustache, quite friendly, told me how to cook seal flipper. You parboil it first, he said, being sure first to remove all traces of fat, which imparts the undesirable fishy flavor, then lard it and roast it for about an hour, making gravy out of the drippings.

St. John's is one of Newfoundland's oldest settlements and has frequently touted itself as "The Oldest City in North America"—a claim that other cities with saintly monikers, such as St. Augustine and Santa Fe, might dispute. Nonetheless, it owes its early existence and subsequent political and commercial prominence to its harbor, created out of one of the world's remarkable coastal configurations. The entrance to the harbor, called the Narrows, is a channel only one-sixth of a mile wide and flanked by steep, rocky cliffs several hundred feet high. When I first saw it, this configuration lent an air of mystery to the harbor, not just because of its dramatic character, but because one could not see the approach of a ship or fishing boat, and so the sudden appearance of vessels coming into the harbor seemed somewhat magical.

The Narrows opens into a protected, deepwater anchorage, shaped like an upside-down foot and nearly two miles long, that was once the home of Newfoundland's great fishing and sealing fleets. In the late seventeenth century, when St. John's was no more than a small cluster of primitive buildings, Portuguese fishing vessels put in here for refuge, repair, and resupply, as they had been doing for at least a hundred years before. The arrival of the Portuguese cod-fishing fleet, known as the Great White Fleet for the color of its hulls, was a St. John's event and celebration in this town for centuries. During its heyday as a seaport in the nineteenth and early twentieth centuries, dozens of the great "wooden wall" sealing ships set sail for the Labrador Front each spring as soon as the ice went out, and each fall hundreds of schooners arrived in St. John's with their summer's harvest of salt cod.

In terms of marine commerce, St. John's Harbour was now only a shadow of its former glory. The large sealers vanished in the 1930s, and most of the fishing fleet, including the famed Portuguese White Fleet, followed in the 1950s with the decline of the Labrador fishery. In the 1960s Canada prohibited foreign fleets from fishing in its waters, so that few international fishing vessels stopped in anymore. Spanish ships, banned from Canadian harbors for infringement of fishing regulations, now anchored at the French port of St. Pierre off Newfoundland's south coast. Only a few local fishing draggers still tied up along the waterfront.

And yet St. John's remained a fairly busy commercial port that I found could easily occupy a pedestrian's interest for several hours. One of the more quietly exciting sights of the harbor was to watch a huge six- or seven-hundred-foot container ship nonchalantly and smoothly dock at one of the piers without the help of tugs. In no other port in North America did the work of a large harbor seem more visible and accessible to the city's population and its visitors.

Although foreign fishing vessels rarely put in anymore, the harbor still boasted a remarkably international flavor. The wharves along Harbour Drive were regularly occupied by large container and tanker ships from Korea, Panama, Holland, Halifax, Norway, Japan, and—somewhat startling—the Soviet Union. During the latter half of the twentieth century, St. John's was one of the few ports in North America open to Soviet ships. After Confederation with Canada in 1949, the federal government imposed restrictions on the movement of Soviet crews, but I occasionally beheld the sight—surprising and vestigially disturbing to one who, as a boy, had read J. Edgar Hoover's *Masters of Deceit*, and whose American eyes still viewed the world through Cold War glasses—of Russian sailors walking nonchalantly along the streets of a North American city. While the Soviet ships were in port, however, the crews seemed to spend most of their time gathered on deck at the top of their gangplanks, wearing sad, impassive expressions. The main waterfront is about a mile long, and it is another mile or so out to the harbor entrance at the Narrows.

The old city rises from the north side of the harbor for about a third of a mile up the side of a steep hill. The main streets—Harbour Drive, Water Street, Duckworth, Gower, Bond, and Military—are roughly parallel to the harbor, intersected and spliced with a bewildering maze of short streets, lanes, and alleys. Many of the short cross streets of St. John's are so steep that the sidewalks have steps, and even handrails. Cars park perpendicularly along these steep streets and look as if they should throw out sheet anchors to landward, especially during the icy winters. Car passengers on the uphill side struggle mightily to open their car doors, while drivers on the downhill side hang desperately onto theirs to keep from falling out onto the street.

In addition to the streets parallel to the harbor and the short, steep ones connecting them, there are a number of diagonal routes—such as McBride's Hill, Feaver's Lane, and Masonic Terrace. These are among the oldest thoroughfares in the city, some of them going back to the seventeenth century and thought originally to have been footpaths or handbarrow lanes. After the Great Fire of 1892 (the third and most disastrous in St. John's history), many of the present wooden houses were rebuilt right up to the edge of these diagonal lanes, creating parallelogrammatic and trapezoidal structures that are among the most charming in the city. There are also a number of pedestrian alleys running north and south that allow one access from one street level to another. Most of these alleys were built after the Great Fire of the 1892, following which a law was passed mandating firebreaks between blocks of buildings at certain intervals throughout the downtown area. The buildings flanking these breaks have some of the few stone and brick walls in a downtown that was, and still is, largely wooden.

The commercial heart of the old city centers along Duckworth and Water Streets. Water Street had been the home of most of the major fish merchant houses—Bowring Bros., Job Bros., Harvey & Co., Baine, Johnston & Co., etc.—whose iron grip on the fishing and sealing industry in Newfoundland remained unchallenged until well into the twentieth century.

By 1987 these old merchant firms were long gone, and two recently built malls had removed most of the commercial trade from downtown. Yet there were still a number of old local businesses and small, quirky shops along Duckworth and Water Streets. These included at least two tattoo parlors (not trendy contemporary "body art shops," but old, run-down front rooms along the west end waterfront, established to serve the seaman clientele); Dicks, a stationery store that had plied its business on Water Street for over two hundred years; and NONIA, the Newfoundland Outport Nursing and Industrial Association, which was established in 1924 to teach and train outport women in crafts such as knitting sweaters and hooking rugs, and whose products were still made by local women. Other distinctive St. John's enterprises included the Mighty Whites Laundromat; the Modern Shoe Hospital (as opposed, perhaps, to cobblers who used leeches?); ABC Sales, selling used stoves, meat slicers, and camping equipment; Family Barber Shop ("Cutting Family Hair Since 1968"); Fred's for the Record, doing brisk sales in Irish and Newfoundland folk music; O'Brien's, a third-generation business that was Newfoundland's main supplier of button accordions; and Wilansky's & Sons Ltd., an old-fashioned men's clothing store on the north side of Water Street that represented the last commercial remnant of St. John's small but once-vibrant Jewish business community. The mannequins in Wilansky's large plate-glass windows were screened from the sun by sheets of orange cellophane, a measure that gave the clothed figures a sepia or underwater quality, as if they were already fading from view.

There were also at least a half dozen diminutive, idiosyncratic taxi stands scattered around the downtown. These consisted of tiny lots, with room for only one or two vehicles, and even smaller "offices," which were wooden sheds surmounted with ancient signs—"Avalon," "O.K.," "Capitol," "King's Bridge," "ABC"—twisted and cracked like old whale baleen, some of them larger than the structures they were mounted on.

And then, of course, there was Ziggy Peelgood's, St. John's signature mobile fast-food outlet. Ziggy Peelgood's consisted of a single truck that plied its wares at various locations downtown: "Ziggy Peelgood's—They Make You Feel Good," purveyor of French fries only, with a soft drink and your choice of ketchup, vinegar, and gravy. The truck also bore the sign "Ziggy Peelgood's, of St. John's and Quito," a perplexing and seemingly whimsical boast until, upon inquiry, I learned that Ziggy's owner, John Hrabowsky, had in recent years sought to escape Newfoundland winters in warmer climes, but his irrepressible spirit of entrepreneurialism had prompted him to set up a franchise in Ecuador's capital once he got there.

The strangest of all downtown enterprises was a small storefront on Water Street surmounted with a cracked blue sign, edged in flaking gold gilt against a red background, that said, simply, "Bartlett's." The store was inhabited by a solitary figure, a Bartleby-like character, a man of indeterminate late-middle or early-old age, thin, with a sharp nose and an angular figure, sparse combed-back hair, wearing a shiny black suit, a white shirt, and a thin early-1960s-era black tie. I was told that he rode his bike in every day from The Goulds, a town about fifteen miles south of the city. His name was apparently not Bartlett, but no one seemed to know what it was. One local writer had dubbed him "The Hunger Artist." He spent most of the day standing on the street in the open dark-red doorway, flanked by plateglass windows that displayed the store's "wares." These were an unrelated and minimalist assemblage of items that, as far as I could see, consisted entirely of a single wooden chair, a secondhand bicycle, a box of pencils, and a hotdog machine. I never saw anyone go into the shop, nor ever met anyone who had. Yet every day, without fail, the dedicated proprietor arrived to open up his store and wait for no one, as if he and it were an example of mercantile performance art.

"The Hunger Artist" was one of several other street characters who called up counterparts from my urban childhood. These individuals— "not homeless, just eccentric" as one local resident put it—included a couple of old fishermen who played their button accordions, made chin music, and danced for change in front of Woolworth's, and a woman known as "the crazy lady" of St. John's. She was a gaunt-faced woman with long, straight, graying dark hair and a long, green skirt, who went about the streets urging people to Jesus and whose hallmark was a long cigarette holder she carried in her left hand. One summer, a friend told me, during a funeral for a local musician in the Anglican church, this woman marched straight up the aisle through hundreds of mourners to the coffin, plucked one long-stemmed rose from the dozens covering the sarcophagus, and marched back up the aisle, rose held high, chanting "On to Heaven! On to Heaven!" as she disappeared out the door of the church.

Though the population of the St. John's metropolitan area was then about 150,000, the central core was still dominated by residential neighborhoods whose streets were lined with the city's characteristic and quirky wooden row houses. These structures are St. John's' counterpart to Manhattan's brownstones, San Francisco's Victorian residences, and London's brick townhouses. Two and, more commonly, three stories in height, they are typically one room wide and two rooms deep, with flat, short-pitched, or French mansard roofs, frequently adorned with bay windows and doghouse dormers with round, tarred roofs. All of the row houses, with their simple windows and doorways, which gave directly onto the street, provided wonderful frames for people standing, leaning, or sitting in them, an occupation very commonly engaged in, especially in summer, that helped to give the city an Old World feel. This sense was reinforced by the general lack of screens on either doors or windows. Mosquitoes were scarce in the city and flies were discouraged by the simple, but remarkably effective, device of hanging a blown-up brown paper bag in the doorway, which supposedly looked like a predatory wasp's nest to incoming flies.

Many of the doorways, windows, and trim were ornately decorated, but the real charm of these buildings lay in the bold and original—some would say outré—use of color. The trim and sheathing on these buildings were painted (traditionally with Matchless Paints, a locally manufactured St. John's brand) in seemingly endless and arbitrary combinations of bright primary and pastel hues. Nevertheless, there was an odd, overall consistency to the effect, creating a set of brilliant variations on a repeated architectural pattern. Edward Hopper, I thought, would have loved this town.

There were little neighborhood stores on nearly every street, too, often two or three to a block—groceries, butcher shops, drugstores, tobacconists, variety stores and novelty shops, locksmiths, tailors, medical suppliers, office supply shops, kitchen supply shops, etc.—all small, specialized, proprietor-owned businesses (often with the owner's family living above the store) that recalled the makeup of the neighborhoods I had known forty years before.

Many of the smaller neighborhood stores were simply the front rooms of people's houses and were marked by nothing more than an ancient Coke or Nehi thermometer nailed beside the door. Some were not even advertised that much. One day, staying at a friend's house on Patrick Street, I went looking for a fuse for a boat electrical system. After I struck out at two of the larger hardware outlets on Water Street, one of the store clerks suggested I might find what I was looking for at "Newfoundland Electronics," which he said was located at 150 Patrick Street, just around the corner from where I was staying. I walked up the steep street and eventually came to 150A and 150B, a duplex that showed no sign of being anything but a residence. Thinking I must have gotten the wrong address, I was about to head back, but glancing down the narrow driveway, I noticed a small shed in back that was, in fact, labeled "Newfoundland Electronics, Limited." It was, as it turned out, very limited. Inside were two men who barely fit among an eclectic collection of electronic fixtures. They seemed to be very busy with very little, but sure enough, they had my fuse. The oddest thing was that my friend, an artist whose pieces involved the use of various electrical elements, had lived only a few houses up the street for twenty years, yet he had no idea that such a shop existed.

Unquestionably, the most unusual and idiosyncratic of St. John's neighborhoods was the Battery, which begins at the east end of downtown and runs along the waterfront toward the Narrows. Here the hill on which the city was built becomes steeper and rockier. The houses comprised a remarkable collection of miniature, motley, and seemingly anachronistic structures, connected by narrow, zigzagging lanes only one car wide, with several fishing stages and boats below them. They seemed to cling, limpet-like, to the nearly vertical rock walls, and some of them were actually semitroglodytic—using the exposed face of the cliff as their back walls. The Battery looked like what it originally was: a jury-rigged fishing village plastered against the flank of Signal Hill, just a few minutes' walk from the metropolitan, commercial, and political center of the province.

At the point where the downtown ends and the Battery begins I came upon one of St. John's more puzzling sights, and a telling example of how things in Newfoundland are frequently not what they seem. About 150 feet offshore, a mysterious, circular slick known as The Bubble welled up from beneath the surface of the harbor. The Bubble attracted a perpetual flock of white gulls that wheeled, hovered, swung down, and plucked at the water. It also attracted a number of tourists, who snapped photos of this intriguing natural phenomenon and graceful avian ballet. Only later did I learn that what they were really taking pictures of was raw sewage disgorging into the harbor through an underground pipe.

Of course, even when I first saw St. John's, the time-warp illusion was imperfect and its unique character was beginning to yield to modern elements. Video and computer stores had already appeared among the more traditional downtown businesses, though these still had the look of mom-and-pop operations. The city had already lost some of its appearance as an old working seaport. Like most East Coast cities, though somewhat later than most, St. John's went through a fever of "urban renewal" in the early 1980s. Many of the old waterfront premises had been torn down, and in their place, massive, characterless piles of banks, office buildings, and chain hotels had been erected, blocking or obstructing the harbor view that many of the residents had enjoyed for decades. (On my first visit I remember sitting in one of those old houses, looking out at one of these abstract monoliths of brick and concrete, and experiencing for the first time the anarchist's attraction to dynamite.) Public outcry, however, seemed to have stopped further monstrosities from proliferating in the past several years, though there were still no stringent design codes or historic structure regulations to preclude other new and equally ill-conceived plans for "modernization." Like Savannah, Boston, and other older seaports in the States, it seemed as if a few irrevocable blots had first to materialize in the St. John's landscape before its citizens could envision what they had to lose.

Despite these architectural and commercial inroads on its traditional character, despite its decline as a fishing harbor, and even more than the many surviving visible signs of its past, what most seemed to place St. John's in a different age for me was its charming lack of self-awareness.

This manifested itself in the way its residents spoke of their city, an attitude that seemed to say they regarded it as nothing more than what it was: a working seaport where cargo ships and trawlers still anchored; a skyline still dominated by church spires and domes; a downtown retail area that seemed, for the most part, merely a larger collection of the mom-and-pop stores found on nearly every corner; and a collage of residential neighborhoods lined with two- and three-story wood-frame row houses that marched in serrated ranks up the steep streets in a jumble of primary and pastel colors.

Moreover, I was struck by the extensive knowledge of its historical past that most St. Johnsmen seemed to possess. Perhaps this was because its past was, after all, not all that distant. St. John's rise to undisputed prominence as the urban and political center of Newfoundland did not occur until the first third of the nineteenth century, over two hundred years after the first English "planters" arrived. And because urban renewal came much later to St. John's than to most North American coastal cities, there were a number of individuals still in their fifties and sixties who had memories of the old densely built neighborhoods (called *cribbies*); of street trolleys and the cobbles that lay beneath the pavement on Water and Duckworth Streets; of the last of the old sealing vessels, Labrador schooners, and rusted hulls of the Portuguese White Fleet docked in the harbor.

And before any living memory, in stories told in pubs and in old houses, I sensed a strong, almost mythic, memory of the city's more distant and more earnest past: of the Irish Catholics who immigrated from Waterford in the late eighteenth and early nineteenth century and were persecuted as severely here as anywhere; of St. John's reputation as a "drinking town," where, less than a century ago, children of ten or twelve years who worked on the wharves were paid in "lots" of rum by the merchants, so that scores of young boys staggered home drunk from twelve-hour workdays; of the sight, straight out of Greek tragedy, on that April day in 1914 of the frozen carcasses of seventy-eight sealers who perished on the Labrador Front and were stacked like so much cordwood, along with the seal pelts being unloaded onto the harbor piers from the star-crossed wooden-wall *Newfoundland*, while Captain Abram Kean, the man responsible for the disaster, not only escaped punishment, but went on to achieve self-proclaimed glory as "the only million-seal captain in Newfoundland history."

All of its history, flamboyant and sad, violent and cosmopolitan, idiosyncratically independent and fawningly currying of commerce's favor, seemed to live more vividly and presently in the minds of St. John's inhabitants than in those of most cities I knew. It was as if the persistence of its wayward, zigzagging streets and narrow public alleys were daily, visible reminders of its origins, when the city was just another outport, a cluster of rude houses and wharves connected by footpaths, sheep tracks, and handbarrow lanes.

One summer evening, perhaps under the influence of these spoken memories and tales, I had my own encounter with what seemed to be an apparition from the city's distant past. As I was walking back from the Battery, there appeared, coming toward me along Harbour Drive, a sight that might have been seen a century ago: a small, towheaded boy of eight or nine, wearing a plaid flannel shirt and worsted trousers and leading a large broken-down Clydesdale by a short length of ship's hawser. The horse, I suspected, was the same one I had seen a couple of hours earlier in the traces of St. John's only licensed horse-and-carriage ride, but I felt no need to inquire of the boy, and he passed me silently with a small smile, thus preserving the illusion of a moment out of time.

Even then, I think I realized that St. John's would and must eventually come to think of itself as a tourist destination or else risk becoming nothing but a hollow urban shell or a depressing chaos of unplanned, large-scale development. Still, at the time, it seemed to me a city in which no *concept* of itself had yet taken hold, so that, for a while, at least, it retained its authentic, unselfconscious character, rooted in a past that spoke of earnest, ongoing history, rather than in a future still unenvisioned and uncontemplated.

Cape Spear

A few miles south and east of the capital city of St. John's lies Cape Spear, a singularly dramatic, treeless, windswept, fogbound headland that juts out into the North Atlantic. It is identified in nearly every tourist brochure and guidebook as "the easternmost point in North America"—one of those abstract, seemingly arbitrary, geographic superlatives that allow one at once to remember a place and to dismiss it without understanding anything of its true distinction.

More meaningfully, from a historical point of view, Cape Spear was the first landfall made by ships coming west from Europe on the Great Circle Route. Thus Cape Spear Light—a curious, white, octagonal, squat, anemone-shaped structure perched on the headland's crest above the pounding Atlantic—has always been of extreme importance to coastal navigation (though its function has now been replaced by an automated light a short distance from the original structure).

Only a twenty-minute drive from downtown St. John's, Cape Spear nevertheless has a climate and a weather all of its own. My friend Penny, a physiology professor at Memorial University, told me that on July 24, 1983, the day the Cape was designated a national park, the temperature in the city was a humid, sunny 80 degrees Fahrenheit. The dedication was quite a special event, as Charles and Diana, the recently married Prince and Princess of Wales, were on hand for the ceremonies. A caravan of buses had been organized to take the local citizenry out from the city for the festivities. Private cars were prohibited in order to prevent traffic tangles on the newly paved two-lane road. Thousands of people from all over the island boarded the buses in tank tops, shorts, sunglasses, and sunblock, expecting a day of sunbathing and picnicking, with perhaps a cooling breeze off the ocean.

When they arrived they found temperatures in the forties, a thick fog swathing the barren, rocky headland, and a raw, bone-chilling wind sweeping in from the southeast off the cold North Atlantic waters. They were there for six hours, with no way back to St. John's except by walking. According to Penny, "People literally huddled together for warmth, like sowbugs under a damp rock. One older woman fell on one of the slippery rocks and cut her leg; she spent the afternoon inside an ambulance, protected from the wind, which she said was well worth the injury."

One Sunday in July a few years later, I made my first trip to Cape Spear with Penny, her young daughter Nell, her colleague Dr. Ken Roberts, and Marlene Creates, a local artist. We took along a picnic basket and kites for flying. Penny was astounded to find several dozen cars in the parking lot. She had last been here fifteen years before, when it had taken an hour's drive along a bumpy, rutted dirt track. She remembered it as basically a place you could come to be alone. Now there was a paved parking lot down below the lighthouse, restroom facilities, graveled walks with railings up to the lighthouse, a small visitors' center with exhibits, and the restored lighthouse itself. "They've ruined it," she said.

It was an unusually clear, sunny day, with a south-southeast wind of twenty-five to thirty knots. I spoke with a young ranger, a St. John's boy going to law school in Halifax who had worked here for the last four summers. He told me that this was a "moderate" day for attendance, and that there were only ten to twelve days a summer out here that were as clear as today. Cape Spear is reputedly one of the best places in North America from which to view icebergs and migrating whales, particularly in late spring, though neither were visible today. Only a few days ago, however, he had seen ten to twelve humpbacks and a few minkes just off the point. He knew of no clear origin for the Cape's name, though he thought it might be because it jutted out to sea like a spearhead.

Though a slight haze partly veiled the distant headlands to the north, we had a panoramic view of St. John's Bay—from Blackhead to the

Narrows and the worn, cannon-capped cliffs of Signal Hill. Beyond them we could make out the sheer drop of the cliffs at Logy Bay, exactly paralleled and slightly doubled by that of Red Head a few miles further on, so that through the haze one seemed to see a repeated image of the same cliffs over and over into the receding distance.

The ranger said that Cape Spear acts as a kind of fog block for the city, catching the cold, vapor-laden ocean air on its sun-warmed rocky ledges, then tossing it, like a gossamer scarf, into and around the bay and out to sea again. Little of the Cape Spear fog threads the needle of the Narrows into the harbor itself, thus accounting for the frequent disparity in weather between the two places. For St. John's to get heavy fog, he said, the wind must come in from the sea some twenty miles to the south and up through a series of inland valleys, which dry out much of the vapor.

It was a place where one could stand and see how encapsulated and contained civilization and its works remain on this island. Though suburbs had gradually spread out over the hills and plains north and west of St. John's in recent years, the city itself was virtually invisible from Cape Spear, only a few miles to the south. Its expansive harbor was cloaked by its flanking headlands like a giant version of the hidden, keyhole harbors of the outports of Newfoundland's South-West Coast.

Despite the "improvements" that Penny resented, there was still an informality and an invitation to self-discovery about the place that was refreshing. The only official sign I saw was a simple one at the point designating it "the Easternmost Point," etc., which had replaced a hand-lettered sign that Penny had seen here fifteen years before that had the distance to Ireland in miles painted on it. There were informal trails and walks over the ledges and hills, with no signs or fences along the sheer drops on the south side. More effective and eloquent than railings or signs, however, were a series of slatted red boxes placed at intervals along these steep rock cliffs, each containing a round life preserver and a long coil of rope.

In fact, there was very little official direction or prohibition at all. At one point Ken Roberts collected a bouquet of wildflowers from the abundant blossoms that seem to bestrew all Newfoundland grasslands this time of year—irises, tiny exquisite blue-eyed grass, buttercups, harebells, red sorrel, etc. He found fifteen species in all. And then, at the lighthouse door, Ken guiltily asked a young woman ranger if what he had done was illegal. "Oh no," she said, with a surprised tone as if she could not possibly imagine why such a thing as gathering flowers would ever be prohibited in Newfoundland (though, in fact, picking flowers in a national park *is* illegal.)

There were no official guided tours offered either, partly because of the perennial budget crunch at Parks Canada, but also because, in contrast to the U.S. passion for "official interpretation," Canadians seem to have a proclivity to allow and encourage people to discover and interpret places on their own. As we approached the lighthouse keeper's house, we were told to "go in, look around, enjoy yourselves, and if you have any questions, ask us when you come out."

The building itself was simply but tastefully appointed with period furniture, tools, and supplies, including an elegant four-poster double bed (or more accurately, a one-and-a-half bed) in the ground floor bedroom, goose-wing dusters in the kitchen (I had visions of wingless geese running about the dooryard), and a room full of flags for displaying weather conditions. Upstairs there was a storeroom full of wooden casks marked for sperm oil, molasses, and olive oil; cases of glass lamp chimneys; a workroom; and a very Spartan bedroom with a single, short bed on a rope mattress.

Once again, I became aware of something that I have experienced at other historical sites and museums: The sense of the past lives lived here was more vivid and present *because* of the lack of labels, signs, and official tours. The purposes of the various artifacts were more clearly and effectively conveyed for our having to read them through the wordless exhibits themselves.

According to the ranger, the story of the lighthouse was this: Early in the nineteenth century, a member of the Cantwell family of St. John's was instrumental in rescuing a Dutch prince from a vessel in trouble near the harbor entrance. Said prince later interceded and secured for this Cantwell and his descendants perpetual custodianship of the light, at the then princely salary of one hundred pounds per annum (roughly equivalent to forty to fifty thousand dollars today) from the Crown. Since then, seven generations of Cantwells had been the lighthouse's keepers, though they now commuted from St. John's to maintain the light, or rather its automated replacement.

The five of us had lunch in the lee of the small new working lighthouse near the edge of the bluffs. The wind, coaxing us always to look north, blew out over the dark-blue white-capped ocean surface several hundred feet below, its textures and details tightened, the motions of its swells slowed to crawls by distance. After we ate, Penny, Nell, and I sent up several kites, which needed no help from us but did somersaults and other acrobatics on their own, swirled up and away and back toward us by the circular currents sweeping over the building.

At one point, as I sat against the lighthouse wall trying to jot down some notes, a maverick gust snatched the piece of paper from my hands and hurled it toward the cliff. I gave it up immediately as a bit of biodegradable litter, but then, caught in a combination of updraft and back eddies created by the structure, it sailed in an arc back toward me, passing within a couple of feet. It raced around again, out over the cliff and back, like some crazy party balloon, in a ring some fifteen feet in diameter, skidding by me three or four times. I reached out for it as it came by each time and was finally able to bring it to ground. I crumpled it and stuffed it under my jacket beside me, but several minutes later, as if with mischief aforethought, another gust popped it out, and this time, its buoyancy reduced, it dropped out of sight over the cliff.

I got up and walked a few hundred feet north of the lighthouse and partway down a slope where there were several old World War II gun emplacements with thirty-foot-long beige-painted cannons ensconced below overhanging ledges—a gift from the United States to Canada at the start of the war through the lend-lease program. These guns had originally been installed in 1896 at Fort Mott, New Jersey, on the Delaware River, to guard the approach to Philadelphia during the Spanish-American War. None was ever fired in either place.

I walked through the circular concrete bunkers and the corrugated steel barracks. The hollow echoing of my footsteps in these deserted garrisons called up the vanished presence of young U.S. soldiers stationed here from 1941 to 1945. The wet floors and dripping walls confirmed an impression of their stay as cold, clammy, foggy, lonely, and miserable.

I met the young ranger again coming off his lunch break and heading down toward the point. The park staff of four or five spent most of their time stationed at various key points—the parking lot, visitors' center, lighthouse, and the point—to provide information and supervision. The last location was always manned because of the danger to visitors on the lower levels. Though the surf that Sunday looked fairly modest, despite the strong offshore winds, I could see that the lower cliff faces were scoured free of any vegetation for twenty to twenty-five feet above the water line. The ranger said that an occasional "rogue wave"—a giant, unpredictable wave several times the height of those immediately preceding it—would suddenly appear from nowhere and "clear the decks" on the lower grassy slopes fifty to sixty feet above the sea.

"We lose one every three or four years," he said, as he left me to resume his monitoring at the point. "We're about due."

Cape St. Mary's

At 6:30 A.M. Penny and I started out by car from St. John's toward Cape St. Mary's, home of the largest gannet colony in Newfoundland and the southernmost gannet breeding colony in the world. The day began in darkness and continued in rain, not a promising start. We swung off the Trans-Canada Highway (TCH) on Route 100 just past the Whitbourne turnoff and continued down the long, empty stretch of highway to Freshwater.

In Placentia we stopped for breakfast at Harold's Hotel, a place that looked as if it had remained stuck in the 1950s. At the counter was a sports trophy naming Harold "Freshman of the Year 1973–74," and also a lightbox projecting a color photo of the town, which we turned on to get the attention of someone in the kitchen. A jukebox in the dining room had the usual mixture of current hits and old country-and-western standards.

After breakfast we began the long and spectacular drive down the coast road from Placentia to St. Bride's, a distance of some forty-six kilometers, through a series of steep picturesque stream valleys, or *barachois* (pronounced, and sometimes spelled, *barasways*), all ending in impounded coves. There were small villages or sometimes only a single house at each of these stream outlets. Penny and I had gone to high school together in West Virginia, and we remarked how much these villages resembled a seacoast version of the hollows and mountain towns of Appalachia.

Most of the houses were one-story contemporary ranches painted in the usual Newfoundland fashion with two or three tones of bright boat paint, primary and secondary colors, often in distinct bands around the house. Penny explained to me the mortgage approval system in Newfoundland, which accounts for so much of the homogeneity of contemporary outport architecture. The Canadian Mortgage and Housing Corporation (a Crown corporation) must approve each house plan before the lender banks give a mortgage. They provide a limited range of approved house plans—fifty or so—or you can submit your own. But since the CMHC plans are free, buddy says, Why should I pay to get my own? Most of these government-provided plans are ranch-style houses from the 1950s, a happenstance that has, over the past several decades, transformed the traditional architecture of most Newfoundland outports into early versions of Levittown as painted by Mondrian.

At St. Bride's, the last town before the turnoff to Cape St. Mary's, the preferred color combination for houses seemed to be brilliant orange and green. Several young people stood by the roadside or next to barns on this Sunday morning with nowhere to go, nothing to do. There was an undistinguished motel in the town called the Bird Motel, but no sign or other indication of where the bird sanctuary itself was. Like so much of Newfoundland, including Saint John's, it seemed to be a place where one must already know where it is in order to find it. Americans do not function well without signs. In fact, on some level we do not believe we are actually in a place—a city, a store, a national park—unless there is a sign to tell us so.

The road out of St. Bride's, shown on the official Provincial Highway Map as "scheduled to be paved" two years ago, soon turned to gravel. The landscape became flat, treeless, boulderless, and grassy. We saw no cars, but at one point a huge toy stuffed bear was propped up against the road, as though hitchhiking. Since leaving Placentia, we had passed only a dozen cars and no hitchhikers (this being a risky activity in most of Newfoundland, where, except for the TCH, traffic is usually so sparse that one risks being stranded out in the middle of nowhere for an indeterminate period).

After three or four kilometers we spotted a single small white sign with "Bird Sanctuary" printed on one side only. From the turnoff it was some twelve kilometers to the lighthouse at the Cape along a potholed one-lane dirt road. Paralleling the road was a single power line, fences, a few cows, and dozens of sheep. Instead of being set in drilled holes, the telephone poles were set in wooden cages full of stones, exactly the same structures used in the underpinnings of wharves to keep winter ice from lifting them. The landscape here was absolutely treeless, but grass, a thick layer of moss, and a few shrubs covered the bedrock.

The wind and rain began to lighten, but there were no landmarks, no sign of any human structures, nothing on the horizon to give any sense of progress, only endless barren moorland. Except for the occasional protrusion of rock and distant glimpse of the dark sea, this could have been Kansas. We began to ask ourselves if we were really expecting to see seabirds here. Bison seemed more likely.*

Slight rise followed slight rise. The wind and rain grew heavier again, obscuring a featureless horizon. We began to wonder if there would be anything to see even if we ever did arrive anywhere. After all, Cape St. Mary's has held disappointment for many visitors—and worse for some.

In 1889 John C. Cahoon, a promising young ornithologist from Taunton, Massachusetts, came to Newfoundland to collect bird eggs and specimens for the renowned New England ornithologist William Brewster. Cahoon was himself a representative specimen of his time, an "ornithological entrepreneur," whose business letterhead listed him as "Professional Taxidermist & Naturalist—Collector and Dealer in All Kinds of BIRDS, NESTS AND EGGS." Though only twenty-five when he arrived on the Avalon's Cape Shore, he quickly established himself as one of the most significant collectors of his time, trapping or shooting (the standard method of documenting birds at the time) the first specimen records for over ninety species of Newfoundland birds.

Cahoon was also a compulsive risk-taker. On July 10, 1889, he visited Cape St. Mary's and, for no apparent ornithological purpose, climbed the three-hundred-foot-high sea stack of Bird Rock, or Bird Island as

---

*And not as improbable as it sounds. For a time in the 1970s, Brunette Island in Fortune Bay was stocked with a herd of buffalo for reasons that remain obscure, though many Newfoundlanders think it was, like the ill-fated Mount Pearl hydroponic cucumber plant outside St. John's in the 1980s, another poorly conceived government-sponsored entrepreneurial boondoggle. The bison died out after a few years.

he called it. He wrote about his feat in dramatic and boastful style to Brewster: "The fishermen say no one has ever before climbed to the top and that two men have been killed in the attempt. The Gannets and Murres nearly carried me off the island and I was obliged to fight my way with a club. . . . The fishermen look upon me as a wonderful man and they may and will do anything for me in the way of helping me to get birds."

The Newfoundland fishermen, who rarely took risks they didn't have to, may also have regarded Cahoon as something of a damn fool. Despite his self-proclaimed prowess, Cahoon could not make a descent off the rock and had to be transported back across the gorge to the mainland by locals using a bo'sun's chair rigged to a block and tackle, during which his grip apparently weakened and he almost fell to his death.

Nearly two years later, on April 26, 1891, Cahoon again ascended a sheer cliff at Cuslett, some ten miles to the north, after collecting raven's eggs on a lower ledge. Apparently he became trapped beneath the overhang. Eventually his grip loosened on his rope and he fell to his death on the rocks below. His bone-shattered body was pulled from the sea the following day.

In the 1960s, shortly before the first road reached Cape St. Mary's, the New Zealand writer Franklin Russell tried to walk there by foot from the outport of Point Lance, some seven miles to the east. He trudged across deep gorges and through unrelenting, driving, bone-chilling mist and rain. He became so cold he could not focus his camera or press the shutter. After several hours of willed forward motion, he finally gave up in exhaustion.

Though it was now possible to drive to the Cape, we had known when we set out that our chances of seeing the birds were iffy at best. Fog was the usual condition on most days, and previous visitors we talked to had told us that they had *heard* the birds clearly, but had seen nothing.

At last the small white tower of the lighthouse appeared above the horizon like a ship. Its glass panels were misted over, blurring the weak beam. We doubted whether this light could be seen from any distance at sea on a day like this, though most lighthouses now provided little in the way of navigational function, since ship orientation was done primarily by radio signals and loran. The lighthouse sat in a small compound of three unmarked, one-story, whitewashed buildings. At one time a wooden fence enclosed the buildings, but several of its sections had tumbled down, and the local sheep roamed and grazed inside its boundaries at will, picking at whatever remained of former gardens tended by the families of former lighthouse keepers.

Except for the light tower itself, the buildings might have been those of a hardscrabble farm, teetering on the edge of abandonment. We saw no bird life, not even gulls. There was a small printed sign beside a garbage box directing us to proceed to the ranger station for information and guides before going on the trail. As we walked toward the station a young man with a mustache came running out of one of the other houses pulling on a woolen jacket. He opened up the visitors' center for us. At 11 A.M. we were the first tourists of the day.

Inside there were a few minimal displays along the wall, a general guide to Newfoundland seabirds, and a visitors' logbook, which we signed. Here, at one of the world's great gannet colonies, the ranger apologized to us: "I'm afraid that all we've got nesting here now is them gannets." We assured him that we were not expecting anything more. He was courteous and helpful, if not particularly informative, a combination I came to expect at most tourist sites in Newfoundland. He offered us rain gear: a bright yellow slicker for Penny, and an old black rubber cloak with galoshes snaps for me.

"The trail starts up there by the garbage box where you're parked. Just follow the metal stakes in the ground. We put them there for people to follow in the fog. It's about a twenty-minute walk. Watch out for the sheep flops."

Most days here have fog. In the logbook, comments of effusive appreciation are mixed with remarks like "Too foggy," "A lot of noise but couldn't see anything," and "We picked the wrong day." But the unpredictability of the place added to its appeal, and a sudden break in the weather made us feel blessed. The rain slacked off to practically nothing by the time we got onto the trail, a dirt path about three feet wide and liberally marked with the droppings of the local sheep.

After a few hundred feet the trail swung over toward the cliff edge. We climbed a slight rise, and all at once, about a half mile off, we saw it: a snow-capped half dome of rock rising sheer up out of the sea for three hundred feet like some miniature Mt. Kilimanjaro. Over its summit swirled a continuous, localized snowstorm of large white flakes. Flanking the rock on either side were small patches of snow-covered slopes sliding down off the mainland cliffs. For a moment we thought that the white on the rock and cliffs was guano from the birds, but then we heard the low distant clattering of the concentrated gannet hordes themselves emanating from the rocks. The snow was birds.

It was already a spectacular scene from this distance, across a gulf of ultramarine waters to the white-headed half dome of Bird Rock. At Cape St. Mary's there are some five thousand nesting pairs of gannets spread out over three miles of cliffs and sea stacks, as well as ten thousand pairs of common murres, a thousand pairs of thick-billed murres (the southernmost breeding colony of these birds as well), ten thousand pairs of kittiwakes, and an assortment of razor-billed auks, black guillemots, herring gulls, great black-backed gulls, and both great and double-breasted cormorants.

To American eyes that are used to having wildlife doled out in tepid spoonfuls, or in the framed reductions of televised documentaries, the initial impression here was that of primal and untrammeled abundance that we associate with "unspoiled nature." In part this impression came from the very scope of the setting, but also from its unannounced majesty, the sense of having *stumbled* onto such prodigality. No signs or guides or boardwalks led us here, only a sheep-shit-lined track bordered by unpainted steel stakes placed every ten meters or so.

The scope of the scene extended far beyond the immediate rocks of the colony. The aerodynamic shapes of the gannets soared widely and effortlessly out over the waters of the bay. It would have been a spectacular sight even without the birds. The rain had stopped completely now and the sky brightened, so that the wet, bird-draped rock seemed to glow with genesis colors. We couldn't believe that we were the only people standing in this place and beholding this sight.

From here the trail swung back from the cliff, and the birds immediately dropped out of sight and sound, not to emerge again until we were almost on top of them. When they did, I experienced the same sense of sudden majesty that I get at home on Cape Cod whenever I come up through the dunes onto the beach, where both the sound and sight of the ocean are muted and hidden until the last moment.

The distant glimpse we had had of the colony hardly prepared us for what we saw now. Bird-sound and bird-sight filled all the space before and below us. The space was mostly down. The rock was separated from the mainland by a sheer chasm three hundred feet deep and eighty feet across. Though we knew the gulf had been created by erosion, the rock appeared to be frozen in the process of breaking itself off from the mainland, as if rocks here calved in late summer the way icebergs do on the coast of Greenland in the spring.

The sight was white, and the sound was dry and white, like clattering bones. It was like entering the diaphanous bubble of sound that spring peepers make on an April night. One was suddenly *inside* what appeared to be a separate, solid mass. The compact dome of birds had dissolved into white particles, a large nucleus of which clung to the top and slopes of the rock, while others whirled and soared and plunged around it, occasionally being drawn into or shearing off from the central mass.

I couldn't get used the lack of any kind of a *frame* for the scene. There were no gates, no fences, and no signs (except for two or three simple "DANGER HIGH CLIFFS" markers on the way out, stating the obvious)—nothing to say *You are here*. Nothing to distract from or limit the birds in any way.

Bird Rock, three hundred feet high, looks twice that height. It is roughly a hundred feet square. The grass across its top and on the tops of the mainland cliffs is thick and a rich green. There are swatches and shreds of it on the rock faces all the way down, giving one the impression of a Polynesian precipice. From this perspective the bulk of the gannet colony, on the rounded, seaward side of the rock, was hidden from us, but there were still over a thousand birds forming a white cap or wig on the head of the rock.

Looking out over the edge I experienced a sudden and shifting vertigo, which came from the unusual sight of gannets soaring through the gap forty to fifty feet *below* me. So motionless and aerodynamic were their sleek, white, black-tipped wings, so smoothly and unerringly did they ride the air, like gliders, that I felt myself riding on their backs, with the dizzying depths of cliff and water rushing past us.

I had read that gannets form nesting territories of approximately nine square feet. They looked more densely packed than that, but one had to remember that these birds have six-foot wingspreads, so that a three-foot-wide space allows them only half a wingspread before invading their neighbor's territory. In other gannet colonies I had visited, the birds spaced themselves out in horizontal rows, like potato patches, but here this was true only on the slopes, where the natural stratification of the rock formed roughly parallel ledges two or three feet apart. On the relatively flat crest there appeared to be a random, helter-skelter pattern. There were no apparent nest constructions, except for bits of green polyester fishnet visible amid the guano and embedded remains of seaweed.

One could not have designed a better viewing arrangement for this colony. The birds on the rock, only eighty feet away, seemed to sense their safety. Unlike terns and gulls, these breeding gannets showed no awareness of our approach. No birds rose toward us in defense or harassment. Their cries already seemed at a maximum, deafening level. Our presence, if noticed at all, was puny, negligible. The birds were wholly preoccupied with their own enthralling presence.

I was surprised to see so many unfledged chicks still in the colony in late July, as many as one to every five or six adult birds. But gannets have one of the longest breeding seasons of any bird, from late April to early October. The young are fed until they reach adult size and then, with much apparent reluctance, they gradually make their way to the cliff edge and leap out into the void. Some flutter down into the water below like wounded birds. But most have an innate mastery of the air from the start. At any rate, all are too heavy at this point for sustained flight. The chicks float on the currents for several weeks, surviving on their accumulated fat, gradually learning to dive for fish and to use their wings. Eventually they rise into the air and follow the adults south across the trackless waters beyond the reach of the winter pack ice.

The young here were in quite different and distinct phases, though all were now nearly or fully the size of their parents. Some still had spiky juvenile plumage on their heads and yellow bills; they were strange gray things that looked like another species, more like miniature ostriches than gannets. Older chicks had smooth, dark gray plumage with white markings reminiscent of loons. Some of the adults were still trying to sit on some of these full-grown birds, providing an example of nature's unintentional comedy. Other chicks appeared dead, absolutely motionless; then one would raise its head, look about, and blink.

It was curious, I thought, that there were no fledged immatures in sight. Had they already left? And though hundreds of adults circled the rock and flew out far over the blue waters, there was no visible fishing going on, none of the spectacular, hundred-foot, lance-straight plunges into the Atlantic on folded wings, throwing up great white sprays of foam. But these birds follow the movement of schools of herring and caplin on a daily basis, and the feeding adults might be as much as forty or fifty miles offshore.

There was not much feeding of the chicks going on, and what there was had a violent, forcible, rape-like quality to it, though in this case it was the parents who appeared to be violated. The chicks snapped regurgitated fish out of the adults' gullets in sharp, repeated thrusts. It seemed to be a quiet time in the colony, though quiet in a gannet colony is only relative. There was a constant surge and flow of motion and noise on the rock. Much of it was adult posturing, or ritualized aggression, consisting of a low bowing of the head and neck, a concave extension of the back and tail, a crossing and extension of the wings, a posture that created a sculptured, boat-like shape. This was often done by solitary birds. The greeting or nest-exchange ceremony was also much in evidence. As one bird flew in and landed next to the other on the nest, each pair extended their necks and heads upward together, rubbing each other's beaks rhythmically and calling loudly.

But there was also much active aggression in evidence: sudden, evil lunges of eye and beak when one adult inadvertently invaded the invisible territory of a neighbor. These birds appeared to bring to an overt climax the structured aggression and anxiety inherent in all colonial nesters, where cooperation seems at best a necessary evil. Whereas most seabird aggression is ritualized behavior that rarely results in injury, gannets often inflict severe damage, and even death, on one another in their courtship rivalries and territorial fights. Yet most of the birds in front of us were, at any one time, calm and quiet. The deafening clattering and the palpable wave of aggression seemed to emanate from the rock itself.

Frequently one of the chicks or adults on the upper ledges of the dome raised its tail and emitted a projectile stream of vile, cream-yellow excrement some four feet long over the edge. Occasionally one of these streams hit an adult on the lower ledge, which the bird shook off with a series of shudders. Was there a hierarchy to the nest sites? Were the lower ledges less desirable? Did the birds there get socially as well as literally shat upon?

People talk about feeling so close to the birds at Cape St. Mary's that it seems they could step across and touch them, an illusion partly due to the gannet's large size. The noise accompanying the birds also makes them seem much closer. In fact, eighty feet is quite close to a bird as large as a gannet. I could fill my 200-mm lens with three or four birds. Through my binoculars I could observe close up the ritual-like markings of the adult gannets: the masked faces and outlined bills; the sculpted, black-tipped wings; the dusting of gold on the heads; the elegant black feet with long, thin green lines painted along the bones of the toes. This ceremonial appearance gave an impersonal, formal quality even to the birds' aggressive behavior, as though it were a sacrament itself, much the way communal human complaints about, say, the weather or the economy have a formulaic, ritualistic element about them.

To our left there was a great gorge nearly two hundred feet across and cutting straight back into the mainland cliffs for nearly a thousand feet. On the far side of the gorge several hundred more gannets, one of the mainland extensions of the colony, spaced themselves out on the slopes. On little ledges protruding from the sheer walls of the gorge were dozens of small gray and white birds that looked like large pigeons. These were kittiwakes (called tickle-aces or tickle-asses by Newfoundlanders), pelagic gulls that also nest here, but whose breeding season appeared done. We spotted no chicks or fledged immatures among the adult kittiwakes, but curiously there were several smashed forms of adult birds on the ledges at different intervals all the way down. The broken bodies looked like road kills, as if they had crashed or been flung into the ledges with great force. What could have caused such naked deaths: natural mortality, chicks trying to fledge, predation from the gannets, adults flying into the cliff faces in the fog?

It occurred to me that we could easily end up the same, smashed on the cliffs below like poor John Cahoon. Here was a place where you could go right up to the very edge of the abyss with nothing to stop you but your will to live. Suddenly Penny and I both had the strange sense that we were being looked at. We turned around and found that the sheep had followed us at a distance. A dozen or so of them rested in the grass about twenty feet behind us, staring directly at us with a conspiratorial look in their eyes. We shuddered involuntarily, remembering all the names of the schoolchildren in the logbook at the ranger station, and carefully began to make our way back, following the metal stakes along the edges of the cliffs.

Cape Pine

Quite unexpectedly, I find I am spending the night with the keeper of Cape Pine Light, one of the more remote lighthouses on the southern shore of the Avalon Peninsula. It is late September and I have spent most of the day driving along Route 10 in a futile attempt to find some of the sizable caribou herds that are said to roam vast barrens of the southern Avalon. About 2 P.M. I decided to see if I could get a bite to eat in St. Shotts, a small outport about fifteen kilometers off the highway. After a kilometer or so, I passed a small wooden sign on the left that read, "National Historic Site—Cape Pine." Although it was not even shown on the map, the turnoff was a gravel road in good condition. I followed it for about ten miles through featureless barrens, with an endless line of spare telephone poles running beside the road, until I came to the light: a tall, round, iron tower about fifteen feet wide at the base and fifty feet tall. It dominated a small complex of buildings—two simple but handsome, traditional wood houses painted red and white; a small shed attached to the light; a foghorn shed; an older abandoned-looking shed; and an incongruous, massive satellite dish—all standing in stark relief against the distant sea like a setting for a Newfoundland novel.

When I pulled up to the house, a large, healthy-looking red fox was standing in the middle of the yard. At first I mistook it for a dog, for it acted quite calm, though it darted off when I approached it. There didn't seem to be anyone about, so I walked over to the edge of the cliffs, which are precipitous and dramatic here, rising sheer for some three hundred feet above the sea.

A loon gave his wail call and a lone gannet flew low over the water, but I saw no other seabirds. The rock cliffs twisted their way down to the sea in contorted vertical patterns. Just offshore, like the dark hulls of grounded ships, massive ledges of slate protruded out of the water, slanted toward the land. These were the infamous and aptly named *sunkers* of the Newfoundland coast, responsible for hundreds of shipwrecks over the centuries. These inert hulks shaped the play of the dark swells that broke over them, a structured symphony of surges, falls, currents, swashes, and white rushing channels of water, creating a complex visual and aural pattern of separate but coordinated rhythms. From that height, the swells far below seemed to move in slow motion, mounting the dark, impassive, uplifted rocks, softly laving and caressing, tugging and sucking at them, spreading their thinning edges over the seams and cracks, and then draining themselves down over their wet sides, leaving the rocks gleaming, still erect and sharp.

As I stood there, mesmerized, I became aware of the fox watching me, hunkered down in high grass about twenty yards off. It was stalking me as it would a bird or a mouse, hunching down in the grass with just its ears and snout protruding, watching me as if I didn't see him, then picking up and moving on. At one point he seemed to be rooting in the ground or gnawing at something with his snout, and he let me get within fifty feet before moving off. When I got to where the fox had been, I saw that he had been trying to loosen some of the turf at the edge of a small boulder in the ground, in the groove of which many sowbugs and insects were crawling.

Then a figure appeared at the door of the house, a tall, lanky man dressed casually in a plaid shirt and woolen pants. He shouted, "He'll stalk you all day if you let him, my son," and invited me in for a cup of tea.

His name is Tom Finlay, and he has been the lighthouse keeper here for the past six years. Born in the nearby Irish community of St. Shotts, he fished for a few years as a young man, but "never saw anything to it." In 1947 he left St. John's on the Newfie Bullet with six other local men, headed for Toronto. It was the first time he had been on a train. He ended up working for the Hudson Bay Company office up near Lake Winnipeg, eventually becoming manager. He was in charge of buying and sorting food, providing the natives and trappers with equipment on credit, a kind of economic feudal system of indentured service that is similar to the one that existed between the Newfoundland merchants and fishermen for centuries.

He was a good company man, and very proud of the way Hudson Bay treated its employees (if not its customers). One time a fire started in the company warehouse and they had to evacuate dozens of barrels of gasoline. But the fire eventually hit the ammunition supplies and "the whole thing went off like a skyrocket." The post lost everything, but the company came right in an "bought us a whole new railroad to bring in new supplies."

He came back to Newfoundland in 1969, and his uncle, who was then the lighthouse keeper, told him that the assistantship position was open, so he applied for and got it. In 1983 he took over as keeper, and his younger brother, David, became the assistant. His brother and his family use the other house in the summer, but in the off-season David commutes from St. Shotts.

Tom's family has been involved with the light for at least four generations on his mother's side, whose family name was Myrick. There is a small white picket-enclosed graveyard beside the road near the house with a single, weather-worn, circular stone inside the fence carved with dissolving letters that still barely read, "Sarah Hewitt / Died September 17, 1889 / Aged 21." This was Tom's grandmother's sister, who lived here at the house. "I found the stone one day down over the rocks and set it up here as a memorial. They said she had diphtheria, but of course they didn't know much in those days."

Tom speaks with the strong Irish accent of the Avalon outports, a much more animated and lilting speech than the West Country growl of Newfoundland's more northern bays. His grammar, too, is different from that of the north; for instance, he does not add an *s* to present-tense first-person verbs or put objective pronouns in the nominative case.

When I tell him I live on Cape Cod and that Myrick is an old Cape name, he laughs, "Ah, small fucking world!" It turns out he has a ninety-three-year-old aunt who lives in Littleton, Massachusetts. He tells me he goes to see her every year, though he didn't make it this year. Years ago he was in New Bedford for his father's second wedding and has two stepbrothers who are scallopers there. He's also been to Hyannisport—"The Kennedys, you know."

"Well," I said, "we're not all rich down there."

He smiles and pours my tea. "We always use canned milk here. I hope that's all right."

I ask him if he has ever been to the lighthouse at Bonavista.

"No, sir. I've been all over Canada, the mainland, that is—and to Philadelphia and New York, Atlantic City, and Boston—but I haven't been anywhere in Newfoundland, and you know, my son, there are some beautiful spots in Newfoundland."

The fox that had stalked me, he says, is one he has tamed over the past several weeks. "I saw some idiot taking a shot at him last summer, so I decided to see if I could keep him close to the house." He beams when he tells me that he has even managed to coax the fox into the house on occasion, and he shows me some photographs of the animal eating from his hand in his front parlor.

Tom offers to show me the light, though he is "on holiday" this week. According to a bronze plaque on the light tower the Cape Pine Lighthouse, or Fer du Cap Pine, stands over three hundred feet above high water. It was built in 1851 by the Imperial Government, when Newfoundland was still a British colony, at a cost of over sixty-five hundred pounds, and thenceforth maintained by the government of Newfoundland. The elaborately constructed cast iron tower, polygonal lantern, and revolving light originally consisting of sixteen whale oil lamps, each with parabolic reflector, were all constructed in England, shipped over, landed at nearby Arnold Cove, hoisted up the rugged cliffs, and transported to the site (in the plaque's typically British understated phrase) "with considerable difficulty."

The light has been modified several times since it was built, and the whale oil lamps have been replaced with a single five-hundred-watt bulb projected through two Fresnel lenses. The beam, aided by prisms, is said to carry twenty-five miles out to sea. "But if you want to see a real light," says Tom, "you go to Cape Race. That light has the largest lighthouse lens in North America. It *floats* in a pool of fifteen tons of mercury to keep it stable and steady, and to clean it you walk *inside* the lens."

The first lighthouse keeper and his family lived in the tower, but according to the plaque, "It soon proved uninhabitable." One could see why. The uninsulated iron walls drip with condensation, a dim light seeps in through two small windows, and the perpetual wind, though mild today, sends a low but constant whine vibrating through the tower.

In those days, of course, there was no road to the light, and supply deliveries by boat were infrequent. The family had to be completely self-sufficient, raising their own food and meat. Tom points out two or three old stone walls in the field below the keeper's house, each about a hundred feet long and three or four feet high, running east to west. He says they were built as windbreaks for the family's vegetable garden, which was tended by his great-aunt Sarah. It is difficult to believe that anything could be cultivated out on this barren, wind-swept plain, but when we walk down to the walls, I can just make out, on the south side of the longest one, the parallel, mounded rows of rocky soil, about two feet wide, that once held potatoes, turnips, cabbage, perhaps broccoli. Even now the wild growth seems greener in these rows, though the garden was abandoned at least forty years ago. A capping layer of moss nearly a foot thick grows on top of the walls, and the browned remains of some irises huddle against their bases, where flocks of snow buntings feed in the lee.

Now, of course, government supplies come in by road, and Tom gets a five-thousand-dollar-a-year allowance for road plowing in the winter. "This road is in pretty good shape compared to the one down to Cape St. Mary's. Oh, my son, you don't want to be taking that one this year!"

There are at present (1989) fifty-five manned lights in Newfoundland, more than in any other North American province or state, but budget crunches are bringing downsizing and automation even to this bastion of local traditions. Tom tells me that twenty-four of the lighthouses are scheduled to be closed down or automated within the next few years. He hopes to retire before they automate Cape Pine, "but the light," he said, "will go on forever. For one thing, it serves as a repeater signal for the entire Atlantic ship network."

I tell him I've been looking for caribou along the highway but haven't found any. He laughs, "Oh yeah, they're just beginning to go back up into the hills for the winter. We used to get some of them in the fall to augment our supplies. In the summer you can see thousands of them down here. They can't be hunted south of the highway now, you see, and most people go for moose anyway. They don't have to go in so far and they get more meat. The caribou also got used to men and the machines when they were building the new highway from St. Mary's, so they're pretty tame, except now when it's rutting season. Christ, last spring they filled the yard out here! I had to make my way through to the light by beating them off with a broomstick. I got pictures of them on my camcorder if you'd like to see them."

I thank him but say I'd rather find the real thing.

His biggest nuisance, he says, are the sheep. I tell him I didn't noticed any driving in.

"No, I run them off. They have lots of sheep over by St. Shotts, and they have an enclosed pasture ground where they're supposed to keep them, but they have to pay a dollar a sheep, and there's one man who has about a hundred sheep that's too cheap to pay, so his sheep come up over the ridge around the light, and when I see them I get on my quad and chase them back. Now when they hear the motor start up they just take off."

Now that they've put a National Historic Site sign at the turnoff, he gets more company in the summer than he'd like. "Had a family from New Bedford camp here last year. Turns out they knew my brothers. How about that?"

I ask him if I might camp in his yard tonight. "Oh, you might as well stay inside. It's just me and there's a spare room with a cot." I accept gratefully, delighted by my luck at being invited to spend the night with a Newfoundland lighthouse keeper. It strikes me that, without design, I have fallen into a position comparable to that of Thoreau 140 years ago when he spent the night at what was then also a remote lighthouse in Truro on Cape Cod, where I live. I calculate this one is even more remote, for we are at least twenty kilometers by road from the nearest inhabited house. I find myself indulging in visions of hours listening to stories of his family history here, tales of shipwrecks and blinding blizzards, while sipping rum with Tom in front of a cozy wood stove.

The reality, however, turns out to be quite different. After supper I sit and watch my host surf through the 105 channels provided by his new ten-foot-diameter satellite dish. Usually, he says, he goes to the States on his holiday, but the dish was just installed last week and he is spending his vacation discovering its marvels. He is very proud of his new acquisition, says it "brings everything to me." "Everything" includes the satellite feed that brings him the news an hour before the rest of Newfoundland gets it, and fewer commercials on the network channels because the satellite signal doesn't carry local commercials.

Though profoundly disappointed, I resign myself to an evening of flipping images of *Golden Girls* reruns, Daffy Duck cartoons, car races, *Cosby* episodes (he gets three of these in a row), talk shows, an old Burt Reynolds movie, etc.—to the 105th power.

Finally, at 11:30 P.M., Tom switches to the local news. The lead story reports the deaths of four men from a freak marine accident at Middle Cove, north of St. John's: A group of seven scuba divers were bodysurfing when one of their number was washed out to sea by a strong, unexpected current. Three Coast Guardsmen in rescue suits went out in a Zodiac to retrieve the swimmer, who was clinging to a rock, when a sudden, freak wave came up and swamped the raft, drowning all the men. Only one body was found.

Unexpectedly, Tom turns off the TV and sits quietly for several minutes, not speaking. Then he tells me of a family tragedy that occurred here in March three years ago. Three of his relatives—a forty-year-old man who was a cousin on his mother's side, a fifty-year-old man who was a cousin on his father's side, and the older man's sixteen-year-old son— had come out from St. Shotts to visit him that day on Skidoos. They left in the late afternoon and were expected back by 9:30 that night, but they never arrived. There was so much drifted snow that it took the search party eighty-four hours to open the road. They found the Skidoos overturned on the rocks below the cliff in the next valley over, but they found only the body of the younger man. The other two, father and son, had presumably been washed out to sea. Tom thinks that probably one of them fell into the water and the others went in to try to save him. He points to the mantel, where he has placed pictures of all three.

Then, almost as an afterthought, he adds, "Those three Coast Guard fellows that drowned today up to Middle Cove? They was the ones found my cousin's body."

Tocher's Pond

The fog and wind that continuously blanket the hills and tablelands of Newfoundland's south coast have created a tundra-like terrain, the most extensive stretch of open, treeless country on the island. These "barrens," as they are known here (the term first recorded in Newfoundland by Sir Joseph Banks in 1766: "For so they Call the Places where Wood Does Not Grow"), are one of the most distinctive and yet featureless landscapes I have ever encountered. The term "barrens," however, is a biological misnomer, for the ground is not barren but thoroughly and thickly carpeted with a luxuriant cover of low growth: dozens of kinds of lichens, mosses, sedges, heath, and bog plants, as well as woody lambskill, called "goowitty"; creeping willow; and sprinklings of stunted spruce and fir called "tuckamore." In places the vegetation forms a mat a foot or more in depth and, in early October, presents a fiery patchwork of autumn colors.

These barrens, like most Newfoundland landscapes, contain an abundance of wetlands—ponds, bogs, and marshes—whose nature reminds me how far I am from home. Back on Cape Cod, everything seeks a horizontal equilibrium. The ponds there are exposed portions of the water table and all of them lie at roughly the same level. Along the bay shore the different salt marsh grasses are arranged in distinct bands of concentric vegetation, each band indicating a particular grass's elevation above the tidal range. In fact, one can get a good idea of the topographic inclinations of a marsh or swamp from the differences in vegetation. The Cape is a land whose appearance is grounded in gravity—fluid and changing, perhaps, but always maintaining a faithful and regular relationship to its foundations.

Newfoundland's wetlands, on the other hand, reflect its ancient, tortured, and complex geological history. It is a land where in places pieces of the earth's mantle have been thrown up, like a breaker over topping a beach, to lie atop relatively young sedimentary deposits; where cliff strata have been wrenched upright and bent over; where the island itself has been ripped apart and crushed back together several times by tectonic forces; where mile-high ice sheets have scraped and scoured and sculpted the rocky landscape into a water-veined labyrinth. What this means is that the distribution and elevation of wetlands is extensive but highly unpredictable. The presence of wetland vegetation reflects subterranean conditions of rock and moisture that are not decipherable on the surface. Mosses, pitcher plants, irises, sedges, orchids, and other bog plants can be found at any elevation. Moreover, they can even form improbable "sloping bogs," where a thin layer of wetland vegetation covers a rocky slope that tilts at a visible angle. In some places these sloping bogs have been known to slide downhill over time, so that the bog has the appearance of a rumpled blanket on its lower end.

These southern barrens are also the favored feeding and calving grounds of the Avalon Peninsula's sizable herds of woodland caribou, the largest of seven recognized Canadian subspecies of *Rangifer tarandus* and the southernmost caribou herds in the world. Several years ago a number of animals from the Avalon herds were airlifted to Maine in an unsuccessful experiment to "reintroduce" caribou to that state. The animals succumbed to a brain infection transmitted by white-tailed deer, which are absent in Newfoundland.

One day I visited the Pleasantville complex of the Wildlife Division of the Department of Recreation in St. John's and spoke with Wildlife Research Manager Sean Mahoney. His office was located in Building 810, and mounted on the wall was the head of a caribou that had been shot between 1920 and 1930. It was a very large head sporting an impressive rack of antlers. A striking feature of caribou antlers is the brow tine, or "spike and shovel," a smaller, vertically flattened antler with short tines, that thrusts forward between the main antlers. This head had two large "shovels," indicating a very mature animal, that extended just over the bridge of the nose, and points that were interlocked across one another like clasped hands.

Sean, a man in his late thirties, sporting a big, black beard and a very furry head of hair, gave me a strong handshake. To my query as to where I might see some caribou, he replied, "Well, it's not the best time of year to see them. In early October they're still in the interior, mostly scattered into small groups. You might see anywhere from three to forty right now. In the spring now, June, say, you might easily come across a herd of three thousand crossing the highways down south." June seems to be the month everything bursts open in Newfoundland: caplin, lobsters, cod, icebergs, irises, caribou, motels, provincial parks.

On a wall map Sean pointed to the area around Frank's Pond, one of the larger lakes in the middle of the vast Avalon Wilderness Reserve, an expanse of over a thousand square kilometers of forest, barrens, and peatland that covers most of the peninsula's southeast lobe. "There was a good-sized herd seen there yesterday," he said, "but it's twenty kilometers off the road and then you've got to hike in for another hour or so."

My rental Escort was hardly suitable for off-road travel, so he suggested that I drive down to Trepassey, where I still might see some caribou from the road. "Rick Taylor reported two to three hundred animals up near Tocher's Pond this week, just a few kilometers north of the highway. It's not in the Reserve, but the caribou don't know that."

He then steered me over to the Department of Environment and Mines (an intriguing political conjunction) in the Howley Building, where I picked up a couple of 1:250,000-scale topo maps of the area and then headed out of St. John's on the Trans-Canada Highway toward Trepassey.

Some of the most impressive stretches of barrens actually occur right on the TCH, near the Butter Pot Provincial Park: absolutely treeless, rocky country with misty ponds lying in shallow depressions like old mirrors and thousands of large, rounded glacial boulders sticking up out of the mossy ground like giant eggs. There were several moose feeding placidly in some of the smaller ponds right beside the highway, but no sign of caribou. At the Holyrood exit I turned off on Route 90 and headed south toward St. Mary's. A few miles on I passed the

Salmonier Nature Park where I could have stopped and seen a number of caribou in the fenced enclosures, but I didn't want my first caribou to be an incarcerated one.

I stopped at St. Mary's, where I bought a pair of Vulcan rubber boots for twenty-five dollars. As the highway began to curve eastward near the bottom of the peninsula, I entered an utterly flat, empty plateau. There is no way to capture on film the absolute flatness and desolateness of these barrens. There are few features to relieve the terrain, to tell itself what it is, only some little boggy ponds, some thin stretches of extremely dwarfed spruce trees with dead tops, and a few boulders.

This stretch of the highway appeared to be new. It was a straight causeway raised an average of six feet or so above the surrounding terrain, so that one had the impression of sliding smoothly through the gently undulating barrens on an elevated track. Small flocks of snow buntings flushed up off the side of the highway as I passed, like little white-and-black stones thrown up into the air. Here and there, off to the side and below, I could see the remains of the road's predecessor: a rutted, wet, zigzagging track running through wet ground, murder to vehicles and maddening to drivers.

Just past Peter's River there was a highway sign: "CAUTION— CARIBOU CROSSING—20 KM." Well, I thought, if they're going to be anywhere, it will be here. But when I reached Trepassey, I had still not seen a single caribou. I got out the topo map and located Tocher's Pond. It was back several kilometers to the west and about two kilometers north of the highway. I retraced my route, looking for signs of a road or track going north off the highway, but there was none. So I pulled into the gravel turnoff that appeared to be closest to the pond, pulled on my new boots, grabbed my camera and binoculars, and set off in search of caribou.

I entered this featureless and seemingly endless landscape on faith and a strong suspicion of misinformation. I took a compass but wondered how much good it would really do me if the fog came in. Men are regularly lost out here in the barrens during the hunting season. Most, fortunately, are found after a day or two of wandering about, cold and hungry, but generally sanguine about the experience, as if they had been caught out in a shower. Despite its flatness it is a difficult landscape to walk through, not only because of the depth and thickness of the ground cover, but also because one never knows, from step to step, at what depth one's foot will strike the hard substrate of limestone and slate that underlies it. Beneath this lush, soft, colorful, sensually inviting landscape, one is always unexpectedly hitting hard rock. Traversing it is a constant series of unpredictable jolts, like walking down a set of steps of randomly different heights in the dark. About a quarter mile out into the barrens someone had carried and set up an official highway sign that read, "Maximum Speed 65 kph."

The land resembled a ragged, multicolored hide, torn in places and abraded through to bare gravel. On foot I could see it was not totally flat, but slightly undulating, like the sea on a calm day. And like the sea, it is a place where light, unimpeded, plays over the surface, illuminating, highlighting, shifting, and changing color, lending it that sense of movement that the sea possesses. The landscape was broken in places by small cones of exposed rock projecting up through the moss, like small incipient volcanoes, or those pyramidal heaves of ice on frozen ponds. Scattered across the boggy surface was an interconnected pattern of lakes, some several kilometers long—all dark, clear, and seemingly empty of life. Their shores were uniformly rimmed with banks of glacial boulders two or three feet high, pushed up against the shoreline by the expansion of winter ice in such regular sloping patterns that they looked like artificial riprap. The shores of the ponds were ringed with caribou trails. In the muddy paths I saw the divided hoof prints that resembled a moose's, though rounder, and ranged in size from that of my closed fist to that of a tea saucer. The two halves of the hoof are designed to spread apart when weight is placed on it, thus increasing the support for the caribou on this spongy, uneven ground.

About two kilometers in from the highway I came upon a small ranger station, located at the head of a long, narrow lake. The cabin was a two-room wood-frame structure originally covered with clapboards and asphalt sheets, and subsequently sheathed in sections of corrugated metal that seemed to have been stripped from various mobile homes. It sat literally in a swamp at the head of the lake. The inside had been substantially trashed and it appeared not to have been used for some time. From there I headed off northerly directly toward Tocher's Pond, another mile or so off, where the caribou had been seen (or at least it was the pond that Sean had identified as Tocher's, though the map had that name attached to another pond two kilometers further north).

Like Cape Cod's outer beaches, the barrens are a place of illusion, even mirage. One of the most prominent features in this area were scattered skeletons of dwarf trees, wind-bleached and sculptured into the fantastic likenesses of humanoid birds with slim, angular limbs and beaks, twisted and posed by the caprice of the wind into strangely suggestive gestures.

All distances here seem vast, for there are no reliable reference points. I walked for nearly six hours, covering some sixteen kilometers. According to the map, I crossed only one hundred-foot contour. The slight change in elevation effectively hides large segments of the landscape at any one point. Not flat enough to reveal everything, the landscape also lacks sufficient elevation to provide a lookout. To gain some sense of progress, I would pick what appeared to be a definite rise, perhaps a half mile off, but by the time I approached it, its altitude would have dissolved into the surrounding landscape. This, combined with the random elevation of the wetlands, made it difficult to tell whether I was ascending or descending.

I saw my first caribou as I came up over an unanticipated rise that suddenly revealed the expanse of what I took to be Tocher's Pond. On the far shore of the lake, perhaps five hundred yards off, a half dozen or so large white forms were moving rapidly back and forth along the shoreline. I thought at first they were birds of some sort, they moved so fast and distractedly, and there was nothing to gauge their size by. Through binoculars, though, I could see that they were quadrupeds with long legs, though I could not make out much else at that distance. They raced back and forth for several hundred feet along the shore of the lake, as if pursued by wolves or blackflies, though the Newfoundland wolf had been exterminated in the 1920s and I had not encountered a single biting insect on my walk (one of the advantages of visiting these latitudes so late in the season). Then, all at once, the animals took off north, away from me. Could they have possibly noticed me at this distance? It was not likely, since caribou are said to have relatively poor eyesight, and the light wind was from the northeast, toward me. They disappeared into one of the invisible creases in the land's fabric in less than half a minute.

After they had gone, I realized that I had heard, or thought I had heard, the distant drumming of hoofbeats as they ran off. Whether or not I did, I was suddenly struck not only by how empty, but also by how *quiet* this place was. There was no sound, no distant traffic, no crashing surf, no birdsong (though I had flushed several small coveys of rock ptarmigan, or "barrens partridge," along the way). There had been a slight breeze through the morning, and gray-bottomed flotillas of cumulus clouds floated in sober procession across the sky ahead of me. Yet I could hear no wind. No spires of soft evergreen rose out of this landscape to card the wind audibly through their needles; no delicate grasses rustled in its passing, or scraped their hardened tips on sand. The low, stiff, but pliant heath vegetation accepted the wind silently.

The only sounds, in fact, were those of my own making. I became intensely conscious of the rhythmic, percussive exhalation of my own breath. As I lurched across the thick ground cover, a continuous soft shadow of sucking, brushing noise followed me. Now that I had stopped and my breathing had returned to an inaudible level, even these self-generated sounds had ceased, and I was aware only of an utter and profound silence, as high and wide as the sky

Was that *it?* I wondered. Was that the "herd" at Tocher's Pond? Or, more likely, did the main herd still lie farther on, at the next pond, the one my map called Tocher's? My legs were already beginning to ache, not so much from the actual impact of hitting the invisible rock substrate beneath the moss, as from the tension of anticipating it. I could stop now and say I had seen caribou. In fact, had I seen nothing, I would probably have turned back at that point, since I was not prepared to hike in another three or four kilometers on faith. But this distant glimpse of the animals had given my mind enough to feed on, had provided a kind of trail snack for the imagination, and so I continued. I bore east to the end of this lake, where it was connected to another by a short, shallow ford about a hundred feet wide. Glad I had purchased the waterproof boots, I carefully stepped across on a series of stones and once again headed north. After another twenty minutes' walking, the whole scene coalesced before me into a discernible ridge, at the crest of which a series of small white crystals stood and glinted in the intermittent sun.

Through my glasses I could make out about fifteen of them, grazing at the very edge of the horizon. They were, if anything, even further off than the small group at the lake, like porcelain miniatures set in relief against a clear blue sky. Absurdly, I snapped a few exposures of these minuscule specks with my telephoto lens, just in case I failed to get any closer.

Then, to my left, down near the shore of a large, deeply indented pond that I now suspected was the true Tocher's Pond, I noticed a pair of caribou less than two hundred and fifty yards off. They were grazing in what appeared to be a section of grassy marsh. I walked slowly toward them. Both were antlerless, and one was considerably larger than the other, with more of a brown saddle, suggesting a cow and her calf. I walked another hundred yards or so before the larger one raised her head and stared at me in recognition. She made no move to run off, and the smaller one kept grazing. I lifted my binoculars and got my first reasonably close look at a living caribou in the wild.

It fit no image of a member of the deer family that I had experienced before. In fact, lacking the antlers, the caribou looked remarkably bovine, stocky and short-nosed, with thick legs and large ears. Their bodies were largely off-white, the younger one's nearly completely so, with a mask of brown around the face and a saddle of brown on the mother's back. They had ridged, parallel markings on their sides that gave the impression of ribs showing through the hide, though their bodies looked sturdy and well fed. Less statuesque than elk, they had a general outline that reminded me more of moose than deer, though they exhibited the alertness and quick movements of the latter. They looked, more than anything, like Brahman cattle, gaunt and off-white, with dark eye rings, dark legs, and extremely large hooves.

When I got within a hundred yards, the mother decided that was enough and began to move off northeast, followed by the calf, up toward the low rise where others of her herd were grazing. When they moved, the image of cattle was broken, instantly and permanently. They moved not like cows, or deer, or moose, or elk, or any other wild animal I had ever seen. Rather, they reminded me of high-stepping show horses. They *pranced* over the barrens, in a kind of delicate, arc-ing trot that lifted each foot clear of the thick vegetation at each step. They seemed to be dancing across my line of vision. Their gait had a rhythmic, resilient syncopation to it, giving the impression that the an-imals were actually rebounding from the elastic vegetation, as if run-ning on a giant trampoline. It was, of course, the perfect gait for this kind of terrain, one that allowed them the greatest progress with the least resistance.

They did not hurry, but moved deliberately up the gentle, sloping ridge to join the larger herd, the mother stopping regularly to look back at me. As I followed them up toward the ridge, I began to see across into a wide, open twisting valley to the east of the next pond. Against the slopes, spread out over perhaps half a mile, were another forty or fifty caribou, clumped in smaller groups.

As I climbed toward them, what I thought were several pair of dis-carded antlers resting on the top of the ridge rose up to become four large bulls, each of which seemed to be shepherding a group of ten to fifteen cows and calves (and one yearling buck with short antlers). The bulls herded their groups off to one side and stood between me and them, regarding me straight on, standing in strange, extended, contorted poses.

Then one of the bulls, larger than the others and with a more devel-oped rack of antlers, including a pair of prominent shovels, moved in and appeared to take charge of the entire herd. He moved with a slow, purposeful, loping gait, breaking up the smaller groups as though de-liberately scattering them, uttering a low, soft, fluttering cough, a sound that did not reach the level of tone, but rather of breathy resonance. Still, though he was now less than a hundred yards from me, I would not have heard it if it had not been so utterly still. Never before had I encountered so many large animals in such a total absence of sound. The circumambient silence, like an invisible ocean, added to the dream-like quality of these animals, moving as they did in such easy, silent grace across this soft, cushioned, insulated terrain.

Then, much to my surprise and consternation, the lead bull began to take deliberate steps toward me. And in that same instant I realized how much I had taken my immunity for granted. I had been seeing myself as an *observer* only or, at most, one who might inadvertently disturb or scare off these magnificent creatures through my clumsiness. It had not occurred to me that I might, in fact, be seen as an *intruder*, one threatening the herd and thus provoking aggressive behavior from the males. As another of the bulls turned his rack of antlers in my direction, I suddenly saw where I actually was: under an unsheltering sky and the gaze of several three- to four-hundred-pound male ungulates in rut. I was at least three kilometers from any road, in the middle of an endless expanse of difficult and treacherous terrain that offered nothing to climb and no place to hide. I hunkered down against one of the small protruding boulders and tried to look like the very insignificant object which at that moment I felt I truly was.

St. John's II:
On Signal Hill

One summer evening during my second visit to St. John's, I walked downtown with my old high school friend Penny and her twelve-year-old daughter, Nell, for some supper. It was Penny's letters, photos, and stories about Newfoundland that had first lured me here. She had come to St. John's in 1970 to do her doctorate in physiology at Memorial University of Newfoundland (MUN), where she now taught physiology. In the intervening years she had also run three gourmet restaurants in the city.

That evening she took us to King Cod on Duckworth Street, which she said had "the best fish and chips in Newfoundland." She was right. The cod was fresh and lightly fried, served in generous portions with hand-cut chips and gravy. Like many of the best little eating places in St. John's, King Cod was an unassuming hole in the wall. Its decor was Early Laminate Minimalist: plastic tables and seats. Penny said that there was "a real sit-down restaurant upstairs with wooden tables, but it costs more and the food's the same as down here in the plastic booths." Across the street was an Irving Gas Station, which, Penny noted, had the best view of the harbor in all of St. John's.

There had been many changes in St. John's since she first came, not just physical ones, but others that suggested a change in the city's own sense of itself. One could see it, she said, in some of the older restaurants on Water Street, such as the Fishing Admiral, which had recently begun adding "Newfoundland decor" to their walls and fronts. Nonetheless, she felt it was still a city that existed more for its residents than for its visitors, where local knowledge was important, where you had to *know* which were the good places to eat, or go for music, or shoes, or seal flippers. It was a place still thin on semiotics.

Moreover, some of the recent changes pleased her. As a restaurant owner, it had been difficult for her to find good fruits and vegetables. Her current restaurant, The Stone House, had a large vegetable and herb garden of its own, the way many restaurants in France do outside the large cities. Still, other than root vegetables and cabbage, it was hard to get fresh produce year-round. Once, she went into a neighborhood store and asked for celery.

"What?" asked the store lady.

"Ce-le-ry," Penny had replied, pronouncing it carefully.

"I had to ask for it several times and finally had to write it down. The woman looked at it and said, 'Oh, celery!' (pronouncing it *exactly* as I had.) 'Oh yes,' she said, 'I know what that is. We don't have any, but I've heard of it.'"

Penny was excited a few years ago when some of the stores and supermarkets in St. John's began importing vegetables and fruits from the mainland. "The checkout girls still don't recognize many of the items, like kiwis. They've never seen them before."

She remembered the first time she bought cherry tomatoes at a mall supermarket. At the checkout counter the girl stared at them, looked up the price, and then, giving Penny a sympathetic look, said, "Oh my dear, I can't charge you full price for them. They's so *puny!*"

After supper the three of us walked along the downtown streets, looking for strawberries for dessert. It was a beautiful, clear evening, the sunlight still bright and brilliant on the simple wood-frame clapboarded row houses, whose eclectic colors and plain, homely shapes I was beginning to love. This whole city was fascinating and likable, once one stopped looking for a city in it. It was, as Penny put it, "well used" by the people who lived here, families and children, despite the recent sprawl of malls and suburbs. Like the Newark of my early childhood, it was still a safe city.

We walked along George Street, now a stretch of new upscale pubs, which, Penny said used to be a seedy back alley with a couple of strip clubs where no one would go. One night fifteen years earlier she and her first restaurant partner, Dell, had been sitting in a car outside what was now Christian's Pub, discussing the pros and cons of purchasing the building, when a policeman came up and demanded to see their IDs and asked their purpose for being there. "He thought we were prostitutes, you see."

As we walked down Water Street, we saw four Soviet seamen coming toward us—young men with hard jaws and short-short hair, carrying nylon ditty bags. Penny said they were loading up on cheap merchandise from downtown stores, mostly jeans and T-shirts. One of them stopped us and, with sad eyes, asked, "Where Hong Kong bank, please?" She gave them directions and they lurched away with that universal sailor's gait.

"The Russians were some of our best customers at Speakeasy," said Penny. "We were the only restaurant that served espresso then. The machine broke down once and we had to send for a man from St. Pierre [a French island off the south coast of Newfoundland] to come and fix it."

At the west end of Water Street we passed the site where three blocks of old stores, houses, and the old post office building had been razed for new development, thus blotting out another chunk of the old city. To the north the new monolithic City Hall sprawled its dark, concrete, castle-like forms along New Gower Street. Scotia Bank had recently raised its facade of reflector windows along Water Street, and next to it Atlantic Place, built a few years before to be the new, large, downtown galleria, sat mostly empty, like an enormous redbrick warehouse. Though Penny regretted the new architectural intrusions, she saw them as part of an inevitable process, one that would likely be hastened by the recent discovery of offshore oil fields.

There were still a few old downtown pubs, like the Orchid Grill on Water Street, that reminded us both of places we had known in Parkersburg, West Virginia, in the late 1950s. Walking up Pleasant Street, we passed an open doorway in which there stood a lovely blond-haired child of four, backed by a wall of sound coming from a turquoise boom box on the floor behind her. Another door opened, and a brown-haired woman in a white cotton sleeveless shirt and brown skirt tossed a handful of bread scraps onto the sidewalk for the pigeons. Two tipsy, rowdy young men hurled eggs into a horse chestnut tree and then bellowed at their witticism.

Going up an alley shortcut, we passed a man in a suit walking his dog, and a teenage boy sitting on a bench in his leather jacket. "It's a foine evening, a'nt it?" said the boy in his Newfoundland-Irish brogue, his face open and pleasant, his words without a trace of adolescent irony.

"Sher is," replied Penny, with a slight West Virginia drawl apparently untouched by nearly two decades among Newfoundlanders. There seemed an almost geological connection between them, as if that continuous seam of Carboniferous coal that stretched from the Appalachians to Newfoundland, that pressed and heated river of buried and transformed plant life, running for more than a thousand miles beneath mountain ridges and rhododendrons, under wide gulfs and cold waters, through rocky headlands and boggy heath, bound them together.

AT 9 P.M. THE SKY was still light, but clear with the first stars. We decided to drive up to Signal Hill to watch the Perseid meteor shower that had been clouded out the night before. Signal Hill is a remarkable resource for the city: a monolithic, treeless, unscarred hump of ancient rock that guards the north side of the Narrows, the constricted entrance to the city's large, protected harbor. Now a National Historic Park, the only structures on it visible from the city are the 1897 Cabot Tower, built to commemorate the four hundredth anniversary of John Cabot's landing in Newfoundland; some Queen's Battery cannon; and a restored powder magazine. It presents a striking background, more prehistoric than historic, to the changing helter-skelter pattern of the harbor and the city. In the daytime it is a tourist mecca, with daily British military tattoo reenactments (many St. John's citizens still seem to regard themselves as more British than Canadian). At night, however, it is transformed into a social magnet of towering importance to the adolescent population of St. John's. Only Cabot Tower is lit up by arc lights, and the dark parking lot, when we arrived, was a constant turmoil of black car shapes and sweeping headlights as groups of the city's youth arrived, disgorged, dispersed, reassembled, redistributed, and left. It was as though there were some huge, unseen drive-in on the premises that they were constantly searching for.

Looking west over the city at night from the crest of Signal Hill, one beholds a vista that rivals the legendary spread of lights across the Los Angeles basin seen from its surrounding hills. St. John's looks bigger at night than by day, the scope and intensity of its lights, flowing in rivers and rising in luminescent layers, belie its modest urbanity. Yet turn east and one encounters the sudden, heart-stopping blackness of the Atlantic void, the city's glow and influence stopped and contained utterly by the immense bulk of the hill.

From the parking lot there are several trails going out onto the rocks and down the steep, almost vertical face of the ocean side. Penny, Nell, and I chose to go north, away from the tower. With blankets and a flashlight, we set off on a trail ambiguously named Ladies Lookout (which leads, even more intriguingly, to Cuckold's Cove). Almost at once the city lights were extinguished behind a ridge, and what human lights remained—those from the Fort Amherst light station across from the Narrows, a freighter far at sea, the distant flashing beam of Cape Spear, and the blinking lights of planes overhead—all became isolated and islanded in the great sea of stars overhead and the deep, rhythmic blackness beneath it. I wondered: From how many other cities the size of St. John's (or one-tenth its size, for that matter) can one see clearly, less than a mile from downtown, the Milky Way in all its splendor?

We slipped down below the trail and spread out our blankets on a ledge of deep thick grass. After a minute or so we heard the murmurings and exclamations of several teenagers, like murres at night on the dark islands of Witless Bay, coming along the trail. A match flared, and four small, round, red glows from the ends of cigarettes were added to the sparse scattering of lights around us. Then the voices lapsed into silence, too, and we turned our attention to the sky.

Almost immediately one of the largest meteors I have ever seen cut an orange scar several inches long in the northeast sky, trailing sparks behind it like a fireworks rocket. None followed for several minutes, but then their frequency increased to one, two, or more every minute. They were widely dispersed, occupying almost the whole northeast quadrant, from horizon to near zenith. Most were smaller blue-white streaks lasting only a fraction of a second. Some cut straight across, others at down-turned angles. Some seemed to come directly at us in a wobbly, corkscrewing course, and some plummeted straight down and out of sight below the horizon, like lit stones.

At the same time this dramatic display of shooting stars was rivaled by a man-made spectacle: great illuminated airships took off from the St. John's airport behind us, sailing east out over the black sea toward Europe. Some continued out, while others slowly banked to the north, circled, and headed back toward the Canadian mainland. They were so low as they passed over us that we could read the writing on their sides, see the rows of lighted windows along their flanks, imagine the faces pressed against them, peering down.

Other planes appeared out of the east from the sea headed toward St. John's, with great belly-searchlights illuminating a silver road of ocean below them and sweeping the dark flanks of Signal Hill, giving us a momentary sense of being terrorists routed out of hiding. This local air traffic was augmented by higher, more distant lights coming back from Europe, or heading out across the Atlantic, planes that make Newfoundland a turning point on their way to London or Toronto or Chicago. In previous decades all transatlantic flights had to land at Newfoundland's Gander Airport to refuel, but I wondered why they continued to go out of their way to pass over the island. Was it, I asked Penny, some kind of aeronautical race-memory?

"No," she said. "It's because the first and last control tower in North America is in Gander. They still get about ninety planes an hour going over."

It was a very busy sky, and yet the airships moved with such grace and dignified motion, anointed with ceremonial lights and trailing robes of sound, that they seemed perfectly natural and admirable amid the celestial display of lights and darkness, something just as splendid and exotic as the night sky, like illuminated leviathans swimming between the islands of stars. We lay on the blanket for a long while watching the needles of light rain down upon us, sometimes illuminating our silhouettes to one another. It seemed as if we could simply stay there, fold into one another, and go to sleep.

As I have felt the growing strength of my draw to this place, this strange and compelling island, I have recognized the need to try to see things without illusions, without romanticizing them, to see only what is there for what it is. Ah, but that night, on the dark slopes of Signal Hill, lying with Penny and Nell beneath an assault of burning rocks from the black sky, with the lighted voyages, arrivals, departures, and extinctions creating a sense of great time, depth, and distance, and with the invisible deep thrumming of offshore ship engines seeming to come out of the earth itself, I felt as if I were plummeting through overlapping and telescoped layers and stages of connection, toward something still unseen and unfelt.

A Newfoundland
Lexicon

> A babel of loud talk, in the half-comprehensible Newfoundland
> dialect, troubled that dim stifling air.
>
> *The Saturday Evening Post*, September 2, 1922.

An Unfamiliar Tongue: *God Stompers, Goowitty, Gallinippers*, and *Scrunchions*

As a first-time visitor to Newfoundland, I found myself stumbling over the thick accents that still flourish around the island. Like most places with widely dispersed and long-isolated populations, Newfoundland has spawned a wealth of local dialects. In St. John's and in most of the towns on the Avalon Peninsula, local speech exhibits a strong Irish rhythm and lilt. In the more remote and largely English settlements of the outer bays, the accent is less flamboyant; but that, if anything, makes it more foreign to an outside ear. Something is swallowed—some say it is the vowels, some say the consonants. To my ear it seemed to be both, so that often what I heard was a seamless, continuous growl, or else a staccato burst of fricatives, plosives, and glottal stops, devoid of any vocalized sound. In fact, I am still not sure whether I eventually came to understand the accent itself or merely began to decipher it from context. In a stable society of fixed activities, individuals tend to say similar things in similar situations, so that, for instance, if I caught

the word "rollin'" on someone's lips in June, I knew it likely had something to do with the annual approach of spawning caplin on the local
beaches, and the rest of the speaker's words clustered around that nexus
of meaning to form a pattern of sense that I "translated" into English—
much as catching a familiar French word might give me a clue to the
rest of a sentence spoken by a Quebecois.

Even as I began to overcome my initial difficulties with local accents,
however, I found myself perplexed by dozens of unfamiliar words, or
words familiar in themselves but with different meanings. Some were
easy enough to decipher. An *outport*, I quickly learned, was any coastal
settlement that was not St. John's. *The Labrador* designated the coast of
the Labrador peninsula, as in "He was fishing on the Labrador." *Stages,
stores, premises,* and *rooms* denoted certain traditional fishing structures
or areas that sat on the *landwash*, or shore. In fact, though fishing had
been on the decline in most places, its rich vocabulary still pervaded the
language. Inshore fishermen still took their *trap skiffs* and *rodneys* out to
catch herring, turbot, plaice, mackerel, lobsters, and crabs. Cod, on the
other hand, had occupied such a central position for so many generations in the life of Newfoundland communities that it was still almost
universally referred to simply as *fish*. To *jig* for cod was to pull repeat-
edly on a line with a jerky motion, using a weighted fish-shaped lure
known as a *jigger*. *Making fish* was the traditional method of salting and
air-drying cod on *flakes*, or ventilated platforms built of poles, boughs,
or wire mesh. Commercial catches were no longer packed in wooden
puncheons or *cantals*, and modern engines had replaced the old *one-
lungers* or *make-and-breaks*, but one still had to be careful if the wind
picked up, for the sea might get *tumbly*, increasing the danger of striking submerged ledges, bluntly named *sunkers*.

People spoke about cutting *aps* and *var*, which I soon realized were
aspen and fir (Newfoundland *f*'s being often pronounced as *v*'s). More
perplexing were references to *sycamore, juniper*, and *palm*, species of trees
that do not grow in Newfoundland, until I realized that they were the
local names for what I knew as red maple, larch, and yew, respectively.
Myrrh, on the other hand, was the pungent resin from a spruce tree, as was
also *frankincense*—a kind of curious blurring of the gifts of the Magi.

Endemic Newfoundland names for familiar things abounded. *Goo-witty* was the Newfoundland name for sheep laurel. *Bakeapples* were the much-coveted, delicately flavored cloudberries found on the *mishes*, or marshes. Birds I knew at home as terns were here called *stearins*, murres were *turres*, *tooting owls* were American hawk owls, and *sea pigeons* were black guillemots, not to be confused with *sea parrots*, or common puffins.

People wore *garnseys*, or jersey sweaters, over their shirts and thick, woolen *vamps* on their feet. On Sunday they put on their *god stompers*, or good shoes, to walk to church. They put new *canvas*, or linoleum, on their floors; made *mats*, or hooked rugs, to cover them; and swept them with *besoms* made from birch twigs. A whimpering or complaining child was pejoratively called a *sook*. Parents used the phrase "my maid" to address their daughter, though it could refer to any younger woman. On the other hand, a sixteen-year-old store clerk might well refer to a septuagenarian customer as "my son," wishing him a "good evening" at two in the afternoon.

On hot summer afternoons a drink of cold water was hauled out of the well with a *spudgel* (a metal dipper attached to a long pole), but on calm evenings the buzzing and biting of *gallinippers* (mosquitoes) plagued the inhabitants who tried to sit out on their *bridges*, or decks. Outport inhabitants might have *toutons* (bread dough fried in fat) for breakfast, *fish and brewis* (cod and boiled hardtack) or *fresh* (frozen, as opposed to salted) fish with *scrunchions* (bits of fried pork) for *dinner* at noon, or a nice (seal) *flipper stew* for *supper* at five, with *figgy duff* (boiled raisin pudding) for dessert. They might also have a *lunch*, or snack, at any time between the main meals.

Christmas in Newfoundland was traditionally a twelve-day holiday, beginning on Christmas Eve and lasting until what was still called *Old Christmas Day*, or January 6, the date on which Christmas was celebrated until the calendar was changed in 1752. During this time, people still engaged in the ancient practice of *mummering or jannying*. Dressed up in *raggy-doos* and other old clothes, masking their faces and disguising voices, the mummers went around to their neighbors, who invited them in, offered them food and drink, and guessed at their identities.

In any case, there were sure to be plenty of *times* during the holidays, where local *fiddlers* played their accordions or, if instruments were lacking, made *chin music* by humming or singing nonsense syllables. At such times, a man might be forgiven if he indulged in more than his traditional *drop* of *screech* (a dark, locally bottled Newfoundland rum). However, if *buddy's** overindulgence led him to behave recklessly or stupidly, he might be criticized for acting like a *stunned bugger.*

In winter most able-bodied men still hitched their homemade *slides* and *cats* (wooden sleds) to their Skidoos (open snowmobiles of any make, as distinguished from *snowmobiles*, which referred to enclosed snow-track vehicles) and went out along the *tractor paths* across the frozen *mishes* and through the thick tangles of *tuckamore* to the woods to cut long *turns* of spruce or fir or short, stove-length *junks* of birch. While at work they occasionally stopped for a *b'il-up* or a *mug-up* of tea, starting their fires with birch-bark *rinds* or thin *splits* (kindling). They talked about the old days, when they camped overnight in makeshift *tilts*, and horses, oxen, or dogs hauled the sleds. Some of the island settlements never had horses, so loads of wood had to be carried out on small sleds called *man-cats*, hauled by men using *harness pads* made by their wives. Almost no one used animals for work anymore, though in recent years it had become popular, among some of the wealthier residents, to breed the traditional island workhorses under the name of *Newfoundland ponies*, a somewhat pretentious-sounding name to those who remembered them as *Torbay nags.*

I also encountered dozens of Newfoundland words and phrases that were familiar enough in American English but had nonobvious and even misleading meanings when used by islanders. *Slipshod*, for instance, was not an adjective describing careless work, but a nicely descriptive noun indicating an old and comfortable pair of shoes. To go *down* or *down-along* the coast in Newfoundland meant (as it does in much of the Atlantic Northeast) to go northward, that is, downwind with the prevailing southwest breezes. *Newfoundland violets* was still

---

Buddy is not a person's nickname, but a term for a generic individual, the equivalent of "someone" or "a guy," as in "Buddy walks into a bar . . . " This anonymous reference has provided a name for at least one popular folk band, Buddy Wasisname and the Other Fellers.

used as a euphemism for the stink created by drying fish. And then there was the lumberman's term *lazy man's load*, which did not denote a light or small load of wood, as one might surmise, but a foolishly heavy one, that is, an attempt to carry more than one should so as to make fewer trips.

Finally, there were many Newfoundland names that struck me at first as purely quaint or humorous, but that I came to learn were actually derived from factual description. A good illustration is *tickle-ass*, or *tickle-ace*, the common Newfoundland name for the black-legged kittiwake. To fully understand the import of this name, one has to know that the bird tends to situate its nests on cliffs enclosing a narrow passage of water, known as a *tickle*, which it is an expert, or "ace," at navigating.

Initially, this cornucopia of strange accents, unusual words, odd usages, rich vocabulary, and colorful and figurative expressions that I encountered gave an exotic flavor to local speech, as if a familiar dish were suddenly served with a rich and varied blend of unfamiliar spices. But as I gradually became accustomed to it and started to investigate its nature, I began to understand that Newfoundland's linguistic heritage reveals a great deal about the island's unique history, character, and worldview.

ORIGINS AND IMPORTS: *Curwibbles, Dumbledores, Roarations,* and *Mae Wests*

The distinctive elements of speech in contemporary Newfoundland English are survivors of a great river of branched and overlapping linguistic waters, fed from many streams, that once flooded the island's shores. Today the tide of local speech is ebbing as Newfoundland and its people have become less isolated from the outside world, but it still saturates the native tongue.

Many local words, phrases, usages, and grammar come from the West Country English of Dorset, Devon, and Cornwall and the Irish dialect of Waterford, brought over from the home country of its early settlers in the late eighteenth and early nineteenth centuries. Some localisms were borrowed from colonial New England and mainland Canada. There are smatterings of Celtic and distorted survivors of

French that are remnants of the long history of Gallic military occupation and fishing along Newfoundland's shores.* There are a few examples of mangled Latin and even more peculiar Newfoundland Latinizations of Anglo-Saxon words. But the great preponderance of terms and constructs that have characterized Newfoundland English, and have rendered it worthy of that distinct linguistic designation, evolved on the island itself, born of four centuries of intense and mortal commerce of its people with land and sea.

The indispensable source and repository of the thousands of words, usages, and meanings endemic to the island is that remarkable work of Newfoundland scholarship, the *Dictionary of Newfoundland English*, edited by G. M. Story, W. J. Kirwin, and J.D.A. Widdowson and first published in 1982. Even a cursory browsing of its more than six hundred pages will reveal many traditional Newfoundland terms and phrases that are, to a stranger's ear, redolent of the earthiness and love of sound we associate with older, rural oral cultures. Irishisms such as *curwibble, flaboolach, glawvawn, kawnya-vawnya, loodle-daddle, noody-nawdy, shabeen, sleveen,* and *pampooty* dance playfully across the palate. Old English words like *carbuckling, calibogus, chuckle-de-muck, cocksiddling, dumbledore, flobber, jillicking, mollyfodge, nuddicks, nuzzletripes, pisswigs, scurrifungeing, snocking, twacks,* and *tallywhacking* seem to belong more to Middle Earth or Harry Potter's School for Wizards than to any actual place, though in fact the lexicons of Newfoundland, J.R.R. Tolkien, and J. K. Rowling all draw heavily on English's Anglo-Saxon heritage.

Faux Latinizations, or the spontaneous yoking of Anglo-Saxon words to Latinate forms, occur in such terms as *roaration* (a great noise), *scrugility* (careful scrutiny), *confloption* (confusion), and *fishocracy* (the mercantile class in St. John's). And no doubt the French must wince at the contemporary renderings of their few surviving contributions to the language of the island: *alley-coosh* (go to bed), *non-plush* (surprise), *saw-*

---

*Sometimes an English phrase becomes so transformed that it is assumed to have a foreign origin. Such is the case for "Good morning, valentine," a greeting that was originally given on St. Valentine's Day in the hope of receiving a kiss or a gift. In time the phrase mutated into such forms as *marnen voleten, mar fallaten, marfoton,* and *mol fol,* which are often mistaken for original "Celtic" phrases. Eventually even its original meaning was forgotten and it came to be used when a trick was played on someone on April 1, "*Mar fauten!*" ("April Fool!").

boo (i.e., *sabot*, a big, clumsy shoe or boot), *barrysway* (*barachois*, a shallow river estuary), and my favorite example, *Bay d'Espoir*—from *Baie d'Espoir*, or "Cape of Hope"—which, in local pronunciation, is wonderfully transformed into "Bay Despair."

In addition to its rich lexical heritage, part of the distinctive texture of Newfoundland English comes from a grammar that is reminiscent of the speech of characters in the novels of Thomas Hardy, which are set in "Wessex," the author's name for the West Country from which many early Newfoundlanders emigrated. In Newfoundland, for instance, inanimate objects commonly acquire male or female genders. The related pronouns are always used in the nominative case, though the genders seem rather arbitrary and often change within the same sentence, as in "*He* was reputed to be a good boat, but I didn't care much for *she*." Virtually all uses of present-tense verbs are given the third-person singular form ("I plans to go up to the hall Saturday night. Is you thinking of coming along?"), except, occasionally, for the third-person singular itself, as in "Tell John to see me when he come home." And if John is late getting home from the hall, he might get a phone call from his wife demanding, "Where's ya *to?*"

A number of Newfoundland bird names were also brought over from England by early settlers and then applied to species found here. *Linnet*, for instance, was the name given to the purple finch, *skylark* to the water pipit, and *nightingale*, quite understandably, to that mastersinger, the hermit thrush. (Americans have done this as well, for instance, in having named our native red-breasted thrush after the English *robin*.)

There is at least one example of a Newfoundland bird name where the bird itself has not survived, although the name has. The great auk was a large, flightless black-and-white alcid that once bred in enormous numbers on the Funks, a small rocky island off the Northeast Coast of Newfoundland. They were commonly known as *penwins*, or penguins, by early explorers and fishermen. Heedlessly slaughtered for food and eggs in the nineteenth century, great auks became extinct in 1843, coincidentally just about the time that the continent of Antarctica was discovered; thus they tacitly bequeathed their name to the also-flightless avian inhabitants of that southern landmass, birds to which they bore a superficial resemblance, though only a distant taxonomic relation.

Several phrases from the States made their way into the Newfoundland vocabulary, largely because of the great numbers of American servicemen stationed at military bases around the island during World War II. The *Dictionary of Newfoundland and Labrador*, for instance, states that *Jiggs's dinner*, the traditional Newfoundland meal of salt beef boiled with root vegetables, was given its name by American soldiers "who noticed the similarity between the boiled dinner served there and the favorite dinner of Jiggs, a character in the American comic strip series 'Bringing Up Father.'" Another example is the American-influenced evolution of sexual imagery found in "The Paps," the Newfoundland name for a mammary-shaped pair of steeply rising islands in Placentia Sound. When the harbor there was transformed into the Argentia U.S. Naval Base during World War II, American troops rechristened these hills "Mae West" in honor of the buxom movie star who also gave her name to the U. S. Navy's standard-issue life jacket.

CHARACTER AND CULTURE: *Strangers, Livyers, Wesleyan Fools*, and *Irish Toothaches*

The Newfoundland lexicon, then, is a distinctive melting pot in which one can taste different inherited and borrowed ingredients. But the bond between self-identity and native ground, always a vital part of Newfoundland culture, is also richly reflected in its vocabulary. A man might have lived in Squid Tickle most of his life, for instance, but he is still said to *belong* to Flat Island if he was born there. A visitor or tourist is almost invariably treated with hospitality, though still referred to as a *stranger* (which, for some reason, is also the name for a duck). Even if a stranger takes up residence in a village, he is a *CFA*, or *come from away*. Someday he might attain the status of a *livyer*, or permanent resident, but he will never *belong*. A half century after Confederation, islanders still talk of *going to Canada* when they travel to their country's mainland, or perhaps they will say they have relatives in the *Boston States*, a term for the United States that developed during the Depression when so many Newfoundlanders immigrated to Boston to find work.

Certain aspects of the traditional Newfoundland culture and character are also embedded in its lexicon. The historical importance of courting rituals, for instance, is illustrated in the term *dumb cake*, a pastry "eaten in silence by unmarried women wishing for a vision of future husbands." The situation of a widow in rural society is reflected in the term *jigging veil*, a humorous reference to the fact that, in years past, wearing a widow's veil was regarded as a means of advertising that one was available for remarriage, thus "jigging" for a husband. And something of the Newfoundlander's ability to make nice ethical distinctions is conveyed in the phrase *second plunder*, which was an approved, or at least a tolerated, form of theft in which one stole goods from a person who had previously stolen them from someone else.

In the past, certain staple household items inspired unusually rich sublexicons. The tea kettle, for instance, perhaps because of its role in the ubiquitous *b'il-up*, or tea break, with or without food, was variously known as *hot-arse*, *hurry-up*, *bibby*, *piper*, *quick*, *smut*, and *slut*.* These kettle variants were traditionally heated on a fire made of *keeps-a-goin's*, or small pieces of kindling that burned hotly, which in turn were lit by *wait-a-minutes*, or sulphur-tipped matches, the local name that one F. Hines of Change Islands explained (with characteristic Newfoundland mingling of verb tenses) as follows: "'Twas hardwood matches at that time, we used to call 'em hardwood wait-a-minutes, 'cause you'd have to scrape 'em on an ass o' your pants, an' he fizz, and fizz, an' by an' by he burn up that brimstone he come to a flame."

Some domestic items whose names seem patently made-up or whimsically descriptive turn out to have concrete historical origins. The Buzaglo, for example, the name for an early wood stove used in Newfoundland, sounds like the inspiration of some marketing department. In fact, it was named after its manufacturer, one Abraham Buzaglo, a versatile Englishman who also published *A Treatise on the Gout* in 1778.

The openness with which most Newfoundlanders treat sexual and bodily functions is reflected in a plethora of vivid words and imagery, often drawn from the natural world. The word *nature* itself, in fact, is often used to designate sexual drive ("It was his nature caused him to run off with that woman"). Male members were traditionally known as

---

*A stranger might have raised his eyes at hearing an outport woman remind her husband to "be sure to take yer slut aboard with ya."

buds, while a woman's pubic hair was known as *king hair*. *Women-fish*, a term I heard in a small outport in Bonavista Bay, is used to refer to female genitals, as in "If we don't get a food fishery this year, won't be any fish around here but *women-fish!*" Conversely, anatomical terms were often applied to natural objects. *Horsefarts*, *crinkly dicks*, *horny whores*, and *whore's eggs* are still common names for puffballs, rock gunnels, sculpins, and sea urchins, respectively.

Arse-bags referred to capacious underclothes, while *bungalows* were clothes worn during pregnancy. *Piss-quicks* are cut-off long rubber boots that you can put on quickly to make a run to the outhouse. Several ponds I encountered are locally known as *piss-a-mare* ponds, after small waterfalls that issue in a fine spray into the water, "exactly like a mare pissing," as an older man once pointed out to me.

A casual or even amused attitude toward unsanctioned sex is suggested in a number of terms referring to fornication. Thus, one might *go on a randy*, or *gulching* in sheltered ravines, *grassing* in a meadow, or *mollyfostering* in the hay. The illegitimate issue that might result from such activities was a *merry-be-got*, a *moonlight child*, or a *moss child*.

And then there is a rather lengthy list of colorful terms for, well, nasal mucus. These include *boo-bugger*, *conkerbill*, and *lamb's legs*. One might be tempted to suspect that Newfoundlanders have an inordinate obsession with this particular substance, but it seems more likely that this snotty lexicon is a product of the Newfoundlanders' environment itself, where a need was felt to vary the references to a very common phenomenon familiar to anyone who has spent much time on the deck of a boat in winter.

Like the inhabitants of most rural subsistence cultures, Newfoundlanders have the capacity for complex emotions toward species on which they depend for survival, a trait that can seem "hypocritical" to societies that have antiseptically removed themselves from the sources of their sustenance. Several bird names, for instance, convey a mixture of pragmatism and affection. One such is *nunchie*, a local name for the dovekie, a small, plump alcid barely eight inches in length. The name, according to ornithologist Bill Montevecchi, is "an allusion to its small size, just big enough for a nunch or lunch."

Given that Newfoundlanders' survival has depended for so long on a knowledge of natural cycles, it is not surprising to find a strong link between time and seasonal events in the Newfoundland vocabulary. Just as *fish* has always referred to cod, *the season* was understood to mean the principal time for catching cod, namely, from spring to early autumn. March was *hungry-month*, the time when harbors were still locked in ice, root cellars and other staples were getting low, and supply schooners had not yet arrived. *Credit time*, or *cropping time*, was the period in spring when fishermen obtained gear and other provisions on credit from the local merchant.

Other traditional terms for seasons were commonly linked to physical activities associated with them. *Rinding time* was early spring, when the sap began to run in the trees, making it easier to strip the large sections of bark, or rind, that were used for covering drying fish. *Dipping time* referred not to sheep dipping, but to the period in late March and early April when young harp seals, or *dippers*, would take to the water. Even references to specific holidays were often activity-related, as in *snap-apple night*, for Halloween, or *bonfire night* (November 5), when *yaffles* (armloads) of *blasty-boughs* (dry fir branches) are still gathered for the celebratory conflagrations.

There are dozens of compound phrases linking the four seasons to specific objects. *Spring var* is a term still occasionally used to describe fir that is cut in spring, left to dry over the summer, and then cut up and hauled out of the woods the following winter. A *summer road* is a road cut into the woods that can be used for cutting year-round, as opposed to most wood roads, which are accessible only in winter, when the marshes are frozen. *Fall fish* described large, fat cod caught in the autumn with jiggers. And *winter's issue* referred to the demeaning process whereby a fisherman who did not earn enough during the fishing season to pay off his previous debts was forced to ask the merchant to issue additional goods on credit to see his family through the winter.

Chronic poverty and the necessity of government welfare, or "the disgrace of the dole," were two constants of Newfoundland life that found expression in language both surprisingly direct and wittily evasive. During the Depression years, most men could afford only tight, ill-fitting *unemployment boots*. Many a day might see only *bare-legged tea* (without food) offered, or perhaps supplemented with *dole bread*, made from coarse, unrefined flour.

The old life was difficult, but the constant change in tasks throughout the year provided a relief from tedium, a change that found expression in the lovely phrase *newfoundland spell*. Moreover, the Newfoundlanders' fatalism and sense of independence helped them face hardships without bitterness, and often with ironic humor. Early, locally built vessels on the island, for instance, were given the ominous appellation of *newfoundland coffins*. *Going in collar* meant signing up for a fishing or sealing voyage (a blunt self-identification with draft animals being put in harness), and *ballroom* was used to refer to the cramped crew's quarters on a sealer.

In many ways the economic hardships in most traditional outports created a genuinely democratic culture, where most had little, what there was shared, and community survival depended on a highly organized system of cooperative labor and communal resources. But societal distinctions seem to be one of the most entrenched of human impulses, and Newfoundland was not exempt from them. As St. John's slowly emerged as the political, economic, and cultural hub of the island, the fundamental dichotomy between the city's urban society and every place outside it resulted in a whole raft of ethnic and cultural slurs. The citizens of St. John's labeled the uncouth inhabitants of the outports *baymen*, *bay-wops*, and *bay-noddies*. In turn, outport sailors on the St. John's wharves derisively referred to the bearded townies as *chin-whiskers*.

Fish merchants lent their name to a variety of descriptive, and often derogatory, phrases: *merchant brig*, *merchant party*, *merchant prince*, *merchant scrip*, and *merchant talk*—this last described as "attempts to explain why the price of fish is low." Distrust and resentment of the St. John's merchant princes, however, did not prevent linguistic xenophobia from growing between the outports as well. For a son to *marry too far*, or to wed a girl from a distant community, was frowned upon: "You don't want to marry too far; you can't trust them."

Religious affiliations also provided a fertile ground for original vocabulary, particularly in St. John's, where the growing political rivalry between Anglicans and Catholics in the nineteenth century often turned violent. As in the States, Irish Catholics were called *micks* by the Protestants; to the Catholics all Protestants were *blacks*. Among

Roman Catholics, a *horse-protestant* was one who was lax about going to church, whereas, among Anglicans, to say that a woman had the *irish toothache* was a euphemism for describing one who had gotten herself pregnant. On the other hand, all human beings were ecumenically distinguished from animals (and Beothuk Indians) as *christians*, as in "When I was going to the seal fishery 'twas dogs then; you were not christians, but all dogs."

Religious slang also flourished in the smaller outports, where three or four different denominations might exist, each with its own parochial school system. For some reason Methodists, or United Church members, were especially popular targets. The more sedate Anglicans looked down upon the Methodists as *wesleyan fools* for their evangelical enthusiasm, or *glory-fits*, while Catholics called them *swaddlers*, the Irish term for hypocrites. There was *wesleyan bread*, or raisin bread, so called "because the raisins, like the Wesleyans, are few and far between;" *methodist feet*, said of someone who couldn't dance properly (since the Methodists forbade dancing); a *methodist hatchet*, which was a two-edged (i.e., two-faced) axe; and the *wesleyan kettle* (so called because, as one source has it, "like the old Wesleyan churchmen [it] heats up quickly and cools off rather quickly").

Most of these linguistic reflections of differences in social position and religious affiliation belong to a time long gone, but the Newfoundlander's talent for original and blunt expression persists, particularly in response to political obfuscation. After the cod moratorium in 1992, the government instituted a form of compensation payments to fishing families under the acronym TAGS. When I asked a local fisherman what it stood for, he said, "They calls it 'The Atlantic Groundfish Strategy,' but we calls it *slow starvation*."

ON THE ICE: *Ballicatters, Bedlamers, Skinnywhoppers,* and *Flipsying the Clampers*

One of the enduring memories of my fourth-grade geography class is Miss Frost solemnly informing us that "Eskimos have twenty-five different words for snow." This factoid was intended to illustrate the point that indigenous cultures (as opposed to our own) often have extensive vocabularies for environmental factors essential for survival. By this measure, Newfoundland's ice lexicon makes a strong claim for indigenousness. There are over fifty terms alone used to describe different types of ice. These include *ballicatters*, a fringe of ice that clings to a vessel or to the shore; *banquese*, spring ice drifting along the Labrador coast; *knot ice*, hard, densely packed ice; *glitter*, a thin sheet of ice formed on objects by freezing rain; *northern slob*, a heavy, slushy, dense mass of ice fragments, snow, and water; and *harp ice*, the ice on which the harp seals whelp—not to mention *jam ice, lolly ice, quarry ice, rot hole, rubber ice, sina* (from the Inuit *sinaa*, edge of ice), and *sish*.

Ice could be *buckly, black, taut, tished, loose, slatchy, slob, way,* and *young.* It could *spawn, calve,* and have a *weather edge.* Work on the ice was made more difficult or dangerous by certain kinds of snow, such as *dead snow*, which is loose and has no firm surface, and *devil's feathers*, which is so deep it hinders movement.

In addition there are several words related to weather conditions on the ice (e.g., *glim*, the shimmer of light over a distant ice field, or *barber*, a cold mist), and there is a whole sub-vocabulary of words related to icebergs, including *islands of ice* (the preferred term of many older Newfoundlanders for icebergs), *rollers* and *growlers* (unstable icebergs, liable to capsize with "a growling sound"), *pinnacles* (large pieces of ice projecting from an iceberg), and *bergy bits*, or smaller pieces of ice broken off a larger iceberg. There are also several dozen compound words and phrases derived from ice, including *ice-work* (the seal hunt itself), *ice-candle* (icicle), *ice-claw* (the grapnel used to secure a vessel to the ice), and *ice-saw.** And finally, if you were a boy not yet old enough to go to the ice for seals, you could still develop your ice legs by *flipsying the tally-pans, copying the clumpers,* or *gallygolting on the tabbies,* that is, jumping from one ice floe to another in the harbor, a game still practiced by young people in the outports.

As several of these examples indicate, the extensive vocabulary for ice in the Newfoundland lexicon is due to the fact that it was the place

---

*This last is the source of one locally told "Newfie joke," in which a man sees buddy sweating away as he cuts a channel through the frozen harbor with his ice saw. "Some hard work, eh?" says the man. "Shut your mouth!" says buddy, "but you ought to see the feller under the ice!"

where the traditional Newfoundland seal hunt took place. Sealing, or *swiling*, was prosecuted widely in Newfoundland from about 1800 to the 1930s, during which time it was second only to fishing in economic importance. The days of the great *wooden walls*, or oak-hulled sealing ships, are long gone, but each March a few hundred Newfoundlanders still go to *The Front*, the leading edge of a massive river of Arctic pack ice that flows down from Greenland along the Northeast Coast of Newfoundland each winter, forming the main breeding ground for commercial seal species. There they still search for *harps* and *hoods* (harp seals and hooded seals) and, when they find the main herds, are said to be *in the fat*.

Judge Prowse, in his magisterial *History of Newfoundland* (1895), felt it incumbent on him to explain to his genteel St. John's readership that "Bloody decks to en!" was "a customary toast of success to the seal fishery, and homicide was not intended." But there was also an almost lyrical quality in some of the terminology as well. Sealers spoke of looking for the *gardens*, or the smooth ice that whelping seals preferred to give birth, or spotting an *Archangel*, a seal "somewhat smaller than the hooded seal." The terms for tools and equipment of the sealing trade were often both colorful and specific; crew members wore *skinnywoppers*, or sealskin boots, which were studded with different kinds of nails, including *sparables*, *chisels*, and *frosters*. Vessels were made fast to the ice with ice anchors known as *devil's claws*. Even religious beliefs were a factor in sealing voyages, giving rise to the term *sunday man* for one who refused to kill seals on the Sabbath.

For commercial reasons, numerous terms developed to distinguish different species, ages, conditions, and variants of seals. The types of harp seals *(Phoca groenlandica)*, always the primary target of the seal hunt, produced a particularly rich vocabulary, including *beater, bedlamer, bitch harp, bleater, cat, dark angel, hair-seal, half-moon seal, heart-seal, laddio, paddler, quinter, ragged-jacket, rusty, saddle-dog, screecher, seal cat, sheeter, smallagen, smutty-nose, turncoat, turning harp, two-yeared bedlamer, voyage seal, white-coat,* and *young fat*.

Names for seals were often appropriated to describe human types. A *bedlamer,* for instance, was a second-year harp seal, and a *bedlamer boy* was an adolescent approaching adulthood. A *beater,* from an old Irish word meaning "a bold, aggressive individual," was a young seal that had just learned to swim and thus was fearless of the sea. Applied to a woman, however, it could suggest one whose behavior was too bold or loose. And *turncoat*, the name for a harp seal whose fur was beginning to take on the darker colors of an adult, could also be used to describe an individual who switched religious affiliations.

FISH: *White-Noses, Poor Jacks, Ghost Fish, and Devil's Thumb-Prints*

Extensive as the vocabulary for ice and sealing was, it was dwarfed by the vast lexicon spawned by the central activity of most Newfoundlanders during their long history, namely, fishing. Consider: the *Dictionary of Newfoundland English* lists over 150 endemic words and phrases related to fish and the fishery, not including all the variants and compound words made from them, which more than double that number. These range alphabetically from *adventure*, an early word used to describe a commercial fishing enterprise, to *youngster*, a term used during the migratory fishery to designate an inexperienced man brought out from England to Newfoundland. (After his first winter, the *youngster* became a *white-nose*, a reference to the case of rhinal frostbite a novice fisherman was likely to experience.)

Most of these fishery terms are names for the fish themselves. *Protestants* were salt herring. Caplin were called *tea-fish*, from the belief that eating them made one sleepy, and so they were not served at the midday meal, but later at teatime. *Rubbish* was the term for all fish species except cod and salmon.

Fish, as has been mentioned, was the universal term for the North Atlantic cod *(Gadus morhua)*. Nonetheless, over fifty words and phrases were applied to this species alone. Some of these designated different local populations, ages, or sizes of cod, but most evolved to distinguish the grades, processing, condition, and quality of the commercial product, a process that was codified in the official categories of the Newfoundland Fisheries Board. This is not surprising, given that cod was a product of global significance, a staple of commerce in the Western Hemisphere for over four hundred years.

Poor jack, or *poor john fish*, an inferior form of Newfoundland salt cod, was known to Shakespeare. In *The Tempest*, Trunculo, on first seeing the man-monster Caliban, describes him thus:

> What have we here? a man or a fish? dead or alive? A fish; he smells like a fish: a very ancient and fishlike smell; a kind of not-of-the-newest Poor John. (3.2.23–26)

Dried cod also figured early on in the West Indian slave trade, where *bim*, the lowest grade of dried cod, often sunburnt and slimy, was shipped to Barbados. *Dun fish* was only slightly better. *Madeira fish*, a better but still inferior grade, was generally sold to the Spanish and Portuguese markets. *Thirds* were "a little worse than Madeira an' a little better than West Indee." *Italian fish* was a superior grade prepared for export to the Mediterranean market, though not as good as *choice italian*, the finest grade of all: firm, dry, with no discoloration. In between there were dozens of intermediate and overlapping grades, such as *puerto rico, jersey,* and *spanish fish.*

Fish could be *leggy, light, bulk* or *cull, damp, glutted* or *green, half-saved, heavy, inshore* and *offshore, pink, pipsi, round, salt, fresh salt,* and *snig.* There were designations for variants, unusual characteristics, and deformities, for example, *tallyfish* (a cod with marks on its side resembling the *tallies,* or groups of slanted, crossed lines used to count fish, said to auger a good catch), haddock with *devil's thumb-prints* (black marks said to be left when the devil grabbed the fish, but let it get away), and *seal-head cod* (a fish with a deformed head*).

In addition there was *grogfish,* the first catch of cod on the Labrador, so called because the crew member who first took these fish out of the hold in St. John's at the end of the season was traditionally required to buy a round of grog for the crew. At the other end of the season there was *lady day fish,* not a tribute to Billie Holiday but the term for cod caught on August 15, the Feast of the Assumption of the Virgin Mary,

---

*I was once told that the residents of Flat Island in Bonavista Bay believed that a *seal-head,* or *swile-head,* fish left on a wharf for some time was *Joner,* that is, a Jonah, or source of bad luck.

when many Irish Catholics gave up fishing for the rest of the summer. *Floater fish* were not buoyant cod but fish caught by summer fishermen in Labrador who stayed on their boats and were thus called *floaters*. A *hungry boat* was one with no fish. *Ghostfish* were those caught by lost fishing gear (*ghost-nets*) that sank to the bottom, a situation that has become a major threat to fish stocks today, especially with the advent of nonbiodegradable synthetic nets. And finally, even fishing did not escape the Newfoundland transmogrification of common Latin phrases. *All quall*, a term used to designate the price offered for an unsorted batch of cod, is said to derive from the Latin phrase *tallis quallis*, "such as it is."

The Theater of Words

In this highly subjective and haphazard linguistic survey, many of the words and usages I have mentioned are no longer in common use, and many others are quickly dying out with the older speakers who learned them in the relatively isolated setting of pre-Confederation Newfoundland. Still, a significant portion of the Newfoundland lexicon has survived into the twenty-first century, helping the island to retain its distinctive character. As much as old fishing stages, ubiquitous accordion music, or the sight of squid drying on a clothes line, it is the persistence in everyday speech of such words and phrases as *fish and brewis*, *scrunchions, figgy duff, pease pudding, goowitty, bakeapples, gallinippers, ballicatters, turres, tickle-asses, mummering, b'il-ups, whore's eggs, devil claws, growlers, bergy bits, white-coats, y's b'y, you got that right my son, plenty o' time b'y*, and *you're as welcome as the flowers of May* that not only delight the visitor but also let him know he has unmistakably *come from away* and has arrived *someplace else*.

Still, the most enduring and distinctive elements of Newfoundland speech may be something less easy to define, something that goes beyond lexicon and grammar. In this book I have made some attempt to reproduce the *music* of the Newfoundland dialect—its accent and cadences, rhythms and sounds—that is so evident to the ear. This is clearly a legacy of the island's long oral tradition, where, among other things, such elements of verbal poetry served as an aid to memorization.

Moreover, there is a remarkable *theatricality* and physicality to local speech, especially in the outports, that is hard to suggest in words. It consists in an instinct for dramatization, a penchant for playful, self-aware exaggeration, and a histrionic use of voice and gestures, so that stories, opinions, or even news of the day are often delivered with finger-poking, arm-grabbing, and shoulder-embracing emphasis. In Newfoundland body and speech tend to combine, much as they did in the singing of sheet-hauling shanties on the old banker schooners. Speech is theater here, and the effect is to re-create to some degree the magic of stage illusion. Whatever is being told or sung or acted out feels as if it were happening in the moment. Past and present blend in the animated telling and vivid use of language. At its deepest level, Newfoundland speech seems to spring from a belief in both speaker and listener that nothing is ever really lost if there are still those who will speak it to life again.

ROADSIDE
ATTRACTIONS

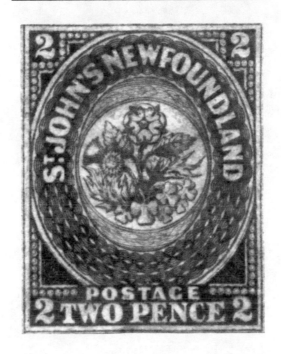

Moose Signs

Though moose were introduced to Newfoundland from the mainland only a little over a hundred years ago, they flourished and proliferated rapidly in a hospitable environment with an almost total lack of natural predators.* The fall moose hunt has become an entrenched part of Newfoundland culture, a rite of passage for every young man (and now a few women as well), enshrined in one of the island's more popular folk songs, "Got to Get Me Moose, B'y!"

Despite the large annual moose hunt, the estimated number of moose on the island ranges from 120,000 to 140,000, or about one moose for every five residents. They are frequently seen feeding beside highways or strolling along the streets of the smaller outports. The summer of my first visit to Newfoundland, a male adult appeared in the parking lot of Churchill Square, a small shopping center on the outskirts of St. John's. He stepped on the entrance mat to the Dominion Supermarket, and when the automatic door opened, he pushed his great rack through the opening, looked around for a moment, and—apparently not seeing anything on sale that interested him—withdrew and headed in the direction of Pippy Park.

One of the favorite places for viewing (as opposed to hunting) moose has been the Trans-Canada Highway, especially along the stretch near Come-By-Chance on either side of the narrow isthmus connecting the

---

*Except for black bears, which will take moose calves. The last Newfoundland wolf was killed in 1927. For years its stuffed body was on display in the Newfoundland Museum in St. John's.

Avalon Peninsula to the rest of the island. Driving this stretch, I often saw them quietly browsing in their cow-contented way among the many marshes and shallow ponds that border the highway there. Perhaps they had learned that the strip of land bordering the highway was, in effect, a hunting-free zone.

Unfortunately, this stretch of the TCH is also one of the foggiest on the island, and the number of moose-car accidents, often resulting in fatalities on both sides, has been substantial, one year reaching over eight hundred. The number of moose-related accidents has been augmented by tourists stopping to watch and photograph these placid, impressive creatures, sometimes without even pulling over onto the shoulder. The result has too often been that the tourists or their cars have been plowed into by oncoming vehicles in the fog.

To address this serious problem, in the late 1980s the Newfoundland Department of Highways implemented a "moose sign" program. This consisted of life-size sheet-metal silhouettes of moose, sometimes outlined in reflective ribbon-tape, that were set up beside the highway a short distance before known moose-watching locations—a semiotic warning system designed to alert drivers that moose, and moose watchers, might be on the highway ahead.

The presence of the moose signs apparently cut down on the number of accidents at moose-crossing and moose-watching sites, but it also had an unexpected and unfortunate side effect. It seems that drivers found the signs *themselves* interesting, and worthy of a slowdown or even a stop for photographing. The result was a rash of new accidents at the moose sign locations.

Sent back to the drawing board by this new problem, the Highway Department came up with a novel solution. Instead of removing the moose signs and replacing them with ordinary lettered warning signs, they placed signs about a half mile or so before the moose silhouettes that read,

CAUTION: MOOSE SIGNS AHEAD

In the years since these new signs have been implemented, the number of moose-vehicle, vehicle-vehicle, vehicle-pedestrians-watching-moose, or vehicle-pedestrians-watching-moose-signs accidents has greatly decreased along the Trans-Canada. But then, so has the number of moose sightings. Whether the moose population along the highway has been decimated by vehicles, or whether the animals have decided that it is better to take their chances in country with the hunters, is a question to which no definite answer has yet been given.

Fogo Island 1988:
The End of the World

Years ago, when I first came to Newfoundland, I spent a few days in the village of Fogo Harbour on the northwest end of Fogo Island. Fogo is Newfoundland's largest offshore island—an island off an island—and off Fogo Harbour are other islands and rocks—Burns Island, Lighthouse Island, Waterman's Ledge, Little Fogo Islands, Barracks, etc.—that seem to recede into the invisible distance, so that if one could stand on the mainland and see forever, Newfoundland and Fogo and its subsequent offshore islands would appear as a diminishing series of skipping stones going off into infinity.

The car ferry to Fogo Island, the *MV Beaumont Hamel*, ran five times a day each way during the summer. The ferry left the mainland from Farewell, an invented designation on the map just beyond Port Albert, consisting of a newly graded, raw gravel road, a docking wharf, and a take-out food stand (plus signs predicting a restaurant to come).

When the ferry from Fogo pulled into Farewell, the back section of its hull, dark blue in color, raised up to reveal a gangplank that extended to admit the cars. The impression was that of a great blue and white whale opening its jaws to receive us.

These local island transportation ferries were not, by and large, designed to make a very pleasant trip. For one thing, they didn't encourage you to stay outside. There were no seats on the deck of the *Beaumont Hamel*, and you couldn't get to the forward part of the deck, so that you were relegated to the rear section where most of the forward view was blocked and you were surrounded by the noise of the motors and the smell of the exhausts. Moreover, the crossing to Fogo is not particularly scenic, just a series of low rocky islands with a few birds on them. In fact the whole design of this boat seemed geared toward persuading me to go inside to the lounge, where most passengers were sitting and watching *Magnum, P.I.*, on the onboard TV, its black-and-white screen filled with diagonal snow and ghostly images that were barely visible.

When the ferry docked at the Stag Harbour terminal, I drove to Seldom-Come-By, one of a dozen or so settlements on the island, to take a look at the fish-processing plant. Seldom-Come-By is one of several examples of Newfoundland place names that appear to mean exactly the opposite of their original designation. Seldom (as it is usually shortened to now) is the last port coming from the north before "the Straight Shore," a twenty-mile stretch of coastline with no sizable harbor available to boats. Thus, it was said, a sailing vessel "would seldom come by without putting in" if there was a storm brewing.

The fish plant at Seldom is part of the Fogo Island Shipbuilding and Producers Cooperative Society, formed in 1967. The Fogo Coop was the first local fishing cooperative in Newfoundland, breaking with the centuries-old tradition of merchant-owned and -controlled fisheries. So successful was the cooperative that a documentary of its formation, made by the Memorial University's Institute of Social and Economic Research in St. John's, has been used worldwide as a blueprint for community self-discovery and organization in developing countries.

But the recent drastic decline in Newfoundland fish stocks had affected Fogo as well and the fish plant was not very busy when I arrived. Most of the boats, I guessed, didn't come in till later. One trawler was unloading its catch of cod with a small crane, dumping the fish into large plastic fish bins on the wharf, which were then carted by forklifts into the plant itself. The plant, visible through the open-sided sheds, showed lines of long, empty, wooden filleting tables constantly washed down by hose sprays. At the rear of the plant three men were unloading gutted cod from the back of a pickup truck onto a wide plank set up on sawhorses, where one of the men was salting them down with fish salt taken from a large plastic bucket. From there they would be taken into the plant, washed, and shed-dried.

The man salting the fish was from Tilting, the only Irish Catholic outport on Fogo, at the east end of the island. He told me they had about three dozen boats go out of here; four or five were long-liners over thirty-five feet, then the twenty-one-footers, which were fiberglass skiffs with outboards. Trap fishing, he said, was a failure in Tilting this summer, but the rest of the island was doing pretty good, though not as good as in past years. Inshore fishing, it seemed, was a very local situation, and varied tremendously from one harbor to another.

I caught most of what the men said when they talked directly to me, but when they began talking among themselves I was generally lost. This seemed to be a common trait among outport people, adapting their dialect somewhat to the person being spoken to, and then reverting to their native dialect among themselves. I wondered if this practice developed from the early Newfoundland settlers' necessary, though infrequent, intercourse with British officials.

The drive up the center of the island was rather unremarkable, except for the general absence of trees, and the dwarfed height (four to ten feet) of the few patches of fir that clung to the rocky, wind-and-salt-scoured hills here.

The entrance into Fogo Harbour, the largest of the island communities (population 1,105) is dramatic. The road rises steadily to a crest about two miles before the town, from which one sees the town spread out around its deep harbor. To the west is the sweeping headland of volcanic rock known as Brimstone Head, which, according to the promotional brochure I picked up on the ferry, "the Flat Earth Society has claimed to be one of the four corners of the world."

I descended the hill and turned west at the harbor, heading onto the main street of the town. It contained traditional structures similar to those found in dozens of other mid-sized outports along Newfoundland's Northeast Coast: the Anglican Church, Our Lady of the Snows R.C., Seaside Retired Citizens Club, the plain and functional white municipal building, clumps of old and frequently abandoned fish stages, and the Fisherman's Protective Society Lodge—this last a massive whitewashed clapboarded structure on wooden posts, abandoned and looming on the hillside above the town. These structures sat cheek by jowl with some of the more recent attempts at commercial development, all housed in variations on that curiously bland style of contemporary Newfoundland architecture: the Scotia Bank, Doyle's department store, a new pharmacy, and a Radio Shack outlet that appeared to have been a short-lived venture, as its plate-glass windows were coated with mud and salt, its shelves stood empty, and the counters were fly-specked.

At a bend in the road I came upon an atavistic scene that, more than anything, let me know I was far from home. On the harborside stood an old fishing stage of dark, red-stained boards, its wide, open maw leading into inner darkness. Around the sloping entrance squatted a semicircle of begrimed, overalled men in their late twenties and thirties. Their attention was fixed on a boat engine suspended from a pulley chain affixed to the gable beam above them, so that it hung about three feet off the ground, like some suspended ark, gleaming in the intense glare of their stares. As I involuntarily slowed, the men turned and gazed as one at me, at my new rented car, my sunglasses and camera case. I don't know which of us seemed stranger to the other.

I continued north on the harbor road, beyond the town center, past the Grenfell Hospital (an old green and white wood frame rambling structure), climbing a gradual rise into what began to have the feel of a different neighborhood, if not community. I passed the new Bleak House Museum, Christine's Restaurant and Take-Out, and one seeming cultural anomaly: Kwang Tung's Chinese restaurant. (Though I did not get to sample its cuisine during my stay there, one local resident offered this interesting recommendation: "It tastes good and it keeps down the stray cat population.")

The road makes a sharp 180-degree turn to the left at the harbor head, and there, at its end, was a large white house with a hand-painted sign on it: "Mrs. John Payne's Hospitality Home—License #453987." Aside from the seedy motel not far from the ferry terminal, this was the only tourist facility on the island, and the one where I had made reservations for the night. Next to it I saw a smaller house with another sign out front that said, "Payne," and some figures moving inside. I took this to be the office and the larger building to be the boardinghouse, but when I went up to the door, the figures seemed to scurry off into the inner recesses. Then a woman appeared at the side door of the first house and called to me, "Wrong one. It's over here. Everybody makes the same mistake." I came to learn that nearly everyone in the neighborhood was named Payne.

Emma Coffin Payne, a dour and tight-lipped women in her early forties, made me feel more tolerated than welcome. Obviously, what we had here from the beginning was a business transaction, nothing more. I came into the large hallway and she told me, "You can take your shoes off there." She was making dinner and did not ask me to sit down or tell me to bring my things in or where to put them. After some flat attempts at small talk I said, "Well, I guess I'll go bring my stuff in." I put my shoes back on, got my bag, came back in, took my shoes off, set down the bag, and waited. Finally, she took me into a small bedroom at the bottom of the stairs, with a single bed and a cot in it.

"You can put your things in here. I don't know if he's coming back tonight. If he does I'll put you upstairs, eh? He's quite a snorer." Later I learned that "he" was her other boarder, a telephone lineman who was regularly on the island for weeks at a time.

It was 5 P.M. I'd been in the car most of the day and said I thought I might take a walk before supper on the bare hills up behind the house.

"We're about to eat."

"We" was her husband, John. John, who looked a few years older than his wife, came in a few minutes later, took off his boots and overalls, said a perfunctory hello, and sat down on the couch in the living room where he appeared to go instantly to sleep. He worked at the fish-processing plant but was laid off this week, on what I gathered was a kind of rotating employment system the co-op members all participated in. He had spent the entire day splitting fir and birch junks from the pile of wood up behind the house. Though they might have modern electric stoves and water heaters, most of the houses in these outports still seemed to heat almost entirely with wood or kerosene.

Supper was at the kitchen table and consisted of sweet-and-sour chicken wings, rice with homemade sauce, homemade white bread with cheap margarine, applesauce, and tea. Mrs. Payne sat between us but had no place setting.

After a long silence of eating, I said, "It's real tasty."

"Hmmph," said Mrs. P. "John's not too fond of it."

"No?"

"But you likes it, eh?" said John.

John gave a little snort, as if contented at having tricked me, and buttered another slice of bread.

"John don't care for chicken much, eh?"

"Oh, what dishes do you like, John?"

"John likes his bread and butter, does 'e."

I thought they were kidding me, but a university friend in St. John's later confirmed for me that bread and butter was the traditional staple of the outports in winter.

John: "You married?"

Me: "Yes, with two kids. But they couldn't come up. My wife didn't get a vacation this year."

John: "You ought to get a Newfie woman while yer here."

Mrs. P.: "John! Would you do that if I stayed home and you went to the States?"

John: "Now don't bother him, let him . . . "

Mrs. P.: "His wife wouldn't like that."

John (to me): "Yeh, but you'd love it, eh?"

Mrs. P.: "John!"

Me: "I've seen some nice-looking women here, though."

John: "Ah-ah-ah-ah-ah!"

Mrs. P.: "You might be sure yer eyes only look."

When I told them I was from Cape Cod, I got blank stares.

"That's south of Boston." More blank stares, which puzzled me since a common Newfoundland term for the U.S. is "the Boston States."

"You know, in Massachusetts?" More blank stares.

I was about to give up, and then it hit me.

"Not too far from Gloucester."

"Oh, sure b'y, Gloucester! Yes, yes."

(For generations on the Grand Banks many Newfoundland fishermen were probably more familiar with the men on Gloucester schooners then they were with people in the next bay.)

"My wife's from Kentucky. Ever hear of that?"

"Oh ya. Is she tall?"

"About average. She comes from a large family—seven kids. She took care of them all."

Mrs. P. (with sudden concern): "Oh, did the mother die?"

"No, she was the oldest. Do you have any children here?"

"One girl—twenty years old, but she's leaving for Toronto in the fall."

They talked among themselves for a while, in a thick outport accent mostly unintelligible to me.

Mrs. Payne, who had not seen the Fogo brochure I picked up on the ferry, began leafing through it with considerable interest. She stopped at the page recounting Fogo's rejection of the resettlement proposals in the 1960s, when government policies relocated the population of hundreds of Newfoundland's smaller, more remote outports. "Resettlement, eh? Hmmph. They should have went ahead with that."

I asked her if she and John still dried cod. "Dryin' fish? I had twelve years o' that, eh? We still puts up a few in fall, just enough for our own winter supply, eh? Hmmph."

John had six rifles leaning against the kitchen wall, two of them muzzle-loaders. "He's just for shooting matches, b'y," he said. "You know, where the women hold up torches and the men shoot them out. Ah-ah-ah!"

A plaque above the stove read, "As For Me And My House, We Will Serve The Lord" (whatever *you* choose to do). In the bathroom the toilet paper holder admonished me: "Don't Sit There All Day–There's Work To Be Done."

After supper I went into the small parlor to make a call to St. John's. On the coffee table a VCR remote sat on top of a large family Bible, in which Emma and John's marriage was recorded in 1962. Beside the Bible was a postcard from Toronto addressed to their daughter, Germaine, dated "8/6/87": "Hi Germaine. How are things? Fine I hope. Both me and Sidney are working we both started work last Monday at the same place. We were to the CN Tower last night and it was so nice looking down on Toronto at night. It's no trouble to miss it, but I don't think we'll be back to dear old Newfoundland to live very quick. Take care—Love, Paula."

On the front of the card was a photograph of the Toronto skyline at night. To one who grew up among these bold and barren headlands, softened only by a thin skin of heath plants and creeping juniper (and an even thinner skin of human claims), the tall illuminated buildings of Toronto at night must be mesmerizing—like the island's Brimstone Head lit up inside and out.

After supper there were still several hours of daylight left, so I set off up into the bare hills behind the house, gently but steadily sloping ledges of red sandstone, the declivities filled with bog and heath plants, including blueberries everywhere. The first several hundred feet of the rocky slopes were covered with a network of black plastic hoses winding down from small natural reservoirs, splitting off at different intervals to supply the houses down below.

Fogo Hill, as this promontory is known, is perhaps six hundred feet tall, though it seemed much more imposing and massive than its elevation suggested. On the north side of the hill there was a vast ravine, with a narrow grassy valley at its bottom that ran out to the cobbly beach. Scattered about were several makeshift wooden structures, fences perhaps. High up on the west side of the ravine I saw a few sheep, some standing, some sitting, on one of the steep ledges. I went the long way around by the backside of the hill, hoping to surprise and photograph them, but when I arrived at the ledge they had disappeared. From this vantage point I could see for some distance in all directions and did not understand how I could have missed them.

When I descended the hill it was about 8 P.M., but there were at least a couple of hours of northern daylight left. I found John back out at the woodshed, splitting more wood. He had just acquired a wedge ax and seemed delighted with it.

Then I noticed a group of children playing softball just across the road on steeply sloping ground. (Softball seemed to be the universal game of choice in Newfoundland, an odd pick given the scarcity of level playing fields in most outports.) They gave me an idea. I went to my car, took out my kite bag, and walked down to the where the children were. I took out the brightly colored nylon wad and called down to them, "Have you guys ever seen a parafoil kite?"

"No!" they all shouted in unison. (As is characteristic of most outport children here, they showed no fear or shyness of strangers.)

"Wanta see one?"

"Sure!"

And that was it. They scrambled up out of the hollow and adopted me for the rest of the evening, a tumbling maelstrom of preadolescent energy eager to show off their neighborhood and island knowledge, and equally eager to learn and see what I had brought them from the outside world.

There were four of them. The natural leader of the group was Angela Payne, a blonde tomboy about eight years old, with an open, intelligent face and a malleable and self-aware manner that could adapt itself to the seriousness of her subject.

Her younger brother, Eugene, curly-headed and freckled, missing his two front teeth, bashful but not shy in demeanor, waited on his sister's cue. Their first cousin, Elvin, was about Angela's age, curious and reserved; and Bradley, the same age, related by a more distant, unspecified connection, was the clown of the group—brash, comical, impulsive. All were Paynes.

"He's a Payne and he's a Payne and he's a Payne," Angela pointed in sequence. Her father, Everett, was an inshore fisherman, and in the winter went sealing with the other men right off the shore here. Her mother, Jo, worked as a packer in the fishing plant in Seldom, on the south side of the island. All of the children told me their fathers were fishermen.

We sent up the kite immediately, and though they all said they had flown kites before, they were hooked by the force of the pull on the fifty-pound test nylon line, then fascinated by the twirler we sent up after the kite. They took turns holding the reel, the turns doled out by Angela, each taking the unknown force in their hands with a mixture of natural confidence and uncertainty, then immediately delighted with their control of it. The pull of the string was like an instant link between us, passed around like a pipe or a joint. I was with them for about two hours, and in that time the kite was on the ground for less than twenty minutes.

They asked me where I got such a kite, and I told them New York.

"Do you know where New York is?" Uncertain nods of the head.

Angela, Elvin, and Bradley told me about their neighborhood. Eugene smiled and was quiet. The sheep I had seen, they said, were from the offshore island in front of us—Burns Island. They had been driven off the island by dogs, swam to the mainland, and now lived up on Fogo Hill. The ravine I had seen from above was known as Frenchmen's Well, named for Frenchmen who used to live there a long time ago and a natural spring a little way up the valley. The cobble beach was important, because the caplin came ashore there to spawn in spring. Years ago whales and seals were brought ashore there for skinning. The Beothuks—the aboriginal inhabitants of Newfoundland—were said to have used it, too. "There are bones in the stones," they said.

They spoke chorally, rather than singly, but there was a dominant voice—Angela's or Bradley's usually—with a secondary commentary—Elvin's or Eugene's—overlapping behind it.* Angela told me there were no moose on Fogo, but in the winter they hunted caribou over by Tilting. And lots of rabbits.

After a while Mark Payne, Bradley's three-year old brother, showed up, a grinning, messy-faced kid in a T-shirt, red shorts, and knee-high rubber boots. Bradley was very curious about how far the kite could go out: "If that kite went all the way out, it would go right through the clouds, eh? Gawd!" When we hauled the kite in from over the sea, it fluttered out of sight just beyond the steep ledges in front of us. Mark went scrambling out over the cliff to retrieve it. Panicked, I yelled, "Mark, don't go near the edge!"

Bradley turned and said reassuringly, "He won't hurt it."

When I protested that it was *Mark* I was worried about, he gave me a contemptuous look and said, "Oh, there's another ledge there" as though I had betrayed my ignorance by suggesting that anyone would worry about children navigating their surroundings here. I was reminded of what I had been told in other outports, that parents here learn early *not* to worry; that children from a very early age are either up on the cliffs or out on the water. There is no other place for them to be.

They spoke with accents as thick as the grown-ups I had encountered, though Angela, I noticed, took pains to speak to me with more

---

*I have found this choral-contrapuntal style of talking common in Newfoundland outports, among adults as well as children.

standard pronunciation, often translating the spontaneous explosions of sound from her companions. I asked if there were any "sterrins" around here.

"Oh, aye, lots of sterrins!" Their eyes lit up at my unexpected use of the Newfoundland term for Arctic terns.

"What about turres [murres]?"

"Oh, aye, the turres—there be every kind of bird about here."

There was no question that these kids were much more familiar with and attuned to the outside world than their parents had been, through TV, radio, and videotapes. The centralized school, I later learned, also took students on regular trips to the "mainland," that is, Newfoundland. Nevertheless, actual physical contact beyond the island was still relatively limited. I took out my cassette recorder and asked Mark if he would like to sing something into it. At first he demurred. When I suggested "Old MacDonald," he brightened and asked, "You know McDonald's?" meaning the restaurant, though there were no fast-food places this side of St. John's. Eugene proudly brought out a peacock feather that he had obtained at the Toronto Zoo while on a visit to his aunt there.

After we got the kite in they asked me if I would like to see Frenchmen's Well. By this time a fifth member had joined them—Ricky, a larger boy of perhaps eleven, another Payne of course, who fitted into the group with that democracy of ages that seems to be adopted naturally in places with limited numbers of kids.

I said I would go, but I didn't want to worry their parents. At this point, in fact, Bradley and Mark's mother came onto the road and called Mark home, but Bradley pleaded to let him come and she acceded. They took me down into the ravine, picking up bones on the beach— dog, seal, and whale bones—and then leading me up to the well, a spring roughly lined with stones, where we all threw pennies in and made wishes. The ground here was covered with large ripe blueberries and another berry Bradley called "blackberries," which grew on a low crowberry-like vine and tasted somewhat like huckleberries. Halfway up the valley there was a trampled area they used as a softball field, with a backstop cobbled together from old boards and fishnets, and a wooden "home run fence."

They all wanted to put the kite up again, and so we did, the erratic winds in the steep valley making it do crazy flips and dips. The boys went off to chase it, while Angela stayed to hold the reel.

"Do you like living here?" I asked.

(Her eyes lighting up): "Oh, yes!"

"Do you think you want to live here when you grow up?"

(Just as definitely): "Oh, no!"

"Where do you want to live?"

(Looking up coyly): "New York."

Then she stood up, handed me the kite, and announced, "This is the end of the world, y' know."

"It is?"

"That's what they say." She gestured up the valley to the hills: "This is the End of the World, and"—turning and pointing offshore—"over there, those islands, that is the Beginning."

"A Half Hour Later in Newfoundland"

During the fall of 1989 I spent a week driving across Newfoundland, exploring parts of the island I had not yet seen. It was the first time I had driven so far by myself, and I decided to see what I could find on the radio. Once I got outside of St. John's there was nothing on the FM dial. When I switched to AM, I got one weak country-western station, and then, surprisingly, a loud, clear burst of sound, a traditional Newfoundland jig, and over it an announcer welcoming me to "The Fisherman's Broadcast." I had found the CBC, Newfoundland.

The Canadian Broadcasting Corporation, established in 1936, is, next to the BBC, the oldest and most widely broadcast radio network in the world. In fact, it has not one but *four* national radio networks: CBC Radio One and CBC Radio Two in English, and La Radio de Radio-Canada and La Chaine Culturelle FM in French. In addition to its bilingual broadcasts, Radio Canada International (the shortwave version of the CBC) provides radio services in Canadian's Arctic provinces and territories in eight aboriginal languages.

The two English-language networks, Radio One and Radio Two, provide different styles and content of programming. Radio Two, or CBC Stereo, as it is commonly known, is largely a music, arts, and culture network, providing classical music during the day and jazz in the evening, with arts reports, recorded concerts, musical theater, global music, and Saturday Metropolitan Opera broadcasts filling out the schedule. Radio One, or simply CBC Radio to most listeners, offers up a smorgasbord of news programs and analysis, radio dramas, call-in shows, literary and scientific programs, radio humor, radio drama, reading-aloud programs, local programming, oldies music, late-night classical music and weekend blues, a few uncategorizably eclectic programs, and a remarkable series called *Ideas*, which has been broadcasting on weekday evenings for nearly forty years. It is a program that lives up to its name by considering every topic from A to Z,* from Glenn Gould to Dante's *Inferno* to the significance of the ocean bottom to the physiology of female ejaculation to a rebroadcast of a 1968 series on "the origins, nature, and history of civil disobedience by Professor George Woodcock."

At the time, on Newfoundland and Labrador, there were over three dozen CBC radio transmitters. Most of them were small, low-wattage FM transmitters with a range of only a dozen or so kilometers, and the only CBC Stereo frequencies were in St. John's on the East Coast and Corner Brook on the West. Still, it was rare, even then, to be out of range of the CBC in Newfoundland, and I usually managed to find a CBC Radio station on long hauls across the island on the TCH or down long, rutted, gravel roads to remote outports.

Listening to the different programs one got a sense, not only of the Canadian culture and society at large, but also of contemporary Newfoundland and its relationship to the loose federation of Canadian provinces it had joined less than a half century before. Here is a sample of CBC stories I heard that week on the road:

> The expected approval of a new NATO flight training base at Goose Bay, Labrador, is being protested by the local Napskaki Innu tribe. Survival International, a U.S.–based Indians Rights group, has expressed concern about the effects of fifty thousand annual low-altitude jet fighter and bomber flights on caribou herds and native peoples.
>
> Three brothers from an outport on the southern shore of the Avalon Peninsula have been arraigned for violation of federal seal regula-

---

*Literally so during several summers when its original host, the British-born radio actor Lister Sinclair, created a series called "A Is for Aardvark," a pastiche of minimeditations on topics beginning with a different letter of the alphabet each night.

tions. Their lawyer claims that a videotape made by the brothers themselves, purportedly showing them torturing live seals, is "misleading and inadmissible." He calls them "the Rodney Kings of Newfoundland."

The recent scandal at the Mount Cashel Catholic orphanage outside St. John's has added to a growing child-abuse problem in Newfoundland. According to testimony by former residents of the orphanage, dozens of children were allegedly abused, sexually and physically, by members of the Christian Brothers order in the mid-1970s. The incidents were apparently covered up not only by the church but also by local police officials. The church has responded by saying that the situation has been greatly exaggerated in the press. According to one bishop, "We've only had eighteen cases of abuse over the past fifteen years." The story has apparently unleashed public indignation not only at the alleged child abuse, but long-standing resentment against the domination of the Catholic Church in community affairs, particularly in the clergy's control of church money. One man from Bonavista, a member of the local volunteer fire department, complained that when the town had fund-raising events, the priest came in and "took his share."

There is a crisis in Newfoundland's inshore fishery, which had one of the worst summers in memory this year. Hundreds of families did not even qualify for unemployment this winter, and for the first time in fifty years many communities do not have winter fish for their own use. The inshore fishermen blame the offshore trawlers, and the trawlers blame the foreign fishing fleets. The Department of Fisheries and Oceans is calling for more studies.

A man in St. John's held his former girlfriend and her sister hostage for over twenty-four hours; the standoff ended when the girlfriend head-butted the man, who was later treated for cuts at the hospital. The man has pleaded guilty to charges of forcible abduction and is being held without bail.

Two wildlife officers investigating an illegal turr-hunter's boat near Wesleyville had a shotgun pointed at them. The suspect surrendered his gun peacefully and was taken into custody. One of the officers referred to it as "an obstruction with a firearm incident."

A thirty-six-year-old Newfoundland man with the improbable name of Kevin Bacon Snow was arrested by the RCMP in Ottawa for scaling the fence surrounding the residence of Prime Minister Jean Chrétien. At the arraignment Snow, described as "a transient living in Toronto with no known permanent address," was reported as seeming "disoriented." Three days later his lawyer said that Snow had been physically and sexually abused as a boy at the Mount Cashel orphanage in St. John's and had been trying to get someone to open his case for years, to no avail. The lawyer said that Snow had consumed "monstrous" quantities of rum and beer and decided to talk to the PM. He got directions to the Prime Minister's residence from the Governor General's house, who notified the RCMP. The RCMP apparently let Snow climb the fence before arresting him and then boasted how swift and effective security was. He pleaded guilty and the judge gave him four days for trespassing, three already served.

There is a squid glut in Black Tickle.

The signature CBC program in Newfoundland is *The Fisheries Broadcast*, a half hour program broadcast daily at 4:30 P.M. from St. John's. The show was originally broadcast on the Great Eastern Radio Network as *The Fisherman's Broadcast*. It is the oldest continuously broadcast radio program in North America, one that predates Newfoundland's incorporation into Canada in 1949.

For most of its life *The Fisherman's Broadcast* was what its name implied: a no-nonsense, nuts-and-bolts, information-oriented program, similar to the wheat price and pork-belly futures reports one used to hear on local radio stations in the Midwest. It was a show designed to disseminate news about the location, prevalence, and price of fish; the coming and going of ships; and the status of lights, buoys and whistles; as well as to allow fishermen to call in and discuss all sorts of related topics, including fishing methods, bait, boats, fish prices, and so on.

Since the cod moratorium, however, there have been few or no fish to report, except for a few weeks each year when the opening of the different bays for crab and caplin are announced. Few ships now enter or leave the capital city's fabled harbor. Lights and whistle buoys that are nonfunctional are still reported, though, with the advent of loran, GPS, and other electronic positioning technology, there are few boats anymore that depend on their signals.

Nowadays the program is "livelier" and covers a much broader range of topics. It is hosted by announcers who sound as if they are emceeing a Kiwanis dinner and have never lowered a jigger or split a cod in their lives. In 1996 the name of the show was changed to *The Fisheries Broadcast* to recognize the presence of women in the fishing industry. Most of the callers are referred to as "fisherpersons," a term the show uses to include fish plant workers.

Still, *The Fisheries Broadcast* has survived and, in fact, has thrived in spite of, or perhaps because of, the demise of the traditional Newfoundland fisheries. Since there are virtually no fish to report, *The Fisheries Broadcast* has evolved into a forum, a kind of daily islandwide group therapy session, during which the collapse of the cod fishery, its causes, the government regulatory, social, and economic policies that have succeeded it, the characters and motives of the politicians that have spawned these policies, the cultural and personal consequences of the moratorium and its aftermath, and all other issues fish-related—which is to say, all things Newfoundland—are discussed, analyzed, debated, harangued, cursed, satirized, and endlessly elaborated with always impressive energy, passion, and rhetoric. On the very first show I listened to, a fisherman from Bonavista called in to complain about federal fishing policies, which, he accurately predicted, would lead to the end of the groundfish fishery: "It's crazy. The government is in cahoots with the big fish plants and their factory ships, stripping the spawning grounds of the last fish. They might as well go out and shoot every pregnant woman on the island and then shake their heads over the declining population. Stunned buggers!"

One of the most popular targets for callers is government policies designed to alleviate the high unemployment in the province. They scoff, for instance, at the money allocated for "retraining" laid-off plant workers. "Retraining for what?" one irate caller wanted to know. "Down in Lawn on the Burin they 'retrained' forty cosmetologists, for Christ's sake! Jesus Christ, man, there ain't forty people with *hair* left in Lawn! What were they thinking, b'y? What *were* they thinking!?"

There is also a great deal of posturing and threatening to "fish any-where we wants, anytime," despite government regulations. On the other side, some callers condemn the fishermen as "freeloaders," living on welfare, who are "equally responsible for their predicament," and suggest that they leave if they don't like things as they are, etc. On both sides there is a Newfoundland earthiness in their language, where epi-thets like "bullshit," "arsehole," and "stunned bugger" are thrown about on the air without censorship or self-consciousness, by women as often as by men.

But what strikes me most about this islandwide "talk show" are not the elements that it shares with most of its talk radio counterparts in the States—for example, passion, strong conviction, and colorful lan-guage—but what distinguishes it from them. The most striking thing about the callers into *The Fisheries Broadcast* is how articulate they are. They tend to express not just feelings that burst unconsidered into lan-guage, but consecutive thoughts, well-reasoned arguments, and often researched documentation. Sometimes the callers seem to be *reading* their remarks, suggesting that they have taken the time to write down those thoughts beforehand, though, again, this could be simply the re-sult of an oral tradition, used to transmitting complex and extended thoughts and information verbally, combined with a formality of ex-pression adopted for such a public venue as a radio broadcast.

One of the distinguishing characteristics of the CBC in Newfound-land is its weather reports; that is, that they are just that, reports, not forecasts, for example, "It's 15 degrees on the West Coast, with light rain and winds of 25–30 kilometers." Sometimes (though not always), a report will venture to report the next day's expected weather, but the kind of three- to five-day weather forecasts that are standard (and usu-ally wildly inaccurate) in the States is conspicuously absent here. Again, the difference seems to stem not from a lack of more sophisticated tech-nology or weather satellites, but from an inherent Canadian modesty or caution, a sense of "Who are we to predict the weather—at least farther than we can see?"

On the other hand, in Newfoundland, the verbal format of the re-ports often seems imported from more cosmopolitan settings, in a not-always-successful attempt to merge network conventions with the realities of the province. For instance, in the summer, one is likely to hear island temperatures given as follows: "Mostly sunny, with highs of 22–24 degrees [Centigrade], except 14 degrees in onshore winds along the coast." This is a dramatic range of variation, something like 18 degrees Fahrenheit. The "except" in such a forecast, however, is less exceptional than it might appear, given that over 90 percent of the island's population does, in fact, live along the coast and therefore will likely experience "onshore winds." Thus, for the sake of broadcast conventions, it seems, the meteorological norm is syntactically marginalized.

When I first began listening to the CBC weather reports, I was struck by what seemed to be very detailed reports for different parts of the island. Not only were separate reports given for seven or eight different regions in Newfoundland, but each report was given by a different announcer from each region. It first seemed like a very Canadian respect for locality, but I later came to suspect this, too, was a result of a network format abstractly applied to local conditions. Even if the weather was identical, or nearly identical, across the province, each region still got to announce its weather locally, with only slight variations in the details:

> "On the West Coast, it's 15 degrees, with light rain and winds of 25–30 kilometers."
> "On the Northern Peninsula, it's 14 degrees, with light rain and winds of 25–30 kilometers."
> "In Happy Valley–Goose Bay and Labrador City, it's 12 degrees, with light rain and winds of 25–30 kilometers."
> "In Labrador West, it's 12 degrees, with light rain and winds of 25–30 kilometers."
> "In Nain today, it's 13 degrees, with light rain and winds of 25–30 kilometers."
> "On the Northeast Coast, it's 15 degrees, with light rain and winds of 25–30 kilometers."
> "On the South-West Coast, it's 15 degrees, with light rain and winds of 25–30 kilometers."
> "And on the Avalon Peninsula, it's 15 degrees, with fog, light rain and winds of 25–30 kilometers."

Thank you, Chet, Kirby, Fred, Kimberly, Dwayne, Ralph, and Bernice.

Despite its conscious attempts to mimic national formats, however, Newfoundland is not likely ever to be completely absorbed, even on radio, by the still distrusted "Canadian wolf," for there is something in its temperament inherently out of synch with the rest of its adopted country. Most obviously, Newfoundland has its own, unique time zone (Newfoundland Standard Time), which is thirty minutes ahead of the rest of the Atlantic provinces. NST was established when Newfoundland was a self-governing Dominion and was retained after Confederation. As a result, whenever the time of an upcoming national program is announced on the CBC, it is always followed by the tag "a half hour later in Newfoundland and most of Labrador." This chronological quirk has messed with the head of more than one CBC announcer. One evening, outside of Deer Lake, I heard the following broadcast announcement: "Coming up at 9 P.M. tonight on *Ideas:* 'The Value of Uncertainty to Individuals and Society.' For those of you in Newfoundland, that'll be at 8:30—I mean 9:30—no, wait—oh heck, you people know when it is!"

A Fine Specimen

One summer afternoon I drove up to Twillingate, one of the oldest and most remote settlements on the island's north shore. Like many Newfoundland names that sound so whimsically English, this one is a corruption of its original eighteenth-century French name, Toulinquet.

Twillingate is part of a complex archipelago of small islands in Notre Dame Bay. It sits in the middle of Iceberg Alley, the local name for the Labrador Current, which brings hundreds of large icebergs down from Greenland each spring. The town was finally connected to the mainland by road about thirty years before, and since then it has become one of Newfoundland's more popular tourist attractions. Local boats now take visitors out to view icebergs and whales in the summer months, a scene cleverly captured in a computer-generated poster depicting breaching leviathans against a backdrop of majestic icebergs and labeled "The Humpbacks of Notre Dame." Though it was now early August, I had come hoping to see one of this summer's crop of bergs.

About three in the afternoon I stopped at an inn in the center of town for a cup of tea. In front of the establishment a trio of bearded men got off their motorcycles and went inside to a table. They turned out to be a land surveyor, an architect, and a doctor, all on holiday from Conception Bay. At another table sat a large, barrel-chested man, clean-shaven, about forty-five, with a crew cut. He ordered by saying to the waitress, "I'd really love a soda pop and—oh, the hell with my doctor, one of those, what do you call them, partridgeberry tarts."

Though we all sat at separate tables, the man struck up a friendly and inquisitive conversation with everyone. It was somehow obvious that he was far from home and in need of company. He told us that he ran a construction business in Yellowknife and was down here buying supplies to ship back home and to recruit Newfoundlanders to work up in Yellowknife.

"The ones who haven't been on welfare are helluva good workers," he said. "I was on Fogo Island last week, bought a used stone crusher from John Burke in Joe Batt's Arm. He and his seven brothers have a combined IQ that's less than room temperature, but they're helluva good carpenters."

He was outgoing and friendly and, like so many people who come from a frontier setting, loved to tell stories about himself. He said he had served in Vietnam in the special Canadian forces "when we were young and killing Orientals—fine specimens of human beings we were. Hey, don't get me wrong, better them than us." Of Americans, he said, "They're a strange people—very generous and kind when they want to be, but with a violent streak in them. They'll nuke your cities, then come in with chocolate bars, just like a big brother, you know, who you know loves you but might just *swat* you if he feels like it. I don't think they like themselves very much, always cutting themselves short."

He likes American music, which he first heard in Nam from a black battalion that used to come down from the hills and play at night. "Best goddam music I ever heard. I go down to Chicago now and then and those black bastards still glare at me when I walk into one of their clubs. I take two white friends with me, real mean fuckers—fine specimens of human beings."

He had only sporadic and oblique knowledge of musicians and bands. He didn't know the Grateful Dead but liked "Lips, you know, 'Satisfaction,' and who's the other guy that died?"

"Cobain?"

"Naw, they made a movie about him. Died in Paris. Not all that music was good. 'California Dreamin'—horrible song—and the girl who starved herself . . . but God, we took it all over there."

He claimed to speak fluent Vietnamese, Chinese, and Malay, and to read some of them, though he said he didn't learn to read until he was nineteen. His father was a Mountie who "had the grace to marry an aboriginal girl before it was politically correct to do so—then he got another girl pregnant—or my uncle did, I was never sure—anyway, I was raised in a Goddam Genuine Canadian Multi-Cultural Family!"

He gave me a running history of the RCMP and their run-ins with the First Nation, or Native Americans. He obviously sympathized with the native side and their fighting ability—"All fine specimens *they* were. Did you know that Charles Dickens's son was an officer in the Northwest Mounted Police?"

He had a twelve-year-old son by his Ukrainian wife whom he clearly doted on. "Very smart, a computer whiz." He said that many of the inhabitants of Yellowknife are descendants of Russian and Ukrainian priests who were abandoned there in 1917 after the Revolution, and who married Inuit and Innu. He also spoke Cree and some Denai.

He told me the story of a "runaway Harvard professor" who showed up in Yellowknife a few years before to "lead the simple life."

"We took him out on dogsleds a few times until he turned blue with hypothermia, then we got him under the caribou pelts and set up a Nunavut shelter as a deflector so the wind wouldn't burn him and got him thawed out. People like him, though; he's good at fixing two-cycle engines. There's a strikingly beautiful twenty-five-year-old Inuit girl who has decided that she wants him, so he's going to be a pap next spring. Of course, he wanted to 'do the decent Christian thing' and marry her, but she said, first, she wasn't Christian, and second, she wouldn't marry him because he was too old and would die too soon. If she married, she wanted it to be someone she could spend the rest of her life with. 'Course, he was choked up for about a week, but he came to accept it. And you know, this is her first, real . . . well, she really wants him, wants to learn everything from him, for when she becomes the first woman president of Nunavut."

Much of this and more I almost missed. The three biker professionals left after he told about his Vietnam experiences. When I got up to go he said there was a large iceberg at the end of the road to Herring Neck on New World Island and he could give me a lift if I wanted to see it. I thanked him but said I had a car and had to be getting on to the ferry to Fogo, which wasn't true. He had a boyish, somewhat shy, and self-effacing manner, but you felt he could snap your neck like a birch twig.

"Well," he said, somewhat crestfallen, "it was just an offer out of politeness."

I drove about a mile down the road with increasing regret, and then turned back with little hope that he would still be there. I asked at the desk, describing him.

"Oh, that would be Mike Black, in Room #1."

When he let me in he had Arctic clothing spread out all over the bed. "I went to Greenland last winter to get warm," he said. "Hell, it was minus fifty in Yellowknife."

He accepted my return without comment as the kind of apology it was. During the drive out to Herring Neck, he told me some of these and other stories about himself.

Herring Neck sits along a marvelously convoluted, long, narrow arm of the sea. Its little clusters of houses are architecturally pure: traditional two-story, flat-roofed or "salt-box" dwellings, with a few older peak-roofed houses. One house had an entire carved miniature reproduction of the village in its yard.

We came up over a rise, and there it was, just outside the arm, about three hundred yards off: a massive three-peaked berg, like a floating ice cathedral, steeply spired, roughly 150 feet high and 500 feet long. It was an utterly alien object, as though it had been dropped here from another world. It seemed to contain and glow with colors that bore no relation to what was around it: a soft, almost Caribbean blue accenting a Styrofoam white. Icebergs morph overnight, not breaking up so much as transforming their shapes, rolling over, and sending out probes toward the rocky shore. This one hovered offshore, as if awaiting further instructions.

We drove down to the end of the road and climbed a hill for a better look, but it was blocked. Mike was out of breath after the climb, saying his lungs had not been good the past year. He apologized for not getting me a better look at the iceberg, and on the way back we stopped at a convenience store, where he went in and came back a few minutes later, telling me that he had arranged for someone to take me out to it if I wanted.

When we got back to the hotel I signed and gave him a copy of one of my books. He asked me if I liked soapstone carvings. "We've got some of the best carvers in the world up in Yellowknife. They're making good money, too. Some earn over a hundred thousand a year. We had one of the best, a twenty-year-old boy, real fine specimen, but he committed suicide last year. Give me an address and I'll send you something from the North."

I've never heard from him again, but when I got home, I checked out his story about Charles Dickens's son. It was true.

Off-Season

In central Newfoundland, just west of Windsor-Grand Falls on the Trans-Canada Highway, is Beothuk Provincial Park. The park contains a family camping area, lake frontage, and a reconstructed logging camp. The logging camp features several log buildings roofed with tarred canvas and chinked with living moss and reindeer lichen, a sawpit, several sledges, and a wooden lake boat under a tarred canvas shelter. I first visited it on a summer morning when the park was celebrating Lumber Heritage Day, with activities for visitors that included a traditional breakfast of toutons and blackstrap molasses, axe-throwing and log-sawing contests, rides on horse-drawn log sledges, and Newfoundland songs and music played by park employees dressed up in traditional lumberjack clothes. It was an enjoyable enough experience, in a generic, detached way, but I had the feeling, without really knowing why, that in trying to "re-create" the experience of this place for tourists, they had sanitized, sentimentalized, and happified it and, in so doing, had removed or covered up any remnant of what constituted an authentic encounter with its true history. Yet I was to learn that, at odd moments, in spite of their shortcomings, such official reconstructions can inadvertently offer up genuine ghosts of this lost past.

Not long after visiting the park, I stopped to visit Mark and Fraser Carpenter, two friends from the States who had resettled in Squid Tickle, a small outport on Newfoundland's Northeast Coast, several years before. During the summers they ran a boat-tour business in nearby Terra Nova National Park, and one afternoon in early November, we drove to the park for a walk up to Malady Head, a six-hundred-foot beetled brow of a headland overlooking Newman Sound. We hiked in through the deep, moss-carpeted, sun-shafted forest of spindly and overcrowded fir and spruce trees, whose dark, bunched tufts of needles at their peaks look more like black mold than foliage, and from whose bare downward-sloping branches hung wispy lime-green beards of lichen, like tattered flags of defeat.

Fraser, who is English, said that the "pine-clad hills" praised in the *Ode to Newfoundland* (the province's official anthem) were probably "a British mistake" for spruce and fir. There never was, she suspected, much pine here. (I subsequently read accounts that stated there were originally substantial stands of native white pine here, but these had been essentially lumbered out by the 1920s.)

We reached the overlook in the late afternoon of a beautiful, late-autumn day. Sitting on a rail fence, we looked out over a great rumpled rug of forested hills, bluffs, headlands, ridges, isthmuses, necks, points, and offshore islands—all interspersed with a tessellation of ponds, sounds, inlets, tickles, and small rivers and streams that compose a vista of well over one hundred square miles. Below us, in Newman Sound, an isotherm of dark freshwater lay like a long, flat crack on the surface of the lighter, crinkled saltwater around it.

"Beautiful, isn't it?" said Mark. "You'd never know it now, but there used to be nineteen different logging firms at one time working in the park, though only one was left when the government took it over thirty years ago. Being so handy to water, it was a major supplier of lumber to St. John's—firewood, wharf pilings, and railroad ties. Before the park came in Bert Burden and Cleves Oldford both worked in the woods here in the winter, building splash dams at the ponds and driving the logs down the small rivers and streams in the spring—just small logs, you know, eight feet long or so.

"There was nothing mythic or Paul Bunyanesque about these woods, no, b'y, just unremitting, almost unimaginable, hard work. Bert's got a crater in his back as deep as my fist. He said it was cancer, but I think it was TB of the bone. He worked for years in the woods here, blood dribbling from his back. He told me one day a piece of bone dropped out of his back on the ground, and he felt better.

"Cleves's older brother Willis was just a young boy, thirteen or so, when he went to work cutting in the woods over there by Wing's Pond. One time the foreman asked him if he wanted to work an extra three or four days. Of course, he said yes, and then set off for home at dark, twenty miles away, arriving in Squid Tickle at dawn, had his breakfast and went back into the woods, and didn't think anything of it."

Mark pointed to the narrows between Southwest Arm and Broad Cove, where a small wooden suspension bridge crosses it. "Cleves worked along the shore down there as a young man. One winter he got caught in a storm so bad that he couldn't go on. Had his two oxen lie down in the lee of their load of logs, then he lay down in the lee of the oxen, and just let the snow drift over them—and that's how he spent the night.

"But hard as this was, it was even harder when they had to work away. The men will never talk about times when they could no longer survive on the land, couldn't get fish or wood enough, and the real world caught up with them."

Mark cited, as examples, the case of a revered schooner captain who was reduced to stoking a boiler in St. John's, and a fish merchant who ended up a church janitor in Halifax. "Bert," he said, "used to live in a tar paper shack over in Gambo for years. The Moss brothers, Jim and John, worked in Gander on the railroad for some years, living off potatoes. Fred and Cleves worked in Toronto during the Depression. Some weren't built for such hard work, their frames wouldn't take it, and it crushed them. They don't talk about it. They'll tell you a hundred stories about fishing on the Labrador or going out on a sealing berth or making moonshine on Flat Island, but you'll never hear them talk about the hard times. It took me years just to hear that much. There's no stories in it, nothing they want to remember."

It was a few years after that, on a cool, gray, windy day in October, that I visited Beothuk Provincial Park again. Like most of the provincial parks in Newfoundland, this one had closed at the end of September. I parked my car at the entrance, stepped over the chain strung between two posts, and walked in. I meandered down a path through the woods away from the campground before coming to the site of the reconstructed lumber camp. This time I was aware of an unnatural orderliness in the assemblage of buildings. The cabins, boats, sheds, and tools were all in perfectly maintained condition. There were no latrines, no middens of cans and broken liquor bottles, no dirt and smell of men living in close, crude quarters together for months on end.

Yet in that altered, late-afternoon northern light, with all interpretive signs removed or covered for the season, no sight nor sound of any tourists or automobiles as far as one could see or hear (only the deep soughing of the wind through the trees and the insistent scolding of a red squirrel from a balsam fir branch), it was possible to sense the isolation and self-sufficiency of such camps, the length and grinding repetition of the work. In my mind's eye I could conjure up the deep aisles cut into these green and gold woods, the ferrying of logs cut the previous winter across the wide, shallow, wind-whipped lake along ice-covered shores. I could feel the loneliness and explosive, diastolic lives of these men, kept in thrall, not to the harsh, economic system of the fishing outports, which put sober, industrious family men in debt to their suppliers all of their lives, but to their own loneliness and appetites, flung from the ox-like oblivion of their work in the woods into brief, violent wastes of spirit, flesh, and wages in Windsor, Grand Falls, Bishop's Falls, and the other logging towns of the Exploits Valley. Here, in the off-season, in these off-hours, in the presence of reasonable facsimiles and natural settings of authentic lives, one could imagine oneself back into the terrible, vanished earnestness of the past.

"We Just Takes Over"

I pulled into Grand Falls last evening about four o'clock, after a day of driving along the Trans-Canada through a landscape strongly reminiscent of the central and northern hinterlands of Maine: long, snag-bordered dark lakes and mountains so worn down that they seemed more like long swells than hills, unrelieved and monotonous undulations upon the land. I was traveling through the logging country of this island, and all day log trucks loaded to the gills passed me in both directions, heading toward the paper mills at Corner Brook or Grand Falls. Long gashes of denuded clear-cuts streaked the hills. In some places there were whole hillsides of dead trees, spruce or fir, killed by some insect pest.

I was tired, but I realized that I did not want to spend another evening in another squeaky-clean, wholesome "hospitality home" where I would be treated hospitably enough but set off to one side like a piece of fragile china or antique furniture, dusted but not used. I wanted something different. I stopped for information at the visitors' info center on the highway outside of Grand Falls and was given a rundown of the available lodging houses. "Mr. and Mrs. So-and-so," the woman said, pointing on the map to one of the newer residential areas in the city, "have just opened up a new H-H. I haven't been there, but we've gotten very satisfactory reports from it." *Great, another night in a suburban ranch house sharing* Wheel of Fortune *with my hosts—no thank you.*

My eye was caught by a listing for the Car-Sans Hotel, both by the name (Did it mean you slept in your car? or that they accepted only pedestrians and cyclists?), and by the rates (thirty dollars a night, Canadian), the cheapest on the list. It appealed to me even more when the woman at the visitors' center directed me to it with a slight but noticeable look of disapproval.

When I found it, it seemed just what I wanted: a large, three-story, dingy-looking, brown and yellow frame building with an attached lounge, a bare gravel parking area outside, and an aura of disreputable promise about it. The only inconsistent note was that it was located directly next to the local elementary school—a planning oversight, surely, but the strict division of what I imagined their respective nocturnal/diurnal operations to be probably kept any conflicts from surfacing. (It recalled to mind the notorious proximity of the city hall and a legendary brothel in the town in West Virginia where I grew up in the 1950s.)

The entrance door had a sign pasted on the window: "DOOR LOCKED AFTER 10 P.M.—USE LOUNGE ENTRANCE AFTER HOURS." Inside was a dark and narrow hallway that served as the lobby. I wandered back along it, noticing posters above the doors and stairways that admonished the prospective transient:

ABSOLUTELY NO NOISE OR VISITORS IN ROOMS
BETWEEN 12 A.M. AND 8 A.M.
—*The Authorities*

and above the stairway:

VISITORS MUST LEAVE ROOM BY MIDNIGHT
—*The Authorities*

and on the inside of the exit door:

LEAVE THE KEY

Perfect, I thought. *Cover yourself legally; then it's the poor slob's fault if he's caught.*

At the end of the dark corridor I came to a closed metal door with a tacked-up hand-lettered sign that said "LOUNGE" on it. I hesitated to open it, and then noticed, on my right, a raised, windowed booth about five feet in height, dark and empty, with a buzzer beside it that had another lettered note: "PRESS FOR SERVICE." I did, and from somewhere in the unseen depths of the lounge a woman emerged: early fifties, peroxide blonde, in a purple dress. "Can I help you, love?" she said, and gave me a key to look at the first-floor room.

It was pretty basic: two single beds with metal frames, a tiny black-and-white TV with a tinfoil antenna, not even a dresser *(Why would you need one?)*. I was somewhat surprised, however, to see, on a pressed-sawdust night table, a gooseneck reading lamp. In all the other Newfoundland hospitality homes and motels I had stayed in, the bedrooms had only ceiling lights. Obviously when you went to bed you were not expected to want to read.

I took a room on the second floor, twenty-nine dollars with a shared bath, and asked the woman in the booth if they would be showing the Series game in the lounge that night. "What Series?" "The World Series." "Oh," she smiled, and said, "I suspect there'll be some of thems watching it" *(if you need to watch something)*.

I decided I had found the perfectly sleazy place for the night (perhaps, in an earlier incarnation, it had even hosted my imagined old-time loggers on their monthly sprees) and looked forward to whatever might transpire in the bar. The game was scheduled to start at 4 P.M. on the West Coast, which meant that it (and likely any other action) would not start until 8:30 P.M. (Newfoundland Standard Time). I decided to go into town to cash some traveler's checks and have supper.

When I returned, about 7:30, I went through the steel door from the hall into the lounge. The decor was Early Newfoundland Plastic: a small, U-shaped bar with a plastic counter and plastic-covered stools; an alcove to the left containing a few wood-grain plastic tables with passionflower plastic chairs; and some large plastic butterflies tacked to the walls. Beyond the bar was the main area, with a dozen or so Formica tables and metal folding chairs. Along the walls were mounted a variety of feed caps, some sort of sports trophy plaques above the bar, and several generic "Newfie jokes," including a length of heavy link chain stretched between the frame of a backsaw labeled "Newfoundland Chain Saw," and the picture of the handgun with the barrel turned backward labeled

"Newfie Hand-gun for Sale—Used Only Once." (As in Appalachia, I find that Newfie jokes and stereotypes are offensive when told or perpetuated by outsiders, but they seem to be happily indulged in by many Newfoundlanders themselves.)

I sat on a stool with my back to the main table area. One of the two women bartenders, nicely attired in a light-brown dress that would have been appropriate in a bank, came up to me: "What'll you have, love?" I ordered a Labatt's and sat quietly drinking it. On another arm of the bar were three or four other men: one a salesman in a black suit who had just checked in, another a local man telling stories in a loud, half-comprehensible dialect. The TV was on, already tuned to the Series game in San Francisco, but it had been postponed by an earthquake that had just struck the area, crushing cars beneath collapsing bridges and highway overpasses. The men at the bar caught me up on the story as it had been unfolding. It felt strange to sense the distance they felt, watching the catastrophe happening in another country, and even stranger to realize I shared their distance.

After about twenty minutes, I heard a commotion suddenly begin behind me: the sound of people beginning to tumble in through the outside lounge door. It was a mass arrival, like a school bus unloading at a McDonald's after a high school game, but the voices were those of adult women. *My God*, I thought, *do they bus them in?* There was the noise of tables and chairs being pushed and pulled about the room behind me in a direct, purposeful manner. The men at the bar looked together at the intrusion, with expressions not of surprise, but of recognition of a regular occurrence. The expressions on their faces seemed to reflect a curious resolve to remain apart, grouped together, not for attack, but to stay out of harm's way.

The women sounded energetically young, but when I turned around I faced a room full of mature females, a few of them twenty-five or thirty, but most in their late thirties to mid-sixties, dressed casually in blouses and pants, sweatshirts and jeans, and running shoes or loafers—dressed, unlike the women tending bar, not for men but for themselves. They moved the loose furniture about energetically and professionally, as if they were here to move the place out. The women began to swarm around me up to the bar, ordering Pepsis and Black Horses and J&Bs. The acrid smell of their cigarettes was already filling the room. Loonies (one-dollar coins with loons on one side) were taken out of purses, counted, exchanged, and laid down on the table.

My face must have betrayed my perplexity, for one of the women— about forty, with short, coifed, dark hair and glasses—glanced at me, gave a short laugh, and said by way of explanation, "Darts, love—we just takes over."

Looking at a Portrait of Mary March (Demasduit)

I am looking at a watercolor portrait of Mary March, a young Beothuk woman in her early twenties. Her skin looks remarkably light, and her short black hair is carefully parted in the middle and combed back around her ears. Her mouth is small and delicate, its Kewpie-doll lips curled in a slight, hesitant smile that reveals a few small white teeth. She is wearing a reddish brown caribou robe trimmed with marten fur, said to be the clothes she was wearing when she was captured. The outstanding feature of the portrait is her large, white, doe-like eyes, in which the dark-brown pupils seem to float upward. She looks just to the right of the viewer, so that there is no way to engage her gaze directly, as if she were looking at something forever out of our sight.

This portrait, a copy of the original painted in 1819 by Lady Caroline Hamilton, hangs in the Mary March Provincial Museum, located in the town of Grand Falls and dedicated to the history and culture of the Beothuks, Newfoundland's native aboriginal tribe. Grand Falls seems an appropriate site for such a museum, for the town was built around the eponymous falls of the Exploits River, the center of Beothuk culture. The Exploits River was the major source of salmon for the Beothuks and served as the main thoroughfare for their seasonal migrations between their summer encampments along the coast and their winter settlements around Red Indian Lake—named after the "red men," the English nickname for Native Americans, which derived from the Beothuks' practice of painting their faces with red ocher.

The museum was originally started in the early 1980s by a group of amateur local archaeologists. When I first visited it in 1988, it had recently reopened after having been taken over by the province and completely renovated. Its new geological, archaeological, and historical displays had been constructed according to the highest educational museum standards and most recent research, and I was told it was now considered one of the finer small regional archaeological museums in Atlantic Canada. One of the most striking displays in the museum was an "encounter passage," where mannequins of a full-sized Beothuk man and a seventeenth-century Basque sailor stood facing each other, with the visitor caught in the middle of their astonishment.

I found that the professional staff, most of them under thirty, quickly distanced themselves from the few remaining eclectic artifacts and displays associated with the museum's earlier amateur incarnation. These included a tiny, ancient, rusting, cast-iron locomotive salvaged from the old narrow-gauge Newfie Bullet; a "National Historic Site" sign placed outside the building with no indication of what it pertained to ("That's the Feds' contribution," a young archaeologist told me. "They felt they ought to be in on it."); and, most egregious of all, the "reconstructed Beothuk village" outside the main building. Going outside, I found that the "village" consisted of an enclosed circle of structures about a half acre in extent, containing ersatz replicas of Beothuk dwellings, cook pits, canoes, and other artifacts. Even I could see that these "replicas" were crudely done and that the site itself—an extremely uneven piece of ground rising in the center to a steep little peak—was an unlikely one for a native settlement. Still, as I walked around, there seemed to be a certain anachronistic authenticity in the presence of some pop cans and plastic trash around the dwellings, serving unintentionally as modern counterparts of ancient Indian garbage middens.

Mary March is the name the English gave to Demasduit, a young Beothuk woman who was captured in March of 1819 on the frozen surface of Red Indian Lake by a group of planters from Twillingate. Demasduit's story is one of the stranger and more tragic "Indian captive" stories, partly because she was one of only two Beothuks whose person and history were known in any detail.

Given that they were among the first American aborigines encountered by Europeans, and that they survived for over three hundred years after initial contact was made, the most remarkable thing about the Beothuks may be how little is known about them. It is possible that their numbers never exceeded five hundred to a thousand individuals. Their lack of contact with the early Basque, French, and English explorers is striking, but it is a lack that seemed desired on both sides. Unlike other native peoples of incipient Canada, the Beothuks had nothing the early explorers and adventurers wanted, and thus there was little motivation to establish trade or communications with them. Unlike the mainland traders, the Newfoundland pioneers were not looking for furs, minerals, or routes into the interior in that ever-elusive quest for the Northwest Passage. The Beothuks had no gold or other precious metals. No settlers sought their land for farming. There was no farming. From its beginning, Newfoundland had only one value—fish—and for that the Beothuks had nothing useful or valuable to teach them or trade with them.

Likewise, the Beothuks seemed to want little from the Europeans other than to be left alone. Like many indigenous North American tribes, they followed the cultural practice of pilfering the few items they found they could use—knives, copper pots, fishhooks—but their depredations were so few that the Europeans generally considered them nuisances rather than crimes or affronts demanding retribution.

Moreover, most of the early European settlements in Newfoundland were along the coast of the Avalon Peninsula, far from where most of the Beothuks lived along the mouths of the rivers to the north—the Gander, the Terra Nova, and, above all, the great Exploits River. With no reason to trade and nothing to compete for, Europeans and Beothuks lived not so much in harmony as in a commensal relationship of largely mutual indifference and nondisturbance, and so little recorded contact occurred for the first two hundred years of coexistence.

It was not until after 1713, when the Treaty of Utrecht solidified British control of the island and residents of the initial settlements on the Avalon began to migrate north into Trinity, Bonavista, and Notre-Dame Bays, that the two cultures began to overlap abrasively. As the

English colonized these areas, establishing fishing rooms and plantations along the mouths of the Beothuks' traditional salmon rivers, the aborigines were driven inland and to less fertile coastal areas. They did not go peacefully, though there are no verified attacks on English settlements. Instead, they engaged in guerilla warfare, stealing or destroying fishing equipment, stages, boats, slips, and traps. By the mid-eighteenth century their actions had grown, in the minds of many settlers, from occasional annoyances to serious threats. Reprisals began. There were numerous incidents, growing in number throughout that century, involving the burning of Beothuk settlements, the destruction of food stores, and, according to documents of the British Admiralty, the occasional murder and massacring of the Beothuks themselves, sometimes "for sport." Such incidents disturbed the British authorities, and they issued edicts forbidding the killing or harassment of Beothuks, but the government presence in early Newfoundland was too small and too far from the distant settlements to prevent further incidents.

John Peyton, Jr., a fur trapper and salmon fisherman, had complained for years to the authorities in St. John's of continuing acts of theft and vandalism committed by the Beothuks. The final straw came in the late winter of 1819, when one of Peyton's boats, loaded with dry salmon for transport to St. John's, was taken in the night by a band of Beothuks. The boat was scuttled and valuable fishing equipment and arms were destroyed. Peyton and a group of other white men set out up the Exploits River in what, he later testified in the official inquiry, was an attempt to establish "friendly and profitable relations" with the Beothuks. Peyton and his companions caught up with the Indian band on the frozen shores of Red Indian Lake. The Beothuks fled, but a young woman, carrying an infant, was unable to keep up. She handed the baby off to one of the Beothuk men, turned, knelt down on the ice, and raised her caribou tunic to expose her breasts, a gesture that Peyton took as a plea for mercy.

When her husband, Nonosabasut, the Beothuk chief, saw that Demasduit had been apprehended, he turned back and confronted Peyton and his men, demanding with gestures and loud voice that she be released. He was an imposing figure, described as being at least six feet tall and very muscular. When he attempted to wrest Demasduit from her captors, an altercation ensued. He attacked one of the men with a hatchet, which another man managed to take from him. He then began to strangle Peyton's father, at which point one of the men shot him dead.

Demasduit was brought back to Twillingate, where she stayed with the Reverend John Leigh for several weeks and was given the name Mary March, because she had been captured in the month of March. Leigh described her as

> Tall and rather stout, having small and delicate limbs, particularly her arms. Her hands and feet were very small and beautifully formed and of these she was very proud, her complexion a light copper colour, became nearly as fair as a European's after a course of washing and absence from smoke, her hair was black, which she delighted to comb and oil, her eyes larger and more intelligent than those of an Esquimaux, her teeth small, white and regular, her cheek bones rather high, but her countenance had a mild and pleasing expression.

In the spring she was then transported to St. John's, where she lived for several weeks at the house of Governor Sir Charles Hamilton and his wife, Lady Caroline, the first governor's wife to actually reside in Newfoundland. It was there at the Hamiltons' residence that Lady Hamilton painted the watercolor portrait of Mary March, which, according to Beothuk scholar Ingeborg Marshall, is "the only fully authenticated portrait of a Beothuk." Two decades later the English artist William Gosse made two miniature copies of this portrait with slightly changed features, one of which is actually thought to portray Shanawdithit, another young Beothuk woman captured in 1823. Thus it would seem that even "the only fully authenticated portrait of a Beothuk" comes down to us with an ambiguous identity.

During the time that Mary March lived in St. John's, she apparently became accustomed to her situation, learned a fair amount of English, and readily identified objects that she was shown with native words, which her hosts recorded, and which supply one of the few sources, though fragmentary and out of any context, of the Beothuk language. She is said to have become a favorite of St. John's society and, clothed in English dress, attended a number of parties and gatherings held in her honor, receiving numerous gifts, which she appeared to relish. Through her "delicacy, intelligence, and proper behavior," she is credited with changing the attitude of most St. Johnsmen from one of disdain and aggression toward the Beothuks to admiration and sympathy, a change that led to the formation in 1827 of the Beothuk Institute, an organization dedicated to locating, befriending, and preserving the remaining Beothuk tribes. It was a change that came too late.

Although she appeared to acclimate herself to life in St. John's, Mary March remained homesick and continued to express an undiminished desire to be reunited with her people. In June of 1819 she returned to Twillingate aboard an English ship, and attempts were made to locate the Beothuk band from which she had been taken in order to return her to her people and to use her as an intermediary to establish peaceful relations with the remaining Beothuks. Glimpses of fleeing Indians were seen in and around New Bay, but Mary made it clear that she had no wish to leave the protection of the English unless she were returned to the band of which her dead husband had been chief. In fact, she showed a peculiar reluctance to leave the presence of Peyton, her captor, whom she seemed to regard as her protector.

Meanwhile, her health had been in decline for some time, probably with pulmonary consumption. In September another ship arrived at Twillingate, this one captained by David Buchan, the English officer who over the previous decade had made multiple concerted efforts to make contact and establish peaceful relations with the Beothuks. Again, efforts to locate Beothuks proved fruitless, and on January 8, 1820, Mary March died. Captain Buchan set out in skiffs with a party of men and transported her body up the Exploits River to the site of her capture on Red Indian Lake. There they found the body of Nonosabasut on an open scaffold in one of the deserted mamateeks that had been converted into a burial hut. They placed Mary's body in a coffin that had been brought with them.

"It was neatly made," wrote Buchan to Governor Hamilton, "and handsomely covered with red cloth ornamented with copper trimmings and breastplate. The corpse, which was carefully secured and decorated with the many trinkets that had been presented to her, was in a most perfect state, and so little was the change in features that imagination would fancy life not yet extinct."

Demasduit's coffin was placed on a scaffold inside a tent, with a Union Jack flying from the top. Many of the presents that she had received from her admirers in St. John's, including two wooden dolls of which she had been particularly fond, were left with her. After Buchan and his party had left, some of the members of her tribe, whose numbers were then probably less than thirty, returned and broke open the coffin with hatchets, removing the clothing and other items. They left the coffin above ground for several months, and then buried Demasduit's remains with those of her husband.

On the back side of the small hill behind the Mary March Museum, a trail wound beside a cross section of a "reconstructed" Beothuk burial cache carved out of the hillside. The opening was covered with a fitted piece of Plexiglas and contained an artificial skeleton of a Beothuk adult in the traditional fetal position, with skin moccasins and a small wooden doll placed beside it. As I peered into the small hillside cavity, its contents obscured in the growing dusk, I saw, or rather heard, a sudden movement inside, a scuttle and then a dark, furry shape with a long, hairless tail that could belong to only one creature. The rat, which appeared to be gnawing on the synthetic skeleton, stopped and looked at me for an instant, then darted out of sight into the side of the cavity. It was an unexpected and no-doubt unintended bit of realism. When I mentioned it to the museum archaeologist inside, he was surprised, and then amused. The subject of discussion in the town all week, he told me, had been an epidemic of rats. The city had recently closed the municipal dump across the highway, but, it appears, with the cardinal blunder of failing to exterminate the rodents. The rats, deprived of the regular nourishment that they had become accustomed to, had dispersed in search of greener pastures.

Two years after Demasduit's death, another member of her band, a young woman known as Shanawdithit, was captured and lived for several years in Twillingate and St. John's. She provided sketches and descriptions that form the main firsthand source of our knowledge of Beothuk culture and the events surrounding Demasduit's capture and the death of her husband. When Shanawdithit died on June 6, 1829, likely of the same disease that killed Demasduit, she was the last of the Beothuks ever seen alive.

On September 14, 1829, W. E. Cormack, the first president of the Beothuk Institute, whose unsuccessful efforts to locate and establish relations with the aborigines had led him to undertake the first known trek across the interior of Newfoundland seven years earlier, published an obituary of Shanawdithit in the *London Times*. It was, in essence, a lyrical eulogy, full of regret and irony, for her people and their strange fate:

This tribe, the Aborigines of Newfoundland, presents an anomaly in the history of man. Excepting a few families of them, soon after the discovery of the Americas, they never held intercourse with the Europeans, by whom they have since been surrounded, nor with other tribes of Indians, since the introduction of firearms amongst them. . . .

There has been a primitive nation, once claiming rank as a portion of the human race, who have lived, flourished, and become extinct in their own orbit. They have been dislodged, and disappeared from the earth in their native independence in 1829, in as primitive a condition as they were before the discovery of the New World, and that too on the nearest point of America to England, in one of our oldest and most important colonies.

Questions of Indigenousness

Indigenous people [are] culturally distinct groups that have occupied a region longer than other immigrant groups or colonist
groups.

—Cultural Survival (organization)

*Questions: Does this mean the oldest known groups occupying a region?
Oldest existing groups? Oldest non-Western groups? Are the English
indigenous to Great Britain? The Micmac Indians from Nova Scotia
supplanted the Beothuks as Newfoundland's resident Native American group in the early nineteenth century, two hundred years after
Europeans first colonized the island. Are they "indigenous"?*

By indigenous, then, we essentially mean early peoples of an
area whose traditional cultures are rooted in particular landscapes with which they are essentially and specifically identified,
whether they are presently living in those landscapes or not.

—From the Introduction to *Family of Earth and Sky:
Indigenous Tales of Nature from around the World,*
edited by John Elder and Herta D. Wong (Beacon Press, 1994).

*Questions: How early is "early"? "Essentially and specifically identified"
by whom? Are sixteenth-generation African-American Chicagoans
therefore "indigenous" to their African homeland? Partly? To what
degree? What about Iowans in California? Or Newfoundlanders in*

Boston, Toronto, or Fort McMurray, Alberta? Do these criteria apply only to intact societies? What does intact mean? Are those individuals or groups whose culture is not rooted in a particular landscape therefore not indigenous anywhere? Can white suburban teenagers be considered culturally indigenous to their particular homogeneous environments of shopping malls and cars? Are there "indigenous" Manhattanites?

Such ideologically deductive and inclusive definitions are at least interesting, in that they state the basic element of connection to a landscape and at the same time, by the use of comparative means of establishing status and defensive qualifiers, show just how slippery that connection can be. We are all, in a sense, indigenous in absentia. Or perhaps one might say that each of us is irrevocably indigenous to his or her own personal history.

The word *indigenous* finds its etymological origin in the Sanskrit phrase *krmi-ja-*, which translates as "produced by worms."

Sweet Cups of Death

I would like to have been at the 1954 session of the Newfoundland House of Assembly when the pitcher plant, a carnivorous angiosperm, was chosen as the official flower of the province. I would like to have understood what they were thinking, what "message" or "image" the lawmakers were trying to send or present. Was it a subtle warning to Canada, which Newfoundland had joined only five years before, to keep its federal claws at a respectful distance? Was it a rough bit of Newfoundland humor? An impish parody of the genteel pretensions being wafted from Ottawa across the Cabot Straits? A refusal by Newfoundlanders to "beautify" with a false image their harsh, rugged land and the hard facts of survival they had become inured to over the centuries?

It was likely none of these, of course, or any other intended message or image. In a culture where plastic flamingos and Smurf cartoon figures are still placed in front yards with no trace of irony, the choice of an insect-eating swamp plant as the official provincial flower was probably no more than a recognition of the obvious. In a land where, during its short summer, a riot of glorious, colorful wildflowers thrives—wild iris, joe-pye weed, rhodora, cow vetch, blue flag, harebell, lupin, goowitty, fireweed, orange hawkweed, and evening primrose, to mention just a few—the lowly and morbidly fascinating pitcher plant is the most characteristic and representative of all. Forced to survive in one of the most nutrient-poor environments of all, it does so by adapting to what it finds abundant there, namely, insect protein.

One sees things in nature for years, and then, for reasons too complex and braided to tease out, one finds oneself finally *looking* at them. I finally

looked at Newfoundland pitcher plants one afternoon in August on
the Great Northern Peninsula. I was exploring an old tractor path into
the woods whose winding and mysterious disappearance into the aisles
of dark spruce and fir had intrigued me. The path was used, in the winter, for hauling out wood, when the marshes, or "mishes," were frozen
solid. Now the path was soggy, and although I had on knee-high rubber
boots, I was tempted to turn back when the track became more of a
flooded ditch than a path, bordered with wild iris pods. But I persisted,
perhaps a third of a mile in, until I came to a large open stretch of bog,
flooded in sunlight and covered with thick mounds of sphagnum. The
bog surface was islanded with clusters of pitcher plant blossoms on long
narrow stems, like bonneted ladies huddled together in gossip.

Although it was still high summer, the bog was ablaze with autumnal
colors. The whitish-green mounds of moss were brindled with scarlet.
The whorls of the pitcher plant calyxes were dyed in purple-red, yellow,
and deep green. Their rosettes of large, hooded, pitcher-shaped leaves
were speckled and streaked with varicose veins and kidney spots—a
vegetable abstract of old age. At the bottom of each pitcher leaf was a
small pool of rainwater, mixed with sweet digestive juices produced by
the plant. Each plant looked as if it had been carved of dull, polished
wax, and from each rosette of leaves there rose a thick, short purple
stalk, at the end of which nodded a single, greenish-red flower of five
petals with a large, flattened pistil.

Surely the pitcher plant is one of the most alien-looking of all flow-
ering plants, something we might have imagined growing on Mars, or
in the nightmare soil of our more lurid imaginings. How do such subterranean colors flourish in sunlight? I stooped to examine a thick
cluster of the plants. Nearly every hollow, hooded leaf sheath had a
small, beetle, fly, or other insect floating in its seemingly benign,
clear, slightly sweet cup of water. One cup I peered into contained a
lovely small white-winged, black-eyed moth that had apparently only
just been trapped. It lay on the surface of the water, beating its delicate, still-dry wings and looking up at me with what seemed a re-
strained poignancy. "I came here pursuing food, or sex," it seemed to
say, "and found death instead."

I pushed my finger into one of the few empty sheaths and felt the soft, dry, fine, down-pointing hairs lining the inside surface. They offered the gentlest of resistance to my finger as I withdrew it, a suggestion of those bamboo Chinese finger puzzles that intrigued me as a child. I have always been amused by the obviously euphemistic common names given to certain flowers by Victorian botanists. Lady's thumb, for instance, an herb of the buckwheat family, possesses swollen stem segments just below the leaf attachments that, in form, resemble the clitoris. Even more obvious is the common woodland orchid, pink lady's slipper, or moccasin flower, whose blossom is not so much a floral mimicry of feminine footwear as it is a remarkably accurate botanical counterpart of the vulva. Its large, semidivided pink flower clearly suggests a woman's swollen outer labia in a state of sexual arousal; the soft, curving platform leading to the stamens and pistils evokes the vagina's vestibule; even the long, spindly, green sepals shading the blossom look like stylized pubic hair.

The long tubular leaves of the pitcher plant bear less visual resemblance to female genitalia than these other species, but they possess a stronger tactile one: the soft, cool outer cowl; the short, stiff front sheath like the hard pubic bone; the moist, delicate, finely haired tube leading to sweet liquor and small deaths.

Seen this way, the pitcher plant seems a highly appropriate choice as the province's official flower. It teaches us that nature is like Newfoundland: We romanticize and euphemize it at our peril, for more often than not, even in its coolest vegetable form, it presents us with undisguised sex and mortality.

Kids

I am spending the night at the Grenfell Louie A. Hall Bed and Breakfast in the town of Forteau (pronounced "Fardo") on the southern
shore of Labrador. My hosts, Peggy Hancock and her husband,
Dwight, were both born in this house—in fact, in the very room where
they now sleep—when it was a Grenfell Nursing Station. After supper
Peggy was telling me about the awful winter here two years ago:

"Oh my dear, there was drifts up to the wires, thirty feet high. You'd
be walking on the highway and if a car come along it'd have to stop and
let you walk around it. It was like walking through a tunnel. They had an
avalanche over to Blanc Sablon, just above the ferry. It just come down
and wiped out one house. The woman there lost her husband and son.
She was saved because she was trapped between the bed and the wall. Her
little one was staying over to her mom's that night, thank God. She was
trapped there for twelve hours—said she could feel her husband's foot—
it was still warm, but then she felt it growing cold. When people finally
come, she could hear them walking over the snow on top of her, said it
was like hearing people walk over her grave. It was packed tight, so she
could hear every word distinctly. They finally heard her and dug her out.
Now the story is that long ago there had been another house built on that
terrace—just a tilt, really—above the ferry, and that another avalanche
had wiped out some people there the same way and no one would build
there again until recently. Her father had built the house they were living
in, and when he woke up that morning he looked out his window and saw
the house was gone—like that, eh?"

It was Peggy's great-grandfather who gave the land for the building of
the first hospital in Forteau, called the Dennison Cottage. It was built in

1907, through a gift by a Civil War veteran who had been abandoned on the Labrador coast by the Southern-sympathizing crew of a Gloucester schooner, and who was cared for by the people here. The current hospital, built in 1946 with lumber cut across the Strait of Belle Isle in St. Anthony's, was the gift of a Miss Louie A. Hall of Rochester, New York, treasurer of that branch of the International Grenfell Association.

Dwight's father had worked here as a caretaker at the hospital before he was married. Peggy pointed out a photo of him on the mantel over the fireplace:

"That firebox was from the HMS *Raleigh*, wrecked here in 1922. The British navy blew it up a few years after because it had all kinds of secret missives on it, but local people had taken artillery shells off it, which they kept in their parlors until several of them turned out to be live. Anyway, one morning Dwight's dad come down and stoked up the stove, a big old woodstove, and sees that there is, like, a covered roasting pan beside it; so when he gets it stoked up, he takes the pan and begins to put it in the oven, when the nurse runs in and shouts, 'NOT ME BABY! NOT ME BABY!' She had delivered three babes the day before, and one of them was a preemie, you see, so she was keeping it in a roaster beside the stove to keep it warm."

There was another photo on the mantel of five young girls from the 1930s. Except for the treeless, barren, rocky landscape behind them, they could have been from Ohio. Even in such an isolated and remote place as this tiny Labrador outport must have been seventy years ago, the dress fabrics, their hairstyles, and even the look of their eyes and the way the girls smiled all seemed to mark them indelibly of their time.

"Three of them is dead," said Peggy, pointing to the picture. "There's my dad's sister—she's dead—but the rest is still alive, far as we know."

She pointed to the girl in the middle, towheaded, about eleven years old, in a long plaid dress with long sleeves, hiding her hands. "Now, we're not sure who this one is. We thinks she's a woman who moved away years ago, but Dad says if he could see her hand he could tell if it were she. One day, when he was six or seven, he was out chopping wood and the girl come over and put her hand on the pile and called him chicken and he come down with the blade and chopped off her finger— just like that. Kids, eh?"

Red Bay

The next day, in dense fog, I drove up the south shore of Labrador some thirty miles from the ferry terminal at Blanc Sablon to the end of the paved highway at Red Bay, population 264. I had come to see the site of the sixteenth-century Basque whaling station that had been discovered there in the 1970s. Unlikely as it seems, this remote corner of a forbidding and unknown coast was once regarded as the "whaling capital of the world." Four hundred and fifty years ago Red Bay harbored up to one hundred Basque whaling ships that harpooned right and bowhead whales from as far away as Greenland. Wharves, tryworks, cooperages, and other structures spread across the north shore of Saddle Island, while living quarters dotted the opposite mainland shore. Dense pillars of black, acrid smoke rose from the tryworks as flensed layers of blubber were rendered down into valuable whale oil, while the massive carcasses of the leviathans were left to rot in the shallow waters offshore.

This daring and difficult industry persisted about fifty years, roughly from 1550 to 1600, and then, like so much early Newfoundland history, disappeared for centuries until the rise of serious archaeology here in the last half of the twentieth century. It was old Basque documents found in Bilbao that led to the discovery of the Red Bay site in 1971, when it was excavated extensively by archaeologists René Beauvoir of Ottawa and Newfoundland's own James Tuck. The visitors' center on the mainland contains a small display of the many artifacts that have been unearthed, among them a number of whaling and carpentry tools, large fragments of woolen clothing, stoneware pots and dishes, and a broken but nearly complete and remarkably delicate drinking glass. Most of the artifacts recovered from the site are in the National Museum in Ottawa and are technically "on loan" from the town of Red Bay.

The site also has environmental significance. A number of ancient algae-covered whale heads and other bones have been recovered. These have proven unexpectedly valuable in the study of the North Atlantic's remaining population of northern right whales *(Eubalaena glacialis)*, a highly endangered marine species. Right whales are large baleen cetaceans, thirty-five to fifty feet in length, with characteristic white wart-like growths called *callosities* on their heads. They were the species of choice (or the "right" whale) during the heyday of North American whaling, for they tended to travel in large pods, were slow and docile when being chased, and floated when dead. As a result of such intense hunting their numbers declined precipitously. Although they've been a protected species since 1935, there are only some 325–350 surviving northern right whales today. In order to gauge the diversity of the remaining gene pool (a critical factor for the species' survival), geneticists have taken DNA samples from these five-hundred-year-old right whale bones to help establish genealogical lines for living whales.

It was late in the day when I arrived at the visitors' center, and I was too late for the scheduled tours to the archaeological sites on Saddle Island; but I managed to get a ride over to the island in an open skiff with Jim Yetman, the local lighthouse keeper. Jim has lived in the keeper's house on the western end of the island for twenty-five years, though the original wooden lighthouse blew down in a storm in 1935 and the "light" is now an automated beacon on a metal tower beside the house on the tallest and most exposed part of the island. His father was the keeper before him, but Jim is the last in a long line of lighthouse keepers. The Saddle Island light is scheduled to be demanned in two years, along with the rest of Newfoundland's remaining manned lighthouses.

I guessed Jim to be somewhere in his fifties, a short, affable fellow with a thick gray mustache and wide, watery blue eyes. Since the lighthouse was automated, his duties are only seasonal, and his wife works in a neighboring town on the mainland. When his four children were growing up, he ferried them from the island to and from the school in Red Bay in his Fiberglas skiff every day. All are now "away," that is, off-island, except for his youngest, David, who is studying biochemistry at Memorial University in St. John's and is employed as a summer tour guide at the visitors' center.

The fog still hung over Saddle Island when we landed and a raw wind blew down over the massive mainland ridges to the southwest. I stood talking with Jim in his boat shed, with life jackets and other marine gear hanging on the plywood walls. He shyly showed me some black-and-white paintings he had done of some humpback whales that had come into the harbor. They were quite accurately drawn. He had seen a minke and a killer whale in the harbor two days before, but it was mostly humpbacks that came in now. There never had been much whaling in the Strait of Belle Isle, he said; it was too difficult for the big boats to maneuver in. Most of Newfoundland's late-developing and short-lived whaling industry was centered further south in the Hawke's Bay area during the 1940s, 1950s, and 1960s—long after most other North American whaling had ceased.

It seemed incredible that the archaeological sites on Saddle Island had been known for only a little more than twenty years. After all, the island's shores are littered everywhere with thousands of fragments of curved red tiles, some of them quite large. These tiles were brought over from France by the Basques as ballast and then used to roof their tryworks and other structures. The name of the town itself is said to have derived from the prevalence of these reddish tiles. Much of the broken tile is heaped in large, midden-like piles on the upper shore. The rest is scattered on the beaches, where the fragments have been rounded and smoothed into flat, brick-red stones by centuries of wave action.

When I asked Jim about this, he said that the people of Red Bay had, of course, always known about the tiles, but they were taken to be just another kind of strange beach stone and they thought no more of them. In other places along the shore I picked up black chunks of what looked like coarse, shiny coke. Jim explained that these were pieces of whale fat that had spilled out of the trypots and into the sand, where they had crystallized. After four hundred years even whale fat loses its smell, and these black chunks, too, had simply been regarded as natural, if unexplained, objects by the local inhabitants.

As we talked, Jim expressed some resentment toward Parks Canada and the archaeologists who excavated the sites. First, he said, they took most of the artifacts to Ottawa and "we don't expect to get them back." All of the digs ceased in 1991 or 1992, and the visitors' center is now owned and run by the community. Parks Canada, he said, has declared Saddle Island a National Historic Site and has promised to build an even larger interpretive center, but plans have been downsized and the money has not been forthcoming. This is the perennial problem facing government-funded projects or enterprises in Newfoundland: brave starts and poor follow-ups.

"It's too bad," he said, "because people are losing their enthusiasm for the project. Either let's get on with it or let us get on with our lives, but don't keep us dangling like a fish on a jigger."

There is not much besides tourism left for the people here except for the caplin fishery, and that has been highly irregular of late. Red Bay is a proud community. It had the first municipal wharf in Labrador, built by the government in the 1950s after a tidal wave swept away most of the private wharves and stages. *National Geographic* did a story on the Basque excavation in 1985, causing attendance to shoot up for a while. But Jim claims Parks Canada deliberately downgraded the significance of the Red Bay site in the *National Geographic* article, in part because it felt the community might not be able to handle the influx of people. "Stunned Newfies, you know," he said with contempt for the stereotype of incompetence that mainland Canadians still hold of Newfoundlanders. Attendance has been slacking off ever since.

Jim invited me up to his house on the hill for tea, but I felt I should use the remaining daylight to walk the island trail, so we arranged for him to pick me up in forty-five minutes at the dock at the other end of the island. I set off along the north shore in mist, wind, and fog, following the original trail used by the whalers, which was now marked with red-tipped white stakes. Everywhere there were printed signs indicating where tryworks, wharves, dormitories, a possible chapel, forges, etc., had been excavated. Other signs indicated the "wooden and stone remains" of wharves and "fat-stained rocks." Aside from the ubiquitous tiles and occasional balls of petrified whale fat, however, I actually *saw* nothing except lichen-covered rocks, mounds of earth and turf, and small nondescript depressions in the indicated places. Without the information I received at the visitors' center, and the interpretive signs lining the trail, I doubt I would have been able to "see" anything more than generations of Red Baymen had.

At the low point of the island's "saddle," several old derelict wooden skiffs had been hauled up and overturned on the shore. Not far inland there was a wooden cabin with a fence made of "longers," or long poles, surrounding it. It had no signs about it and did not appear to be an exhibit. I could see a Skidoo and a sewing machine inside through the missing door. Abandoned garden mounds outside might have been ten, or a hundred, years old. As at so many historic, even "officially" historic, sites here, it is often difficult, if not impossible, to tell which of the elements in a place are identified with past use, and which with present.

Despite the obvious attempt here by archaeologists and government officials to create a definitive, linear story line of history, there was a flattening out or confusion of time in the literal landscape, which reflected and enforced the lateral concept of time I had discovered among the older Newfoundlanders. In one place, for instance, a large, rounded grassy mound was vaguely labeled as "a nineteenth-century Inuit site." It was odd, and strangely compelling, to gaze on an aboriginal habitation that had *supplanted* an older European one. After all, in how many places on this continent have early European settlement sites been subsequently, and nonviolently, occupied by Native Americans? It added to the posthistoric quality of this place.

As I neared the eastern shore of the island, I came on a sign indicating the most spectacular of the finds made here in the 1970s: the hull of a 1565 whaling galleon, resting in silt in about twelve feet of water just offshore. Although centuries of winter ice had eventually caused the hull to collapse, splaying its ribs out like a fan, it had been otherwise perfectly preserved. The ship had been carefully excavated underwater. Among the more dramatic finds were a wooden compass with a brass gimbal, a brass sandglass frame, and a plank bearing a scrimshaw carving of the ship itself. There were tens of thousands of codfish bones still bearing the marks of the splitting knives, and some delicate bones that were later identified as those of the European black rat, which a faunal analyst commented might be "the earliest black rat ever recorded in

North America." The archaeological team had made a rubber mold of the ship's hull, from which a scale replica had been made. But what struck me as most remarkable was that, once the excavation had been completed, the ship hull had been reburied and left to slowly decompose in the frigid waters where it first sank nearly four-and-a-half centuries before.

Of course, I could see nothing of this with my own eyes. There was no visible evidence that I was looking at a major marine archaeological site. Without the interpretive exhibits and signs, there were only the featureless, dark, frigid waters of the Labrador Current. Once again I saw these things only through the archaeologist's imagination, illuminated in images and photographs reconstructed and displayed in exhibits, giving me X-ray vision through this thin soil and barren rock into the hidden past.

The most moving site of all, however, was at the far eastern end of the island: a rock-bound point facing the open Atlantic with waves crashing and exploding against the "sunkers" just offshore. Here are some sixty-eight Basque burial sites, most of them multiple graves of two, three, and even six bodies together. Many are thought to be those of whaling crews who drowned or died in some accident at sea. The graves are marked only with lines of small glacial stones. Photographs of the excavated (and then reburied) bodies show that they were laid out with their heads to the west, perhaps so as to be able to look back toward the home country. Their hands were crossed over their lower abdomens as if in modesty. (Were their clothes removed before burial, so as to be used by those remaining alive?)

One body had been buried outside the perimeter of the cemetery. Where the other graves were quite shallow, less than a foot deep, this one was nearly a meter deep, and the skeleton had an eight-inch wooden cross on his chest, indicating, according to archaeologists, that the deceased was not of the Catholic faith, or perhaps had committed suicide.

Suicide may have seemed like a rational option to some of these men. In one place six unburied skeletons had been found, some in a sitting position, amid the rotting remains of an ancient wooden shed. Over the long centuries, sod had grown up over their bodies, and roots and tendrils had woven themselves through their mold-green bones, eye sockets, and nose holes. It is not known what happened to these men. Like the early cod fishery, this was a migratory whaling industry, and each fall the boats would return with their harvest to their European ports. Perhaps these men had been chosen by lot to remain behind, like the early English "planters" in Newfoundland, to care for the premises, waiting for a ship that might or might not have returned the following spring.

From these grave sites it was a short walk out to the dock where Jim Yetman would pick me up and take me back to the mainland. Standing there, in the gathering darkness with a raw wind coming off the ocean, I thought of those six men, huddling and starving through the long sub-Arctic winter, looking futilely seaward each darkening, shortening day for help that never came. And so there may have come a morning when they decided, or perhaps simply tacitly acknowledged to one another, that there was not sufficient reason to get up and go outside anymore.

As Jim ferried me back from Saddle Island to the visitors' center wharf, he tempered somewhat his earlier remarks about the government's handling of the archaeological project here in Red Bay: "I will say this for 'em, Tuck and the others. They sent all the kids in this place to university. Before the archaeologists came, kids here never even thought they could go to college. Then they put them to work, you see, with the digging and the making the docks and such, and encouraged them to get more learning, and now there's not a one of them doesn't want to go to the university in St. John's. Oh, I'm not saying all of them makes it through. Some of them comes back after a while, but they all goes, they all tries it. They were inspired, you know. They never thought they could go, and now they do. I'll say that much for them, my son. Pretty soon there'll be none of us here but old folks. And then"—here Jim gave a wry grin and cocked his head back toward the windswept headland behind me—"we'll all join those poor boys in the ground. Y's b'y."

The Log of Voyager

The South-West Coast of Newfoundland rolls like the cracked and rumpled skin of some enormous walrus for nearly two hundred miles from Port aux Basques on the west to Terrenceville on the east at the top of the Burin Peninsula. Its cliffs are among the most consistently high and formidable along the island's entire unforgiving shoreline. Averaging five hundred to six hundred feet in height, they form a constantly changing tapestry of bold headlands, beetling bluffs, sheer drops, treacherous reefs, and offshore islands.

The coast's majestic length is sliced and crenellated with long, deep fjords, the work of Ice Age glaciers, which scoured all the soil from the hills and tablelands of the interior, making much of Newfoundland's southern coast a barren, treeless landscape, a tundra-like terrain that is home to moose and caribou, snowshoe hare and rock ptarmigan, and some of the world's greatest concentrations of nesting seabirds. What impoverished the land, however, enriched the sea. The glacier-scraped soil was deposited over a vast area of shallow water south of the island, which helped to create Newfoundland's Grand Banks, the most productive cod-fishing grounds in the world for over five hundred years.

These rocky headlands, so empty and forbidding to the casual observer, nonetheless contain numerous deep and well-protected harbors, through entrances often so narrow as to be undetectable until one is almost upon them. Even then it seems improbable that there should be any communities sustaining themselves in such remote and inhospitable settings. Yet this coast is the home of several dozen of Newfoundland's extraordinary outports, some of them over two hundred years old, ranging in size from a few dozen to several hundred families. Their houses are perched like wooden limpets on steep rocks that circle small, deep harbors at the base of sheer cliffs, or else fringe the landwash (as the shoreline is called in Newfoundland) of small islands hugging the coast. Narrow passages, or "tickles," between the islands and mainland provide anchorage and protection from the frequent ocean storms.

As it has for centuries, as it did for the Basques, Portuguese, and French who preceded the English and Irish, the inshore fishery of cod, halibut, mackerel, lobster, and squid remained, until recently, the basis of the local economy for most of these South-West Coast communities. And though the artifacts of twentieth-century technology—TV satellite dishes, telephone transmitters, and radio equipment—have brought them into direct informational and cultural contact with the rest of the world, a dozen or so of these outports remain physically unconnected by any road to the outside, reachable only by seaplane, by helicopter, or—as they have always been—by boat.

I first visited the South-West Coast outports in 1987 aboard the *Marine Runner*, the mail and passenger boat that made a daily one-way run from Terrenceville to Port aux Basques. It was both a fascinating and a frustrating trip, for the boat tied up at the government wharf in each outport only long enough to take on or let off passengers, drop off and pick up mail, and unload food supplies or mail-ordered items ranging from ammunition to large appliances. I barely got a glimpse of the curious faces of the inhabitants and the strange topography of these mysterious, roadless places—Francois, Grey River, Rencontre West, Ramea, La Poile, Grand Bruit—before we pulled away and the intersecting planes of the high coastal cliffs closed like sliding panels across the harbor entrances as though they had never been.

So when, a few summers later, I was invited to join a sail from New York City to Newfoundland's South-West Coast, I jumped at the chance. The idea of revisiting this stretch of coast by sailboat, with both the time and the independence to explore, at some length, some of the most spectacular coastline and singular communities on the shores of the western North Atlantic, was irresistible.

What made the offer even more intriguing was that the vessel I was asked to crew on was *Voyager*, a classic John Alden fifty-foot gaff-rigged wooden schooner. Originally built in Maine in 1929, she went aground on a jetty during a storm in Newport in 1954, after which she was rebuilt and then sold to her current owner, Peter Phillips of New Rochelle, who had sailed her for the past thirty years. In 1972 he had her hull rebuilt again along original lines in Lunenburg, Nova Scotia. Fitted out with modern navigational equipment, she had made several transatlantic crossings and had won racing trophies in her class up and down the Northeast Coast; but she had never been to Newfoundland.

I had been, and this, I was sure, was the main reason I was invited along. However, I had never been aboard a sailing vessel for more than a few hours, and never on one this large and complex. Most of the other crew members were far more experienced in sailing than I. They included the captain, Peter, a man in his fifties, with thick gray hair, a carefully trimmed beard, and George Clooney good looks; his wife, Jeanette (a certified captain in her own right), slim and athletic, with long brown hair that cascaded around her face and half-hid her large, soft eyes; Paul Bradley, the first mate, a cabinetmaker from Mattapoisett, Massachusetts, a wiry, muscular man in his late thirties who nearly always went barefoot and had sailed with *Voyager* for thirteen years; Jim Mairs, my New York editor, a man with a deep, soft voice and an open, midwestern face who had often crewed with Peter and Jeanette; Jim's younger wife, Gina Webster, a professional photographer, a petite olive-skinned woman with classic Italian features who had had only slightly more experience sailing than I, but who made up for it with a natural self-confidence and quick intelligence; and Eric Swenson, a publishing colleague of Jim's, a tall, older, white-haired gentleman who had also sailed on *Voyager* before. Peter, Jim, and Gina brought the boat up from New York to Mattapoisett, just south of the Cape Cod Canal, where Paul and I boarded. Eric and Jeanette were to fly up to Halifax and join us in Lunenburg when we stopped there for supplies.

Log (Supplemental):
July 19–July 29—Cape Cod to Newfoundland

From Cape Cod it took us nine days to reach the coast of Newfoundland. We sailed through the Cape Cod Canal, rounded the tip of

Provincetown, and set a straight course for Lunenburg on the southern coast of Nova Scotia. From there we hugged the shore east to Cape Breton, went through the locks at St. Peter's Canal, and sailed into the broad, protected waters of the Bras d'Or Lakes. After stopping at Baddeck, we went out through St. Andrew's Channel at the eastern end of the Bras d'Or, then headed north-northeast across the Cabot Straits toward La Poile, the westernmost roadless outport on Newfoundland's South-West Coast.

During the first few days at sea, I gradually came to perceive and appreciate the profound difference between sailing and any form of motorized travel over water. Like most landlubbers I have always, if unconsciously, assumed the main difference was speed. At sea, however, the main difference is sound—not the total lack of it, but the contrast. Instead of the obliterating and monolithic roar of a motor, a wooden sailboat emits a spectrum of various but related sounds: the creak of the rigging, the hull settling in its ribs, the clanging of the staysail back and forth along its metal traveler in a shifting wind, the gentle *shuhh* of following seas against the stern, the harsh side slap of choppy seas. One morning Jim Mairs commented on how the ship's sounds were "very human sounds."

"Well," Peter replied, "she's a very human ship. She has her own mind. She can be contrary, stubborn, buoyant, sluggish, responsive. She's taught me a lot."

On the first leg of the voyage, a two-man watch system had to be designed for our crew of five, a mathematical problem whose solution was a twenty-four hour schedule of staggered three-hour watches pairing those least familiar with the boat with those most familiar. This arrangement allowed each crew member to share his or her watch with two others, as each member's watch was rotated back three hours each day, allowing seven and half hours between watches. Despite its seeming complexity, the schedule worked well.

As the least-experienced member of the crew, I was initially matched with Peter, the captain, a bit of good fortune in that it put me on a fast learning curve about boats at sea, or at least *this* boat. Peter, a soft-spoken man with a gentle manner, lived with Jeanette aboard *Voyager* all year, berthing it at New Rochelle when they were not at sea. He had taught architecture for twenty-five years in New York, but they were now planning to take a five-year sail around the world.

A schooner like *Voyager*, Peter explained, is made to sail *with* the wind. The gaff rigging provides maximum sail area, especially when sailing wing-to-wing, that is, with the sails on opposite sides of the boat. Because she is low-centered, she doesn't need as deep a keel as a Marconi-rigged (triangular-sailed) boat, which is made more for beating up against the wind. Although we didn't encounter any heavy weather on the trip up, we occasionally experienced some ten- to twelve-foot following seas, which the boat's flared stern flattened out and transformed into a series of gentle, rolling surges forward.

As we sailed across the Gulf of Maine, the winds were light and out of the southwest. The second night out of the Cape Cod Canal we sailed on a broad reach with five sails—main, fore, forestay, jib, and topsail. Paul, the first mate, scurried barefoot up the main rigging and out on the gaff to rig the topsail. In his workshirt and jeans, he looked like a friendly blue monkey as Gina photographed him from the deck. I stood a midnight-to-0300-hour watch with Peter and took the helm for the first time, sailing wing-to-wing—the mainsheet on a starboard tack, the fore on a port—the boat swinging back and forth easily as we began to sail before the wind. With the light on the peak of the foremast illuminating the main and topsails like a great Japanese lantern, we rolled ahead, the great sails on their Sitka spruce booms and gaffs swaying and yawing, jibing and lifting, like Robert Frost's silken tent, in loosely held bonds, a symphony of sails and spars.

At first, the surface life of the open ocean seemed remarkably thin. We occasionally spotted an individual whale at a distance, or a few dolphins shadowing the boat, but the bird life was fairly monotonous, consisting exclusively of two species, greater shearwaters and Wilson's petrels—plus a bedraggled and exhausted migrating cowbird that spent the night in our bow, and that Paul christened Birdy and fed dead flies from the galley.

But rather than being disappointed at the comparative dearth of bird species and the numbers of cetaceans, I began to notice how adept and fitted to their environment the birds were, and what different approaches they took to it. The smaller petrels lifted and dropped over the swells, almost as if they were bouncing on a silky trampoline, expertly attuned to the rhythm of the watery surface. The shearwaters, on the other hand, exhibited the accuracy of their common name, skimming and arcing across the surface, appearing to dip the tip of first one wing, then the other, into the water itself, as if they were showing off, like a world-class skater or trapeze artist, or drawing momentary hieroglyphs on the water itself.

As we crossed the Gulf of Maine, the numbers of whales and dolphins did not increase much, but I came to see them differently than I had on whale-watching trips at home. They were no longer just objects for my observation, zoo animals in a somewhat larger pool, but denizens of a world I was merely passing through. They were in their own element, and the infrequent sightings came to have more significance, as if they were favors bestowed upon us, audiences granted. Peter maintained that cetaceans are much more likely to approach a boat under sail than one under motor. Whether or not this is true, we were certainly more aware of some of their visits than we might have been otherwise. Early on the third morning, at about 0400 hours, while I was on watch with Paul, we heard several soft but expansive exhalations—*P-H-h-u-u-h!*—off the starboard bow. The blows stayed with us for five minutes or so, coming within forty to fifty feet of the boat, and gradually dropping astern. We could only vaguely make out their black shapes, but they seemed too large to be porpoises or dolphins.

After a few days, I found the measure of the weather and the immediate environment shifting from myself to the boat as a whole. I learned how the different sails played off one another, that each sail was not simply *more* sail, but acted in concert with the others, catching wind funneled or sheared forward by others, blocking wind for others if not properly rigged. The nautical phrase for adjusting sails and stays, "tuning the rig," with its metaphoric overtones of a properly tuned instrument, took on literal appropriateness. I found I liked the set of the boat best when she was on a starboard tack, on a broad reach. I liked to stand in the bow and look back through a billowing, overlapping set of sails—jib, staysail, foresail, mainsail—that seemed to be straining the wind like the baleen of a great whale.

After picking up Jeanette and Eric and reprovisioning the boat in Lunenburg, we crept slowly along the southern coast of Nova Scotia toward St. Peter's Canal. The five-man watch was revised to a seven-man schedule: three hours on, seven and a half hours off, alternating new people every one and a half hours. On the first night out of Lunenburg I drew the 0130 to 0430 watch (the worst) with Paul. It was mild, perhaps sixty degrees, but even sixty degrees seeps into your bones after three hours sitting at the helm or sitting on the main boom trying to keep it from flopping about in a near-nonexistent wind.

A full moon remained hidden by a light cloud cover, and we could see two or three fishing lights to port as we headed even farther offshore. Paul told me that he had sailed with Peter since 1978, when he was twenty-four. They went to the Mediterranean in 1984, Nova Scotia in 1986. He met his wife, Monique, when a boat he was on beached and wrecked in a hurricane near her home in northern France. They have an adopted four-year-old Tahitian boy named Daniel. Now he does woodworking in Mattapoisett, where he grew up, and mostly crews in schooner races with Peter.

"Yeah," he sighed wistfully, "with a wife and a kid at home, it's hard to get away much anymore."

Paul was relieved at 0300 hours by Peter, who asked me if I could handle the boat alone for a few minutes while he searched for some of the new charts we would need going through the Bras d'Or. We were on a straight course sailing directly before a moderate wind, but being alone at the helm for the first time gave me an enormous sense of responsibility, not only for the boat but also for those sleeping below. I suddenly felt a shadow of that ultimate responsibility that every captain of a boat or ship must feel, the responsibility from which there is no appeal.

My senses, already sharpened on the voyage, had become even more intensely aware of every nuance around me. Although I cannot claim to have done more than begin to perceive what a good sailor must be aware of, I had at least come to appreciate the truth of Peter's gentle reproof to the landlubber's complaint that sailing consists mostly of "nothing going on."

"I've never understood that attitude," he said. "For me, nothing could be further from the truth; being at sea is endlessly fascinating. Every day, every hour is different. Something is always changing, the wind, the current, the colors of the water."

This was no mere aesthetic appreciation, but stemmed from the *necessity* of such awareness at sea, especially in a sailing vessel, where the lack of keen awareness can have serious, even fatal, consequences.

It suddenly occurred to me that all of the sights and sounds around me—the various voices of the boat itself; the gentle pitch of the hull as it evened out the following seas; the rush and swash of the swells around us; the various arcs, parabolas, and ellipses traced by the masts in the skies; the symphonic movement of the clouds; even the cries of the seabirds around us—were all *connected* in a visual harmony and rhythmic relation that was immensely satisfying and pleasing in itself. Because the boat was a human artifact controlled by humans, it required constant attention and adjustment to maintain that harmony and synchronization. And yet we were being *driven* by the direct and universal forces we could observe around us, rather than by the product of immense and removed economic, technological, industrial, and political systems. There was also a kind of abstract exhilaration in realizing that, when under sail, we were moving dozens of tons of wood and iron hundreds of miles while using up absolutely no fossil fuels, creating absolutely no atmospheric pollution, and spending not one cent for the propulsion. Even the breathing of the whales I could hear intermittently in the dark seemed to be coordinated with the rhythms of the waves and the rigging of the boat, so that we both seemed to belong to the same element. We were all working the same waters.

The next morning we passed through St. Peter's Canal, at the southern entrance to the Bras d'Or Lakes and headed toward Baddeck, where we had our first dinner ashore and spent the night tied up at the main wharf.

As we cruised the "lakes"—actually, a large, nearly landlocked body of saltwater—toward Baddeck, Paul told me that sailing on *Voyager* had "spoiled" him for other boats, especially smaller ones. That this was a special boat was not an opinion held only by its crew, but one that also seemed reflected in every port we visited. In Lunenburg, for instance, many of the older men had recognized her as a locally built (or rebuilt) boat and were understandably pleased at her return to her home port. While we were tied up in Baddeck, the owners of contemporary yachts came aboard to admire her sleek racing lines and teak deck.

On Sunday morning, eight days after I had come aboard *Voyager*, we sailed east through St. Andrew's Channel, leaving the Bras d'Or and entering the Cabot Straits. We were now on a thumb line of 69 degrees across the straits to La Poile Bay, Newfoundland, a distance of about a hundred miles. It was a beautiful morning of full sun, with a nearly calm sea. The Cabot Straits crossing is often a rough one, with fog, strong winds, and cross currents being common, but ours was a smooth and clear passage before a light southwest wind. Dolphins occasionally played in front of the bow, and I observed some darker seabirds, Cory's shearwaters, sailing low between the swells. Shortly after entering the straits, we saw, off the port stern, the distant shape of the North Sydney-to-Port-aux-Basques ferry gradually gaining on us, a huge new diesel-powered ship, the *Joseph and Clara Smallwood*, named after Newfoundland's first premier, still alive at ninety-four, and his wife. Our courses were intersecting ones, but the ferry quickly gained on and then passed us long before we crossed her wake.

By nightfall there was a distant cloud bank far ahead that Paul said was sitting over land, but it was not until one o'clock the next morning that we finally saw the lights of Port aux Basques, some thirty miles west of our destination at La Poile.

LOG: Monday, July 29, 1510 Hours—
La Poile, South-West Coast

By dawn the coast of Newfoundland was clearly in view: that convoluted, complex, layered coastline of rock and sparse vegetation, with low correlative clouds hanging just above it. It was another clear and beautiful morning, a light west breeze keeping us almost at four knots, the sun just a couple of degrees above the horizon on this eastern land. Out here, far from the mainland, the water is bluer and foamier and the swells are wonderful. They approach the boat from behind and seem to play with it, like dolphins, before sending us sliding down their transparent foreslopes.

We have set our clocks and watches one-half hour ahead to Newfoundland Daylight Savings Time. But if clock time has advanced, other signs suggest that we have emerged into a land still perceived through the eyes of the past. Even our navigation charts reflect a sense of time warp. In his cabin, from beneath the stack of contemporary charts we had followed all the way up, Peter now drew what looked like a batch of old treasure maps. Though recently printed, the charts for the South-West Coast of Newfoundland are based on British Admiralty Surveys of 1871 and 1872, drawn and lettered with the elaborate cartography and calligraphy of the era. The charts are sprinkled with names that also speak of an older and more colorful era, submerged ledges known as *sunkers*, rocks with names like Bad Neighbor and Blow Me Down Peaks. I half expected to find sea monsters and mermaids drawn in the margins. The charts strike me as aesthetically appealing, but Peter is concerned about their accuracy, though the soundings have presumably been updated over the past 120 years.

As the morning brightened on crisp, deep-blue seas, the coast continued to slip by us some three miles to the north. Rumpled, tortured, beetled, and serrated, the lower rock faces are as cracked and dry as the skin of an alien from a sun-dried planet, the sloping terraces and plateaus above thick with lush, low green vegetation, with occasional thin waterfalls crevassing the rock faces.

Because it has so little revealed history (and therefore identity) this coast reminds everyone on the crew of some other place they have been—Gina of Scotland, Jeanette of Caribbean islands, Paul of Tahiti, Eric of Italy, Jim of Venezuela—and by the irreconcilability of these various analogues it proves its own individuality. It is a somewhat paradoxical landscape, at once ground-down and defiant, compressed and abraded by the weight and rasp of countless glaciers and millennia of erosion. Yet the impression of this scroll of worn rocks is not that of *remnants*, but rather as if all that wearing away had only revealed some inconsolable, tempered core of itself. And what the frozen seas of eons past have carved into the countenance and contours of this land, the rolling seas we ride on still breed in the people who inhabit it.

At 0900 hours we motored into La Poile (rhymes with "coil"), an outport of about seventy residents, and tied up at the government wharf. As usual, a group of men and boys materialized almost instantly and showed intense, if largely silent, interest in *Voyager.* Here, in this small Newfoundland outport, the general curiosity that locals have taken in *Voyager* in previous ports has taken a different form. It seems more personal, especially among the older men. One grizzled old fisherman paid her a puzzling compliment when he growled, "Is she a Newfie boat, b'y?" At first I thought his eyesight must have dimmed considerably, mistaking this cruising vessel for a one-time working schooner, but a man on the dock told Peter that twenty years ago, most of the fishing boats out of here were schooner-type vessels with two twenty-foot dories that they would take with them and lower over the side to handline for cod. It occurs to me that for many of these old-time fishermen, many of whom worked the old banker schooners that used to sail these coasts, our vessel must seem a visible symbol of their past, representing, without literally being, one of those hundreds of wooden sailing vessels that only yesterday were such a constant part of their horizon and that must seem to have vanished mysteriously like fog during their lifetimes. They must have wondered how anything so substantial, so omnipresent and integral in their lives could have disappeared so utterly. Where would it have gone? It is cataracts of disbelief, not of corneas, that makes these old men see *Voyager* as proof that the ships they knew and sailed on are still out there somewhere, and that our boat is a symbol and an envoy of their continued existence.

I have seen this behavior elsewhere. One day several years ago on Cape Cod, I drove into Hyannis and saw a dozen or more cars pulled over to the side of the road at the Barnstable County Municipal Airport. The drivers, all men over sixty-five, had gotten out of their cars and stood peering through the chain-link fence. On the runway was a World War II troop transport ship painted in camouflage colors. I realized that the men were staring at their own near but irretrievable past, a past that had formed them into the men they were, and that it didn't matter whether or not they had actually ever flown on a transport plane.

Voyager, then, is not only a sailing vessel, not only an object of great beauty and strength, but a talisman of memory as well. When the local men and boys gather like moths at the government wharves as we come in, they are not just showing interest in a strange vessel or admiration for a well-designed and well-built one. She is, for them, young and old, a living and visible reminder of their racial history, an embodiment of their source or emergence, prompting them, clearly against knowledge and recognition, to ask, nonetheless, "Was she a Newfie boat, then?"

The architecture of La Poile, like that of most contemporary Newfoundland outports, is composed largely of prefab, single-story tract houses, a recent, inexpensive, practical approach to housing in these remote places, and certainly, for their residents, an improvement over the indigenous dwellings that characterized the outports only twenty or thirty years ago, when the only affordable source of lumber was the stunted spruce and fir trees of the sparse forests.

The exceptions are the boats themselves and the fish stages. Like most of the boats I have seen in these outport harbors, from dinghies to dories, from the common trapboat to small long-liners, the vessels in La Poile are nearly all wooden and built along traditional lines. The stages are individual wooden docks where the fish are brought in and cleaned—and small sheds holding the owner's fishing equipment. Most of the stages appear (and smell) coeval with the land itself: ancient, seemingly rickety structures that appear to have been passed on, intact, with necessary repairs, from generation to generation. The waters beneath these wharves are arctic-clear, though considerably less than immaculate. A mix of fish heads and fish guts, discarded boat engines, and less-identifiable metal objects lie submerged among the golden tresses of seaweed. Below one dock I saw a rack of caribou antlers, green with algae. I fished it out with a jigger and a line and have set it out on the bow to dry and air out.

Fish flakes—slatted wooden platforms that once served as the main structure for curing and drying cod—are only rarely found in Newfoundland today, but the practice continues among many of the older residents. One woman here in La Poile has rigged a fishnet over her small root vegetable garden, on top of which she is drying a few dozen fish (and, perhaps not inadvertently, adding a bit of fertilizer to her garden). In another yard I saw dozens of cod fillets drying on the clothesline alongside the family wash.

The houses are bunched on rock outcrops sloping down to the harbor in a hodgepodge fashion. A variegated blanket of wild flowers—buttercups, thistles, bluebells, goowitty, and others—covers the rocky hillsides, and the footpaths between houses are often lost in thigh-high grass. There are no streets to speak of, only a maze of cart paths, some of which have been marginally widened and cemented over to accommodate several three-wheeled ATVs and small dock tractors. The town's one "road," a dirt track wide enough for a few local pickup trucks, runs for a few hundred yards along the shore from the government wharf to the dump and the cemetery at the other end.

Each of these roadless outports has a village store or two, whose shelves are generally stocked with a narrow choice of a few staples, some root vegetables, packaged snacks, and, occasionally, some overpriced and rotting fruit. In La Poile there is also the inevitable fish-and-chips take-out that serves as the main gathering place for the youth of the village. Looking forward to a taste of fresh Newfoundland cod, we ordered some for lunch but were disappointed to find that the cod were processed triangles of frozen fish that tasted like cardboard.

Despite the fact that fishing remains the staple of the local economies, there is little fishing activity in evidence here. Inshore stocks have declined drastically along most parts of Newfoundland in the past several years, and most of the boats in La Poile are tied up or hauled out for repairs or repainting. Salmon is plentiful in season in these waters, and the South-West Coast is world-famous for some of its salmon rivers. In fact, an important source of supplementary income derives from guided fishing expeditions, with outside parties flown in by seaplane or helicopter. In order to "protect" the salmon for tourists, however, local fishermen are not permitted to fish them commercially, which is a source of widespread and vocal irritation. In a few weeks, however, the squid are due in, and the men express hope that they will bring a renewal in activity along the shore.

LOG: 2340 Hours—White Bear Bay

In late afternoon we sailed east from La Poile under a fair southwest breeze of fifteen knots, green-blue swells slipping under the stern with so little motion that they, or the boat, seem insubstantial. We decided to make time under this wind, heading for White Bear Bay, the largest and deepest of the fjords on the South-West Coast, some forty miles away. Porpoises leaped and crashed on their sides along our bow, and swam visibly from side to side beneath it in the clear green waters.

An hour or so before sunset, as the low light cast blue shadows of the stays against the white mainsail, we passed the long archipelago of low rocks that surrounds the town of Burgeo like a broken fortress floating on a swirling, misty sea of acrylic blues and reds.

A few miles beyond Burgeo we saw the plastic and mutating shapes of the cliffs of Ramea directly off the starboard rail: tall, dramatic islands that formed a single mound of stacks, pyramids, and mesas before each finally resolved into its particular shape.

We came about on a new course, heading now toward the looming shape of Deer Island, an enormous six-hundred-foot-tall rock at the entrance to White Bear Bay. As we did, the westerly winds shifted north, coming straight off the land. An incongruously warm river of almost tropical air, carrying a deep resinous fragrance of conifers, flowed over our faces. It was an unexpected shock to the senses, something like what the *Niña*'s crew must have experienced on that October day in 1492 when, after more than five weeks at sea, they *smelled* the as-yet-unnamed island of San Salvador before seeing it. Off to the right, a blood-red moon rose over the hills to the east as we entered the bay, a fjord nine miles long and over six hundred feet deep, walled in by thousand-foot-high cliffs. The warm black wind continued to pour down the fjord, and the sanguine moon skipped along the ragged tops of the lower hills to the east as if trying to outrace us.

We motored up the bay for eight miles before we found water shallow enough to drop our hundred-fathom anchor line. Since it was now completely dark, Peter navigated the boat up this black chasm from down in his lighted cabin, watching the sonar screen for uncharted rocks and ledges. Finally, near midnight, we dropped anchor, chain, and line in about sixty fathoms of water.

The wind has stilled, and the moon has broken free of the cliffs and hangs like a silver beacon in the sky, flecking the surface of the black water with a trillion silver minnows.

We sit on deck, saluting the night and our splendid isolation with Newfoundland rum and Havana cigars purchased in Lunenburg. Paul takes out his guitar and we improvise some suitable lyrics to the tune of "On Moonlight Bay:"

ON WHITE BEAR BAY
We were jiggin' for cod
On White Bear Bay.
We could hear the Newfies singing;
They seemed to say:

"You have stolen my fish,
Now please go 'way."
As we jigged all night for cod
On White Bear Bay. (On White Bear Bay)

Now the rest of the crew has retired, but I am too exhilarated and restless to sleep below, so I spread my sleeping bag on the forward deck. The water gently laps against the planked hull as I lie looking up at the brilliant stars. We are at least thirty kilometers from any human settlement, farther than I have ever been from any inhabited place on this continent. It startles me to see the Big Dipper hanging over me, just as it does at home. It seems odd and inappropriate to have the same constellations hanging over such a remote and exotic place as this. The patterns of the stars ought to be as strange and new and dramatically impressive as the scene over which they hang. There is nothing new under the moon, either, the stars seem to say.

LOG: Tuesday, July 30, 0730 Hours

I am lying on deck, at the head of White Bear Bay, with the sun now just shining full on the great beetling bulk of Blow Me Down Point on the west side of the fjord. The sheer cliff walls on the east side are still in the shade of dawn. The spiraling calls of numerous hermit thrushes, like overlapping coils of the thinnest fly-fishing lines arcing over a stream, go bouncing off these sheer rock walls, walls that drop unvegetated for three to four hundred feet before meeting an unlikely line of spruce growing upon the talus of previous rock slides. The trees form an uneven band one to three hundred feet wide and, in places, reach down to the water. There's a roaring on the western wall that I first took to be the wind carding through the short, stiff branches of the spruces, but now I see it comes from a long narrow waterfall, or "piss-a-mare," cascading down through the cliff face.

A small boat is coming up the fjord toward us. It seems incongruous to see any human presence other than ours here, yet this morning, when I first woke and looked up the bay, I saw a small house, or camp, at the very head of the bay about a half mile away. The boat is probably that of the cabin's owner, come out for a short getaway. His approach is a rebuke to last evening's easy sense of exotic isolation. I stand at the rail and relieve myself over the side. My God, I think, what emissaries we are! We come to a new and fabulous place like this, and what's the first thing we do? Piss in it.

LOG: Wednesday, July 31, 1930 Hours—
Grey River, South-West Coast

Despite the decline of fish and fishing in recent decades, the South-West Coast communities have retained a healthy population of young people. Where lack of work has drained off the younger generation to the cities from most Newfoundland outports, leaving them essentially geriatric communities, these roadless outports, lacking easy connections to the outside world, have thus far held onto their children, who seem to thrive in the closeness and security of their continuity. The reason is largely the reversal of the provincial government's policy toward its rural outports over the past twenty years.

During the 1950s and 1960s, under the leadership of Premier Joey Smallwood, the Newfoundland government regarded these small outports as "obstacles to progress" and instituted a widely resented policy of "resettlement" of their inhabitants to designated "growth centers." Smallwood's administration "encouraged" abandonment of the more remote outports by offering small stipends and withholding vital government services, including ferry service, electricity, and medical care. Then, in the 1970s, in the wake of the economic failure of this social engineering, a new government decided that the traditional outports were "cultural resources" and not only reintroduced government-subsidized services to the communities but began advertising them as "destinations" for tourists.

From the time they can walk, outport children live on or near the water, in part because there is so little land for them to play on. At several outports we have seen them diving off wharves into icy water that our tender skins could not have endured, rowing skiffs and dories expertly between the tied-up boats, standing about with their fathers, and shyly but assertively looking over this strange apparition from the outside world that has sailed into their harbor. Like their ranch-style houses, their outward garb, from U-2 T-shirts to neon running shoes, mark them as Children of the World, but the ritual of their days, and the literally all-encompassing presence of an untamed and majestic natural environment, still shape their outlook. The sea is still an early, powerful, and, sometimes, fatal presence. Yet most of the mothers of these outport children learn early not to worry about them. As one woman said to me, "We can't keep them inside all day now, can we, m'dear?" Still, few of the outport people seem nostalgic about the "old days," which were filled with grinding poverty and material hardships that are difficult to imagine.

Last night we moored in Grey River, another roadless outport about twenty miles east of Burgeo, though one of the inhabitants we talked to told us it had had at least two previous names: "It was, let's see, I believe it was called Garrett's Cove, and then 'twas Little River for a good many years. Then, early in this century, there was a real sickness and we asked for the boat doctor to be sent in. Well, b'y, he got sent to the other Little Bay, about sixty miles west of here, and so we changed our name to Grey River in the hopes we'd get him next time. We still don't have a doctor, though."

Even among places of extraordinary locations, Grey River is exceptional. Visually, it represents the extreme of outport isolation. From outside, the entrance to the harbor is virtually invisible, barely two hundred feet wide and marked only by a small light set on a wooden tripod on the face of the bluff. The town itself is a good mile inside the entrance, on the west shore of the fjord, flanked on three sides by high, steep hills seven to eight hundred feet tall. The only access to the interior is a long, steep ravine, from which a stream flows down through the town.

Grey River, about midway along the South-West Coast, is one of the oldest of the roadless settlements, though just how old none of the residents seem to know. The surviving gravestones go back only to the beginning of the twentieth century. But its early settlement and remarkably concealed location make me wonder if it was the place referred to in a diary I once read that was kept by one of the French Acadian refugees from Nova Scotia in the eighteenth century, many of whom took refuge from their English pursuers on this remote shore. She referred to the desirability of the harbor they had taken refuge in by remarking that it was so remote that they could light a fire in winter without danger of the smoke being seen by British ships. Think about that.

While we were ashore today, I made the acquaintance of Freeman Young, a man in his late fifties who is a lifelong inhabitant of Grey River. His surname, like several others in Newfoundland—Myrick, Snow, and Payne, for example—has its counterpart among the old families on Cape Cod. Most of the early settlers, or "stationers," in Newfoundland came from Devon, the same part of the West Country of England from which the Plymouth Brethren came to Massachusetts in 1620. Like virtually every other man here, Freeman Young has done some fishing, but his main job is running the town generator, which brought electricity to the outport about twenty years ago. Located in the very center of the village, the generator runs twenty-four hours a day, producing a considerable, constant din. When I asked about the noise, Freeman said, "I don't even hear it no more, nor does any of us, I guess."

He invited me back to his house, a small but neat cottage finished inside in Formica and Masonite and with a view of the harbor out of the open kitchen door. He pointed out a scraggly cottonwood tree next to the front stoop. It was perhaps fifteen feet tall and half dead, and strung with Christmas lights. "Tallest tree in Grey River," he said, proudly. "She's not doing too well now though, is she?"

Inside I met his wife, Hazel, a short, plump woman in her early thirties, originally from Hermitage, and their boy, Carl, eight or nine, who kept exclaiming, "Maw! Maw! I can *so* go aboard that yacht!"

Freeman showed me pictures of himself and Carl on their Skidoo at his cabin on the "main river," some fourteen miles up the fjord, where he goes to do some hunting in winter.

"Do you hunt caribou?" I asked him.

"Oh yes, b'y. It's not legal for us, but we wiggles one every now and occasionally."

He played for me a tape of one of his favorite "Newfie songs." It was called, I think, "Don't Bring the Beeper Home, B'y," and concerned a caribou poacher who was caught because the animal he killed was wearing a government tracking collar that he foolishly left on the animal, rather than disposing of it. When I left, Hazel gave me two loaves of fresh home-baked bread for the crew.

Outport people no longer freeze or starve during the winters, but life can still be hazardous. Despite diesel engines, modern navigation and communication equipment, and Newfoundlanders' born-and-bred knowledge and respect for the ocean, the sea still claims lives. This afternoon Paul and I walked on a cart track up to the cemetery outside of town, a quarter mile up the hillside and several hundred feet above the harbor. This is the third cemetery in the town. The first two, about the size of backyards, are located in the center of the town. This one is no larger than the other two. It has a chain-link fence around it, but the gate was unlocked. Like many Newfoundland outport cemeteries, it looks untended, though the graves are all ten years old or less. One read, "Amanda Lushman 1979–1988," and next to it, "James Young, 1897–1986."

A new, crated marble stone was lying in the tall grass on its side, apparently having only recently been delivered there. It was a double stone, with the names side by side:

E. David Young   Jason P.C. Farrell
1981–1990   1980–1990

Above the names was the legend, "We Loved Thee Well But Jesus Loved Thee Best," as though it were a contest that Jesus had won.

Here was a small mystery: two young boys who had apparently died together. Were they friends? Brothers? (It was quite possible one was adopted.) Did they drown? Or fall through the ice? Did they die in a Skidoo accident? I did not feel as if I had the right to inquire. Down below us in the harbor, framed by the cloaked stone mountains of the fjord and the bright jumble of houses along the curved landwash, *Voyager* appeared regal and commanding. From someone's pickup truck on the wharf a country-and-western song boomed up clearly.

On the way down we came upon a crew of young men installing new water pipes. They were chopping up what looked like a newly cemented lane. "It's the same everywhere, isn't it?" Paul quipped. "Pave the street, then tear it up to put in the mains."

We stopped in the store, just around the corner from the wharf, to see if we could restock the ship's dwindling supplies with something for breakfast. While the young girl there flirted with Paul, I checked out the meager inventory: a few packaged staples, chips and Pepsi, last year's turnips and potatoes, a freezer half full of salt beef, salt cod, pork shoulder, what looked like pressed frozen chicken, and several boxes of slightly mildewed raisin muffins.

Log: Thursday, August 1, 2200 Hours—St. Pierre, France

Left Grey River last night about 1900 hours on a run to St. Pierre, where we hoped to replenish our depleted stores. Fog came in heavy after midnight and stayed with us all the way. Gina got me up for the 0430-hour watch. I took the helm while Peter stayed at the radar and

Paul stood in the bow guiding us into the harbor channel at about 0530 hours (0500 hours St. Pierre time).

We are tied up at the ferry dock in front of customs. The *douane* official (thereafter referred to by us as Dwayne) came aboard at 0730 hours. We indulged in fresh croissants and baguettes from a patisserie across the square and a thermos of espresso from Hotel Robert (courtesy of the owner, J. P. Andrieux). We all took showers at the St. Pierre Yacht Club and then enjoyed the impossible delicacy of crepes for lunch at La Maringuoin'fre ("The Mosquito") restaurant. Then a nap, followed by an unusually long and leisurely cocktail hour below decks, and a two-and-a-half-hour dinner at La Caveau. There were stuffed squid, lamb chops, cod Provençal, and three bottles of blanc de blancs. It is hard to believe we are only fifty miles from flattened frozen chicken and moldy muffins. Everyone retired by 2200 hours. Tomorrow we head for St. John's.

Log: Friday, August 2, 1140 Hours—St. Pierre Harbour

"The weather has caused a change in plans." Can there be any more common log entry on a sailing vessel? An easterly blow of twenty-five knots or better came up during the night, making passage toward Cape Race impossible this morning. Our original plan was to sail completely around the Avalon Peninsula and into St. John's Harbour, from which four of us would fly home, and Peter, Paul, and Jim would sail *Voyager* back. But we are already several days behind schedule, and still at least two hundred nautical miles, or a minimum of three days' sailing, from St. John's. Gina, Eric, and Jeanette are scheduled to fly out of St. John's back to New York on Monday morning, and the three men who will make up the skeleton crew for the return trip are anxious to head back before the main hurricane season is upon us. Therefore, Peter has decided that as soon as the weather breaks we will head for the ferry terminal at Placentia on the west coast of the Avalon Peninsula and take a bus or taxi to St. John's on Sunday morning.

In the meantime, we all agree that there are worse things than being stuck in St. Pierre for an extra day. Commonly and erroneously de-

scribed as the last French possession in North America, the small islands of St. Pierre and Michelon lie about forty kilometers off Newfoundland's South-West Coast. They are, in fact, not possessions but
actual *départements* of France (as much as Hawaii is one of the United
States), with full political standing and representatives in the National
Assembly in Paris. St. Pierre *is* France, in law, language, culture, customs, money, and attitude. Though the landscape is the same as that
along the rest of the South-West Coast of Newfoundland and the architecture is similar to the wooden townhouses in St. John's, most of
the shops close in the afternoon in European fashion, and at the yacht
club little *enfants français* take sailing lessons in identical little sailing
boats wearing identical sailing outfits with white short-sleeved shirts
and blue ties.

Not surprisingly, many of the residents of St. Pierre seem somewhat
snobbish about their Frenchness. I spoke to a concierge at one of the island's two hotels and learned that a large group of tourists from Montreal were arriving the following week.

"You must be happy to be getting some guests who speak French," I
offered.

"Pah!" she replied, with haughty disgust, "Zey *sink* zey spake
Franch!"

One anomalous chink we have noticed in the armor of the French
culture here is the presence of a number of vintage Wurlitzer jukeboxes
and John Deere lawn tractors around the town. The somewhat bizarre
explanation lies at the entrance to the harbor in the form of the huge,
rusting hulk of a German freighter that sank there in the 1950s. The
ship was carrying a cargo of some five hundred jukeboxes and three
hundred lawn tractors, which, in good maritime tradition, were salvaged by the populace. Though lawns are nonexistent here, residents
use the tractors like golf carts to get around town.

As the last remaining French presence in the western North Atlantic,
St. Pierre is of extreme importance to French fishing rights on the
Grand Banks. In the 1980s, during the so-called fish wars, Canada de-
clared authority over a two-hundred-mile fishing zone off its coasts.
France did the same, and President Mitterand, in a histrionic display of

saber-rattling, sent over a battleship that circled St. Pierre. Because of its strategic importance, St. Pierre is heavily subsidized by the home country. St. Pierre children go to Paris universities on scholarship. French wine, meats, and fresh produce arrive regularly by ship, and public works projects are funded by the French government. For example, St. Pierre is currently in the midst of a multi-million-dollar project to construct a large rotary right in the center of town, whose sole purpose appears to be to allow its citizens to speed into town, zip around the rotary, and race back out into the narrow side roads without decelerating at all.

Though there are only a few miles of vehicular roads in St. Pierre, the locals are just as obsessed with driving as their Parisian counterparts. At the public pier, we have encountered a characteristically Gallic variation on the general interest that *Voyager* has sparked on the entire trip. Instead of walking down to the boat, the citizens of St. Pierre *drive* onto the pier in their Renaults, Citroëns, and Peugeots, keep their motors idling as they peer at *Voyager* out of their windows with studied indifference ("Alors, c'est un bateau de Terre Neuve, n'est-ce pas?"), and then roar off again at top speed.

LOG: 2315 Hours—St. Pierre Harbour

Easterlies and fog continue. I went into town this afternoon to buy some bottles of wine for friends I would be staying with in St. John's. When I got back, Paul was talking with a large, thick-set, round-faced man in his mid-thirties who introduced himself as Bob Appleby of Burin, one of the main fishing ports on the Burin Peninsula just east of St. Pierre. He is captain of the forty-foot trawler *Stephen & Elizabeth*, which came in about noon from having set gill nets and longlines off the tip of the Burin this morning. He let his crew go home and is now waiting for his wife to come over on the ferry for "a little vacation" until the blow is over.

"Had the hull made and sent over from Lunenburg in 1988, and finished her off myself," he told us. "Teach navigation in the winter. My family come from three men who jumped ship from the English back in the 1800s. They lived, you know, like animals. My father was only five-foot-four. I fished with him for eight years. Died at fifty-eight of a massive heart attack. He left us kids $350,000, but he never had a day of pleasure in his life. I figure I'll not last much past sixty years, on account of my size. I can't do much about it. So I figure to work five more years and then retire. Continue to teach in the winter and enjoy my boat in the summer."

I told him I had heard that there are no fish anymore and that the government is about to impose a moratorium on cod and other groundfish.

"Well now, sar, I think that's just crying wolf. They's fish there if they'll just go get 'em. I can get ten thousand pounds of flounder in a week, sell them at twenty-eight cents a pound—they gets fifty to sixty cents in Nova Scotia—and clear twenty-eight hundred dollars. But some of them's lazy, that's the *troot* of it. Some of thems just fishes to get the stamps."

Bob also told us that Newfoundland schooners were derived from Nova Scotia boats, which in turn were derived from Gloucester boats. If true, this suggests an actual family resemblance that would give a less symbolic explanation for the serial recognition *Voyager* has received all the way up the coast. He invited Paul and me onto to his boat to show us all of his up-to-date high-tech equipment: fish finder, loran location plotter, computerized charts, etc. His cabin in many ways is furnished like a new Newfoundland house: lots of Formica counters and Naugahyde lounge chairs, even shag carpeting. There are four forward bunks, one of which has a specially fitted compartment for Bob's bible.

Log: Saturday, August 3, 2100 Hours—Argentia Naval Base

To the surprise of all of us, we have ended up on American territory. We left St. Pierre this morning, rounding the long, narrow, boot-shaped Burin Peninsula (the "Italy of Newfoundland"), then crossed Placentia Bay, intending to seek a mooring in Placentia Harbour near the eastern terminus of the ferry from North Sydney, Nova Scotia.

When we reached the entrance to Placentia Harbour late this afternoon, however, we discovered that *Voyager*'s mast would not fit under the highway bridge at high tide. Rather than wait six hours for the tide to go out and then risk being trapped inside when he wanted to leave, Peter decided to continue a few miles north to the old Argentia Navy Yard.

The U.S. Naval Base at Argentia Bay was created in six months during the winter of 1940–1941 under the Lend Lease Atlantic Pact agreement that had been signed by Roosevelt and Churchill only a few miles from the base. It was an enormous complex, and after the United States entered the war, it contained some forty thousand naval personnel, hundreds of ships, and a half dozen runways. Today the base has lost its strategic importance, and a mere skeleton crew of about five hundred U.S. personnel are still stationed there. Moose graze on the empty, overgrown runways, and the word is that the base will close in a few years.

We sailed into Argentia Bay, a capacious harbor protected by two symmetrical, rounded rocks that were dubbed "Mae West" by the GIs when they arrived, a name that has stuck among Newfoundlanders. When we arrived at the thousand-foot-long wharf, there was not a single vessel in port. Peter, as a former U.S. Navy captain, has managed to secure permission from the base commander to tie up here for a few days.

"Professional courtesy, you know."

LOG: Sunday, August 4, 2320 Hours—St. John's

This afternoon the entire crew—minus Jim Mairs, who has developed back troubles on the last leg of the trip and has volunteered to remain on the boat—took a taxi to St. John's, where we checked into the Hotel Newfoundland, the splendid new incarnation of the city's old Newfoundland Hotel. After two weeks at sea almost any accommodation with real mattresses and hot showers would seem like nirvana, but the Hotel Newfoundland has surpassed everyone's expectations. When we trooped into the elegant lobby—a ragtag group of unshaven, unwashed, wild-haired sailors lugging duffel bags, boots, and a rack of rather odiferous caribou antlers—the staff didn't blink an eye. They were, in fact, highly efficient and professional, and yet personable, composed primarily of Newfoundlanders who exhibited the genuine friendliness toward strangers that the province is famous for.

I contacted my friends in St. John's, with whom I will be staying for a couple of days before flying back to the States. Then, as I was running late to meet the others for dinner, I simply threw all of my filthy gear on the bed, stood in the paradise of a hot shower for five minutes, put on my one set of clean clothes, and went down to the restaurant. Later in the evening we all came back up and had drinks in the private lounge overlooking the harbor. From there we watched the ship traffic passing in and out through the Narrows: the local fishing fleet, container ships from Korea, factory ships from Halifax and the Soviet Union. At about eleven I returned to my room and found a note, with two chocolates, on my pillow. The note read, "Dear Mr. Finch, I am sorry I was unable to turn down your bed this evening because of your personal belongings. The Night Maid."

Log: Monday, August 5, 2200 Hours—Argentia Naval Base

Gina, Jeanette, and Eric flew out of St. John's this morning, but Peter, Paul, and I (they called me "Mary" for the duration) spent several hours walking St. John's—far too little time in a city of such color and character—but we luxuriated in using our land legs after nearly two weeks at sea.

Because of an unusually cold July (strawberries were just now coming in) we were able to witness a few of the dozens of icebergs that have been drifting down past St. John's all summer. One large berg was reported just offshore at Blackhead Cove, a small community about ten miles outside the city. I borrowed a car from a friend and the three of us drove out to see it.

At Blackhead we pulled into the yard of a house on the shore at the end of the lane. An old man was chopping up kindling in the yard. He seemed singularly unimpressed with both the iceberg and those who had come to see it, their appearances or disappearances. It turned out he had been a member of the carpenters' union for forty-eight years and had helped to build Strain Memorial Hall at the Argentia Naval Base. In one of the small windows I noticed an old woman, his wife, white-haired and thin-faced, shyly pulling back the curtains and looking out, a young smile on her face, at all the new faces. Her expression seemed to say that at last the world had come to her door.

The iceberg was about a hundred yards offshore, a frozen sculpture over a hundred feet high and about three hundred feet long, bearing an uncanny resemblance to a ship under sail. Several small "growlers" had broken off the main berg, and one was beating against the rocks on the shore. Paul and I shied some rocks at it, trying to knock off some pieces. After risking a cold dunking in icy waters, Paul finally succeeded in retrieving some chunks. That evening we had drinks with iceberg ice, which, because it is formed under enormous pressure on the Greenland ice cap, expands and crackles dramatically when dropped in liquid.

When the three of us took another taxi back to Argentia this evening, we brought a small piece of the iceberg with us as a treat for Jim. When we arrived, Jim was taking a nap. We woke him up and handed him a glass of vodka with some of the ice in it. Jim took a sip, then sat peering steadily at the glass, saying nothing.

"Jim," I said, "you're not being very appreciative. After all, Paul risked life and limb to get that. That's ten-thousand-year-old ice you're drinking."

"I know," Jim replied. "I'm quite impressed. I'm just checking it for mammoth shit."

Log: Tuesday, August 6, 1600 Hours—St. John's

Last night I slept aboard *Voyager* for the last time. We woke before dawn to find ourselves pinned to the wharf with an easterly gale blowing thirty-five knots against the starboard bow. We pulled the bow off the pilings, reset the fenders, and waited for a lull. It finally came about 0830 hours. Seizing this window for departure, Peter quickly started the engine and ordered me to the wharf to cast off lines. *Voyager* slowly began to motor her way out of the harbor, moving toward the Mae West rocks. Jim shouted at me, "Be sure to thank the Navy!" Peter, anxious to get out of the harbor before the wind picked up again, raised his hand without turning. Paul, standing on the cabin deck, gave me a mock-formal salute, in imitation of John Mills's loyal fool character in *Ryan's Daughter. You're right, Pete,* I thought. *She is a very human boat.*

As the boat slowly grew smaller and finally disappeared from view behind the massive wharves, I realized that, in a small but real way, *Voyager* had become for me what she was to the old men of the outports along the South-West Coast: a touchstone releasing history, personal and communal, an object of great memory, telling us who we are, or were, or might even be again.

AFTER THE MORATORIUM

The Newfoundland
Conundrum

Everything was better back when everything was worse.
—**Caption on a** *New Yorker* **cartoon**

I once knew a writer who came to Newfoundland in the 1960s. He came to write about birds and instead wrote about the people here. Twenty years afterward he talked about his experiences. He had a more complex idea about finding "salvation" in nature than most writers I know. He said he found more terror and horror in wilderness than he did in Manhattan, where he lived. Yet he had been terribly discontented in the city and had made what he called a "cross emigration" to Newfoundland. He spent three summers there, mostly in remote outports with strong, distinct personalities. They became a kind of symbol of salvation to him. The Newfoundlanders, he found, had a supersensitive, almost metaphysical relationship to animals and nature, similar to what he had encountered in older indigenous cultures, a kind of psychic contact with the physical world that made him wonder if modern man had lost senses we'd once had and no longer use, such as telepathic powers and the ability to see the future.

He was no mystic, however. He admired the Newfoundlanders for their "animal adaptation" to the world, and a kind of "sublime peace" they possessed. You see, he put great store in the ability to adapt. Man, he maintained, is a gregarious and technological creature. Our future, he believed, lay in more, not less, technology. The speed of technological development is so fast that we cannot predict its future, he used to say. People who cannot adapt to it go into a profound depression, or even madness.

There was a conundrum, he believed, in the traditional life of Newfoundlanders that recapitulates the history of our race. (He used the term "race" in the older sense, to mean species.) On one hand, the old life here was tremendously difficult, so full of suffering and constant labor that it was only natural they would try to escape from it when they could. Confederation represented escape from that extreme hardship. It was, by and large, the people in the rural outports who supported Confederation with Canada in the referendum of 1949. The relatively sophisticated urban populace in St. John's opposed it in the name of preserving "independence" and the "right to determine our own future." The outports were right, he maintained. In the weeks before the referendum the Canadian government had assembled seaplanes loaded with food to deliver to the starving outports if the vote was favorable. That's how bad it was.

But they did this, he said, they voted to escape their suffering, not knowing that their life here represented the true, evolutionary state of man. It is our business, he believed, to suffer and endure; it is what we were made and selected to do. It is all perfectly dreadful, of course, a thoroughly bad life, and yet, like the animals, primitive man was not neurotic or psychotic. There was a kind of satisfaction in it not possible in an air-conditioned apartment in Manhattan. This, he said, had nothing to do with "natural" versus "artificial" surroundings. In fact, he liked living in Manhattan; it was his favorite city, very convenient to get around in, full of interesting and agreeable people and places, that huge oasis of Central Park, and so on. No, he said, our modern neuroses have nothing to do with pollution or crowding or the supposed "isolation" and "hectic pace" of urban life, but rather with the very fact that technology has made our lives so easy. Our dilemma is that we are constitutionally unable to take satisfaction in that, yet also unable to give up those very amenities and conveniences that make true satisfaction impossible. We are, in a profoundly metaphorical sense, caught between a rock and a soft place.

After he left Newfoundland he traveled all over the world seeking to repeat the experience he had found there. He wrote numerous books about the relationship between animals and human beings, some of which won prizes and became quite well known, but he never found anything else "so well wrought," as he put it, to write about as Newfoundland. Nevertheless, his experience there had somehow allowed him to accept his fate and his own death. There he had seen life reduced to its most basic terms, didn't particularly like what he saw, but found a measure of peace in knowing the truth of it. Few of us manage to do as much.

Fogo Island 1995

It has been seven years since I first came to Fogo. The mainland road to the ferry slip at Farewell has now been paved and a restaurant with a pool table built beside it. I came over with my minivan on the 8:30 evening ferry. TV reception on the boat has improved. I watched a *Seinfeld* rerun and found myself wondering what Newfoundlanders make of such a narcissistic, nihilistic, irony-drenched portrait of life.

On the ferry I found a flyer for an "Irish/Newfoundland" night at the Castaway Lounge in Joe Batt's Arm on the north side of the island. When we landed I drove over there, but at 10 P.M. there were only four people in the lounge. I was told that the crowd would come in later. Compared to other outports I have known, where most people are in bed by ten, things start late here.

I played a game of pool by myself. Two women in their forties sat on stools nearby watching me. One said to me, "Here's a partner for you," indicating the other, a blond-haired woman about my age, wearing a flower-print dress. I offered her a game. She sunk the eight ball on the break, and then I had a run of seven or eight balls. When I finally missed a shot, she said, with gentle sarcasm, "Oh, do I get another turn?" It was not the way to impress a lady, I suppose, but I was not trying to.

After the game I bought them both drinks. They were from Tilting, the Irish village on the east end of the island. The woman I'd played pool with was Mary. She still lives there, she said, though like almost everyone of her generation in Newfoundland, she has spent some years in Toronto. The other woman, Colleen, was a businesswoman who lives

172

in Ottawa. She is part owner of two businesses, a trade exhibit firm and something she calls "taxes for fishermen."

Mary told me that this past spring, in late April or early May, a polar bear floated into the harbor at Tilting on an ice floe. It landed in their backyard, where it attacked their German shepherd behind a shed. She heard the ruckus, came out, and at first didn't know what it was. She wondered what a large gray horse was doing in their yard ("They gets dirty when they comes on land, you see"). The bear was standing on its hind legs, tossing the dog up in the air with one paw and catching it with the other, then tossing it up again. She called her husband, who came out and shot it and "h'isted him up on a t'ykle." After a few days the government took it away. It was the second bear to come ashore on Fogo that year.

On Cape Cod, where I live, it is not uncommon for a whale to wash up in your backyard. Such strandings used to be regarded as windfalls by the local people, but now they are occasions for earnest, organized rescue efforts, often involving extensive and expensive rehabilitation. But whales do not attack your dogs. I realized that, for all their modern appearance and appurtenances, these people still live in a much more direct, confrontational position to the natural world than I do.

That night I slept in my van in a gravel pit. In the morning I went out to the fishing wharf in Joe Batt's Arm and met a one-armed man who told me that since 1992 most fishing here now is snow crab and some "experimental trap fishing," three days a week. The crabbing was finishing up now, he said, to be followed by some trawling. The cod moratorium has hit the Fogo communities particularly hard because they were so independent and proud of their fishing cooperative. Then, as if he felt he were being too morose, he said, "Tell me, sar, does you know how to get a one-handed Newfie to fall out of a tree?" I said I didn't. "Wave to him."

I have come to Fogo this time to see the Brimstone Head Folk Festival, which started in 1984. Like most places in Newfoundland, the only apparent future for Fogo seems to be tourism, though the residents are still touchingly informal in how they go about it. The previous weekend I had tried to get some information on the upcoming festival. First I called the 800 number for Tourism Newfoundland and Labrador on Saturday and got an apologetic woman who told me that she was the answering service and that the tourism office was not open on weekends. But she managed to find a number on Fogo for the festival, which I dialed. A young child answered. When I asked to talk to someone about the festival, he shouted, "MA!" and a woman came to the phone. She told me it was mostly music, very traditional, with a square dance at the Lions Club Friday evening. When I asked about a ferry schedule and whether I needed a reservation for my car, she said, "Just a minute, it's down on my refrigerator. Nope, no reservations, it's just load and rode."

I drove from Joe Batt's Arm over to Everett Payne's house at the end of the road in Fogo Village. As I drove through the town I noticed that there were no small children on the road, as there had been on my previous visit. I had written the Paynes ahead of time to let them know I was coming, and they greeted me with affection and pride in the fact that someone from away would make the effort to look them up again. It has been hard times for them since I was last here, seven summers ago, though they have a nice ranch-style home with modern appliances, wall-to-wall carpeting, color TV, chintz curtains, etc. Now in his late thirties, Everett, as well as his three brothers, are, or were, nth generation fishermen from Fogo. Until the moratorium they earned their living long-lining and trap-fishing cod. He proudly showed me a photo of them taken several years ago by a writer: "He got it into *National Geographic!*"

His wife, Jo, a handsome, curly-haired redhead with freckles, is from Stag Harbour, a village on the south shore made up mostly of families resettled from the Indian Islands. She still works at the Fogo Coop plant in Seldom.

"But it's hard, y'see," she said. "We're hit double, eh? When Ev was fishin' and me workin' at the fish plant, we was doin' all right. Now there's only the crab fishery, and Everett only worked eight days at it this season. We wants to send Angela to Europe for her junior year, but it's hard now, eh?"

Everett mows his lawn a lot, washes his car, sits and talks to his friend Keith, who is visiting from the Burin Peninsula, and, in a concession to changing roles, helps Jo with the dishes. He is a serious man, concerned about not only himself but also his community and its future. He is on the Fogo Island Development Committee and responded thoughtfully to my suggestion that a seal product industry might be developed locally. Currently, he said, sealskin pelts sell in stores on the mainland for fifty dollars a square foot, compared to a dollar fifty for cowskin, though the hunters only get one or two dollars a pelt. Keith, a secondary-school teacher, was wearing a $180 pair of sealskin boots and left his own job last spring to go sealing.

"I guess it's just in yer blood," Keith said. "Come March yer blood just start b'ilin'. I don't care what noise those Greenpeacers makes. I'm proud of my country!" he said, meaning Newfoundland.

I asked Everett if it would be all right if I camped down in French-man's Cove.

"Help yourself, b'y," he said.

As I was unpacking the van at the head of the old road that goes down to the cove, John Payne came out of his house and greeted me. He remembered me from when I had stayed at his wife's guesthouse on my first visit here.

"What brings you back, b'y? You run out of women fish back home?"

I told him I was here for the festival. When I asked him about Fogo's fishing situation, he replied in typical Newfoundland fashion by way of a long, roundabout story. It concerned a friend of his who left Fogo Village one winter day in the early 1950s on foot across the ice to go scaling over at Barr'd Isles, about two kilometers east by water and practically next to Joe Batt's Arm. There were no roads then, and only two phones on the whole island, one in the old post office in Fogo down by the Grenfell Hospital and the other at the "C&T" telephone office in Joe Batt's Arm. He kept trying to reach someone at the C&T office to find out if his friend had arrived safely, but it was three days before they found out that he had.

"Now see," he said, "it took us three days then to find out about a few miles, and here you can come from Massachusetts to hear our music. We're all linked up now, and yet we're dependent on the government for everything—the ferry, the hydro, and if that UI [unemployment insurance] check doesn't come, what have you got? Oh yes, b'y, times was hard in the old days, all right, and in the Depression, you know, we didn't have nothing, but we didn't owe anybody nothing either. All we had us was a pair of boots, a jar of jam, and a little bread, and sometimes we didn't have the jam. But we had our boats, and we had our wood, and we had our fish. Yes, b'y, we had the fish."

The "road" that runs from the paved road down to the cove is built of roughly laid rocks and has become thickly grassed-over. Except for a sizable boulder near the top, one could believe it was some ancient wagon road. It was actually constructed so that the women of the village could haul water up in buckets from the old Frenchman's Well in the valley below in the days before they dug artesian wells or built reservoirs into the hill. Local people still come down to get some water for drinking, though it used to be much more important.

I set up my tent in the cove on Friday night, on a grassy shelf just above the beach. It is now Sunday morning, and for three days a strong fresh southwest wind has blown constantly down this broken, glaciated valley, rippling the seedheads of the grass like watered silk, bending the bluebells and the starlike yellow composites. The sides of this valley, which rise several hundred feet to the crest of Fogo Hill on the west, are upended walls of dark metamorphic schist, creating miniature palisades with small skirts of talus at their base. The hillside ground cover is creeping juniper, blackberry, partridgeberry, Labrador tea, and small blueberry plants with minute, flattened leaves that hug the ground. Everett Payne told me that "we don't eat them," but I have found the dark blue, dusted berries delicately sweet to the taste.

On the tops of the ridges scores of rounded, light-colored granite erratics perch like abstract sculptures, or giant dinosaur eggs. These glacial boulders do balancing acts all over the surrounding ridges and hills. I cannot help but wonder what the people here thought of them before Louis Agassiz developed his modern glacial theories. Probably what most of them think now: leftovers from the Great Flood, perhaps, or, more likely, simply features of the landscape so common as not to need any explanation.

The valley, perhaps a half mile in length, ends in a long, low mound of cracked rocks. This is a "storm beach," piled up over the centuries by storm surges and waves. The top of the mound is covered with rippling grass. Below the steep berm is a jumble of rounded granite boulders, beige and dark pink, and broken, staggered ridges of schist. A pair of snipe perch on the rocks and have been calling with their high, tubular whistles almost continuously since I arrived.

Offshore are the small, rocky islands where the goats were pastured in summer on my previous stay, though I have seen only gulls there this time. Small white waves caress their sides and fling back their seaweed tresses like endless desire meeting endless resistance.

Though I am less than a quarter mile from the nearest house, I might as well be camped along some wilderness shoreline in northern Labrador for all I see and for all that come to see me. Aside from the gulls and a few other birds, the only wildlife I have seen are some lovely small orange-and-black butterflies that cling to the golden heads of the crowds of yellow flowers.

The scenery is alpine and littoral all at once, though less the former now as there are no longer any sheep hiding among the hills. A new iceberg, enormous and far offshore, has appeared this morning. It has turned and shape-shifted all morning: now a crouched panther, now a ship with sails lowered, now a group of whales. The one-armed fisherman I talked to in Joe Batt's Arm told me, "Oh, he's been out there since early spring. He started up at Change Islands and worked his way down here."

MY FIRST VISITOR arrived on Saturday morning: a short, bearded, middle-aged man with glasses who walked down the road to the cove. He seemed a little shy and was startled to find me here. He is one of Everett's brothers and told me he once weighed 283 pounds. He has walked much of it off. He walks at least three hours a day. He said there is little else for him to do.

Later, a little before noon, Angela Payne came down the stone steps to my tent with Shadow, a black poodle-terrier mix. She carried a pot of moose stew for me from her mother. I spread out the blanket for her next to me, but she stood off to one side, speaking shyly, hesitantly. She is a cheerleader now, going into the eleventh grade next year. I asked her if any other of the children I flew kites with on that summer day seven years ago were still around.

"Mark, you remember him, Bradley's little brother? Well, he died of meningitis a year or two after you went away."

"I'm so sorry."

"He went almost overnight. The funeral was bad. All of the aunts and everybody was crying, wailing, really, in the church. There are so few of us young ones now, you see, it hits them harder."

Later that afternoon, when I was back up at the car getting something, a strapping young man walked up and said, "Remember me?"

It was Rick Payne, one of Angela's friends who had flown the kite with us, now nineteen and a student at MUN. He accompanied me back down to the cove and I asked him if he would walk up the valley with me to help me find the old well again.

"Sure, b'y, but I haven't been up there for some year."

Nevertheless, it didn't take us long to find the well. It is only a crudely dug, three-foot-wide depression, maybe eighteen inches deep and ringed with sharp broken rocks, but it has always been full of good, clear water, even in drought years. Rick told me that there were once many gardens down here—before his time, but his father and uncles talk of it. The low mounds of rocks scattered in the lower valley, he said, had been removed from the garden plots.

He pointed out where the ball field used to be: "We plays basketball in town now," he told me. "Look at the grass—she's finally growing. She never used to get that tall with the kids running all over it."

Sheep, gardens, ball fields, kids. Nothing keeps the grass from growing here now. Gulls call from the rocky islands like cranky, scolding, posthistoric ghosts.

Later in the afternoon Everett, Jo, Angela's younger brother Tyler, and Shadow all walked down the path to visit. They have been kind to me, feeding me whenever I have stopped in, giving me moose stew, jars of moose meat, fish and rice, and a couple of moose steaks (from animals Everett shot on the mainland last fall) to take back with me. Jo Payne pointed to the protected cove of water just off the beach. "We used to let the kids bathe there. Mark liked to go after the little fishes there. We calls 'em 'barneytickles,' but there's not so many now. Since the caplin is gone, the gulls have been eating the barneytickles."

When I got back home, I looked up the word *barneytickle* in the *Dictionary of Newfoundland English*, but it was not there.

On Saturday evening I headed off for the festival, which takes place in the municipal park at the base of Brimstone Head. Though this was the biggest tourist weekend of the year, there were no signs on the main road directing visitors to the site. At the park I found several hundred people, most of whom appeared to know one another. There were puppet shows and games for the children, a spaghetti dinner and a square dance in the pavilion, and live entertainment on the central outdoor stage. In a smaller pavilion there was a display of paintings of Fogo scenes by a Quebec artist named Danielle Loranger. She was not there when I went in, but a handsome man in his late thirties with a strong Newfoundland accent was actively hawking her paintings like a carnival barker. We struck up a conversation, and I found out he was Danielle's husband, Wade Kean, originally from Wesleyville and a surgeon at the hospital in Clarenville. For the past two years he has been posted at the small hospital on Fogo. Danielle, a self-taught artist, became intrigued with the life of the local people and began a series depicting many of the traditional activities: hauling up the trap skiffs at the end of the season, bringing in wood on horse-drawn sleighs, going mummering at Christmas, jigging for fish through the ice, boys playing hockey on the ponds, etc. The drawings were at once idealized and realistic. The poses were formal and iconic, but the details were painstakingly accurate, for example, hockey goals fashioned from torn fishing nets, mummers' costumes made from old sheets and dresses. It was clear from the wondering faces of the people seeing themselves depicted in the paintings that they had never thought of themselves as subjects for representation before.

At dusk I wandered over to the base of Brimstone Head and began to ascend a complex system of spidery wooden stairs and platforms that stretched up and out over the entire Brobdingnagian length of this ancient volcanic upthrust, ending in a viewing platform that provided a spectacular vista out across the ocean to the Change Islands and beyond. Traversing the route, I spotted dozens of young couples hidden in the rocks' crevices and ledges like limpets clinging to one another.

Returning, I walked over to the main stage, where the star attractions of the evening's entertainment were beginning to perform. There was a folk-rock band from St. John's, a comic storyteller from the Clarenville area, and a few other imported acts. But I was pleased to see that, as the woman on the phone had said, it was mostly a local festival, and it was the local acts that received the greatest applause.

The pride of the festival, in fact, was a local group of five teenage girls, all fourteen years old, called the Fogo Accordion Group. They played in unison, without chords, but were impressively synchronized. Two men accompanied them on guitars, one of whom was their high school music teacher and was listed on the program as their "trainer."

But there are signs that the strategies of modern marketing are making inroads even here. The Fogo Accordion Group already has two cassettes and a video out, which were for sale at the festival. The first cassette, made the previous year when they were thirteen, is called *Reviving a Way of Life*. It shows the girls, still kids, wearing blue T-shirts and beige pants, all smiling guileless smiles against the background of a fishing boat. The video and second cassette came out this year, and on the covers the girls are wearing lavender, cut-leather vests and short skirts. They look directly at the viewer with the self-aware self-possession of models and a conscious pose of arch, adolescent sexuality. The title of the new album is *Pushing All the Right Buttons*.

A Time in Petty Harbour

T he fishing village of Petty Harbour is probably the most photographed town in Newfoundland and is generally regarded as
the Classic Newfoundland Outport. Only ten miles south of the capital of St. John's, its setting is extreme and picturesque. This, along with
its proximity to the provincial capital, has made it a favorite site for
filmmakers as well, most notably for *Orca*, the 1977 killer whale rip-off
of *Jaws*.

Petty Harbour possesses a deep, keyhole harbor that offers good protection from storms. It has a rough-and-tumble appearance, surrounded on three sides, like a West Virginia hollow, with sullen,
stubborn, burnt-over sandstone hills. To the south, west, and north,
these steep, barren, rocky masses rise six hundred feet above the clusters of small houses surrounding the harbor. A rapidly flowing river
tumbles down out of the hills through a steep valley, cutting the town
in two, a physical division that used to mark the religious divide between the Roman Catholic and Anglican neighborhoods here. Just
across the bridge spanning the river, a prominent rocky knob rises
abruptly to the southeast. In winter the sun does not appear until after
10 A.M., after which it rises halfheartedly until the lower hills in the
south and southwest intercept it again at about 2:30 P.M.

Much of Petty Harbour's reputation rests on the renowned prowess
of its local fishermen. There are several good fishing grounds just offshore, which are especially favorable for small-boat and inshore fishing.
Going in and out of their protected harbor in trap skiffs and small long-
liners even in the roughest weather, the men of Petty Harbour have

always brought back the big catches, at times enough to supply the whole Avalon Peninsula. Even when cod stocks declined seriously in the late 1980s, Petty Harbour boats always seemed to be able to find fish and return with their holds full.

Not even the fabled resourcefulness and skills of the local fishermen, however, could withstand the groundfish moratorium in 1992. It hit Petty Harbour as hard as it hit all the outports, and perhaps harder, because the community had managed to weather every setback except an outright ban on fishing. For several years after the moratorium, the prospects and mood of the town were at an ebb. Many of the local fishermen had sold their boats or put them in dry dock. Eighty or ninety small boats still went out of the harbor, though they went now not for fish, but for snow crab, a species that had not yet emerged as a major economic crop and so was regarded with some disdain and embarrassment by a people who had lived by catching cod, the "king of fish," for several hundred years. Though the federal and provincial governments were offering "retraining" programs for out-of-work fishermen and processors, there was at that time a sense of uselessness and a resentment against an authority that most Newfoundlanders believed had destroyed their livelihood.

Some of my friends in St. John's regarded Petty Harbour as something of an "outlaw town," suggesting that there had been a rampant increase in drinking and divorce, and a flagrant disregard of the law that went beyond the venerable outport scofflaw tradition of occasionally poaching a moose or "wiggling" a salmon or two out of season. Others denied this, saying that social ills and illegal behavior in Petty Harbour were no worse than anywhere else. This seemed more likely, but it was also true that because of Petty Harbour's stature as a model Newfoundland outport, incidents that occurred there tended to get more publicity. Recently, for instance, there had been a highly publicized occurrence involving the three Hearn brothers, who had been arrested for violating sealing regulations— specifically, for "torturing" young seals on the ice. What was remarkable about the incident was that they had made a home video of it. A copy of the video was apparently made by a friend and sold to the International Fund for Animal Welfare (IFAW), which used it in its zealous campaign to eliminate the Canadian seal hunt. Some locals told me that the "torturing," actually consisted of tossing dead seal bodies around and gaffing them in a joking manner. They seemed to resent not so much the Hearns' illegal and reprehensible actions as their stupidity in filming themselves, which resulted in bringing down the law on their community and giving it unfavorable publicity.

It was during this dark period in the town's history, at the darkest time of the year, that I had an opportunity to stay in Petty Harbour for a couple of days. I was visiting friends in St. John's over Christmas, and my friend Simon, who owned a house in Petty Harbour, offered me the use of his house while he was away on business. Curious to spend more time in this town of recent notorious repute, I accepted Simon's invitation. On the evening of January 5, when I arrived in Petty Harbour, I found the houses on the streets and the hillsides still festooned with Christmas lights and displays. Because most Newfoundlanders still celebrate "Old Christmas," or the Twelve Days of Christmas from December 25 to January 6, not only the holiday lights but also the local parties were still going at full wattage.

Simon's house is a small ninety-year-old flat-roof structure that sits in the very center of town, mashed against a wall of rock right next to the bridge on the north, or Catholic, side of the river. In front of the house is the most striking and anomalous feature of the town, one that rarely appears in any photographs or scenes that have been filmed there. An enormous, above-ground steel pipe snakes its way down from the hills nearly half a mile from the west, following the course of the river into the middle of the town. This is a conduit for water from a series of inland ponds that provides power for an electric generating plant that sits at the base of the hills at the edge of town. It was the first power plant in Newfoundland, built in 1898 to provide electricity for St. John's.

The huge, black corrugated pipeline, some eight feet in diameter and bound with braided steel ropes, feeds water into the turbines of the power plant, and then carries excess water a hundred yards further, where it stops almost literally at Simon's doorstep. The power plant still serves as a recharging station for St. John's, and runs intermittently. When it does, as it did my first night there, the river pours loud and full out of the turbine outfall. The feeder pipe must remain full at all times, and it apparently leaks profusely, for this time of year its dark, ribbed sides were slathered with ice-drapery, and small spouts of water sprung here and there all along its spine, giving the whole thing the impression of some enormous mythic black Arctic worm, frozen in its own progress.

My next-door neighbor, Simon had told me, was a man named Tommie, in his mid-forties, who lived with his mother and aunt in a two-story flat-roofed house built about a hundred years ago by his great-grandfather and neatly painted sky blue. Though he has a boat, Tommie is not primarily a fisherman. He is a skilled mechanic and welder who works on all sorts of motors, marine and terrestrial. When I arrived at Simon's house, I saw Tommie in the open door of his garage, bent over some kind of engine suspended on pulleys, while a covey of three or four other men, ranging in age from sixteen to over sixty, huddled around him, all of them hatless and in rubber boots. Simon had told Tommie I was coming, but they seemed engrossed in their work, so I did not go over and introduce myself.

That evening I stayed in reading, playing Simon's piano, and missing the familiar social scene of St. John's. Shortly before eleven o'clock, I decided to take a bath and go to bed. Just as I was coming out of the tub, there was a loud, insistent knocking on the locked front door. I hastily put on my sweat pants and opened the door. There stood Tommie, a short, thick-limbed man with large facial features, steel-gray hair in a long flattop, and a clenched-tooth grin—a little bundle of exploding energy in a red pullover, light gray overalls, and dirty-white boots. With him were two of his cousins—Jonnie, a taller, younger man who was a carpenter, and Earl, a bearded fisherman. They were smashed, and knew it. Tommie, with a half-empty bottle of beer in his hand, said, "Bob, b'y—Bob is it? Could you give us a lift around the harbor so we can get some more beer? We can't drive."

"I just got out of the tub," I protested, but he was insistent.

"It's not far, b'y. We got keys but as you can see we can't be driving."

So I put on Simon's boots and my coat, and Tommie and I got in the front of his jeep while the other two crammed themselves in the back. I drove across the bridge to the store on the south side of town.

"My father," Tommie said, "used to be afraid to walk over to this side of the harbor at night for fear he'd get a rock thrown at his head by some of the Protestants. But that's all changed. Now everyone respects everyone else's religion, or the lack of it."

Jonnie offered a less ecumenical explanation. "It's because of the diddlers at Mount Cashel," he said, "those fucken pervert priests who went at those poor orphans. That did it, that finished it. The Church, God damn their fucken eyes, the Church here is finished!"

When we got to the store, the front was dark, but Tommie got out, leaving me holding his bottle of beer. He went up a side set of stairs to the upper story and emerged seven or eight minutes later with a six-pack of Black Horse Ale under each thick, short arm. "Got us a couple of brewskies," he said. I took him back around to the house of one of his cousins and let the three of them out. He invited me in, of course, but this time I declined firmly, went home, and crashed.

In the morning I stoked up the woodstove and walked up to a grocery store on the hill above the house to buy some supplies. The town was covered with "glitter" from the previous night's ice storm and looked like some Christmas scene in a glass ball, with a black snake coiled through its center. The harbor was frozen over and the fishing boats had been hauled out for the winter. The "store" was a dilapidated, weather-beaten dark-green wooden building that, except for its setting, could have come out of a Bernard Malamud story, as could its proprietor. Her name, she said, was Irene. She was a small, wizened old woman who looked as if she had had little pleasure in life. She looked at me and said, "You're not him, is ye?" I didn't know who she was referring to, but I felt confident replying in the negative.

The space within was no more than eight feet by twelve feet, much of it taken up with a large, glass-fronted Pepsi case and shelves of tinned goods. Apparently there was more room elsewhere, for when I asked for milk, she went to a back room and brought back a half gallon. The printed hours for this minimal enterprise were a surprisingly generous 8 A.M. to 11:00 P.M., though a hand-lettered notice next to the posted hours said that as of January 6, the evening hours would be cut back to 10:30 P.M.

"There's not much business this time of year," she explained, "and last year someone came in with a bread knife looking for money. He was some junkie from St. John's. I never had but six dollars in the store, and he didn't take that. He didn't even take so much as a muffin—that's why me brother put that electronic buzzer in. It goes off when the door is opened, you see."

There was a single copy of the *Evening Telegram*, the St. John's daily paper, on the counter. I asked if it was hers and she said, "Yes, me son, but I don't read." I asked her if she would sell it and she said she would.

Guessing that the house would probably not be warmed up yet, I walked down the hill and stopped for coffee at the "Petty Harbour Cafe—Also Convenience" beside the harbor below. At 9:30, I was obviously the first customer of the day. The proprietor, a man in his forties, was alone in the place. He brewed some coffee for me and continued watching the news on the TV. Sonny Bono had been killed on a ski slope at Lake Tahoe the day before, just days after Michael Kennedy had bashed his brains out against a tree in Aspen playing touch football on skis with a snow-filled water bottle that his mother, Ethel, had just brought up on the ski lift.

"I'm not having a good day meself, b'y," said the man, though I couldn't tell whether he was referring to the lack of customers, the deaths on TV, or some other, more general source of woe or disappointment.

After breakfast I crossed the bridge and took a stroll through the south side, the old Protestant side of town, where half the fishing fleet stood in dry dock. Most of the vessels appeared to be twenty-two-foot wooden trap skiffs with small pilothouses forward, but several had no cabins at all and were just open boats with tillers to steer by. They looked at least a half century old, but all were in good shape, well painted with hulls scraped clean. On the boat slip a huge hooded seal lolled on the concrete ramp. He had apparently been there for two months. At first people thought he was sick, but he just seemed lazy. People had taken to feeding him, and he was looked on as a minor winter tourist attraction that brought a few people out from St. John's to photograph him. Lately, however, he had gotten testy and impatient when he wasn't given food, and parents were beginning to worry about their children. Soon after I was there someone shot him.

Walking back to the house, I was almost run over by a small group of adolescent girls who came barreling down from the grocery store with their candy bars and pop. As we passed, one of them pushed another over toward me. She let out a sharp, savage growl, then laughed hoarsely. They all looked me over briefly and passed on. I felt as if I had been brushed by a dark wave of sexual aggressiveness.

That night about 9:30 there was another knock on my door. It was Tommie again, this time relatively sober, inviting me over to his house to have a beer and "meet me mum."

The scene I walked into seemed, at first, like a David Mamet version of the traditional Newfoundland "time," or house party. Tommie's thick-limbed black Lab, Dutch, greeted him at the door. In the kitchen were four men and two women. I recognized Jonnie and Earl as two of the men. Jonnie and one of the other men were plastered and nearly incoherent. Earl, in a mustard-colored coat and boots, was mopping up something that had recently been deposited on the floor. Tommie introduced me to his mother, Grace, a pleasant-faced woman, taller than her son, in her late sixties I guessed, with wiry light brown hair. She sat at the kitchen table against the wall holding a Chihuahua and wearing a red bandana and a pained expression on her face.

"Watch your language!" she exclaimed whenever one of the men used the word "fucken," which was almost every sentence. Across the table from her was a smaller, plump, hunched older woman. This was Tommie's Aunt Mary, who said nothing but kept a look of severe disapproval on her face. It was clear the boys were the worse for wear at the end of a twelve-day holiday binge, and I suspected behavior like this was not usually tolerated in the house.

On the kitchen counter was an aquarium with two large African red-eyed turtles in it, a male about six inches long and a female about eight inches, which Tommie's girlfriend had bought as babies from a local pet shop. He carefully lifted them out to show them to me. The female, he said, once locked onto his lip and it was an hour before they were able to remove her.

The kitchen had an electric range and baseboard heat, but the interior of the house looked much as it probably had for the past century. Tommie took me into the parlor, where he pointed out his brother, Jack, asleep or passed out face down on the couch. The walls were covered with family photos, including black-and-white ones showing his grandmother as a young wife in the 1930s, and his mother's wedding dinner in the 1950s ("That's she on the right, and me dad next to her, short—like me"). Both pictures had been taken against the same floral wallpaper on which they were hung, so that the figures in them looked as though they were cutouts pasted on framed portions of the wall. The ceiling was covered with the original, dark-stained, beaded pine paneling. A neatly and densely decorated Christmas tree glowed in the next room, where a dusty ten-pound family Bible, dated 1865, lay open on a pedestal.

When I came back into the kitchen, Jonnie came over and handed me an open can of Black Horse.

"So, Bob," he asked me, "is you married?"

"Well," I replied, "I was, yeah."

"Shit, b'y," he said, placing his lanky arm around my shoulder, "we all *was* married!"

St. John's III:
"The Colour of My Voice,
the Colour of the Land"

It's mid-March and I have taken the daily bus from Gander down to
St. John's to visit my artist friend, Marlene Creates. As I walk from
the station to her house through blowing snow and icy streets, cars inch
their way over the edges of the steep streets, like kids on sleds at the
brink of hills, not sure if they want to risk it. On Water Street the wind
is so strong and the sidewalks so icy that I am involuntarily blown along
the street, sliding on my feet like an iceboat. Such storms around the
vernal equinox are known by St. Johnsmen as Sheila's Brush, named
after the folk figure who is identified in the *Dictionary of Newfoundland
English* with admirable ambiguity as "the wife, sister, housekeeper or
acquaintance of St. Patrick," and whose birthday is celebrated on
March 18, the day after that of the patron Irish saint.

St. John's—lovely, old, quirky St. John's—continues to change, gradually, but inexorably, into Any City, North America. King Cod is gone.
Dicks Stationery, after two hundred years on Water Street, has moved
to an industrial area, replaced by a coffee bar.

Wilansky's, the last of the Jewish-owned downtown stores, has
closed, its undraped mannequins still behind the orange-cellophaned
windows, looking unseemly and forlorn. The mysterious Bartlett's has
closed, too—or, rather, is completely empty—and dark, the haunting,
emaciated figure of its proprietor vanished, its blue-on-red sign peeling.

The old fishermen who once busked in front of Woolworth's for spare change have vanished, as has, for that matter, Woolworth's itself.

Although a few of the old local businesses—Mighty Whites Laundromat, Modern Shoe Hospital, the Family Barber Shop—remain, Duckworth and Water Streets have become dominated by restaurants, bistros, coffee bars, banks, and upscale clothing and sports stores—just like any other mid-size city downtown that managed to survive the urban flight of the 1970s and 1980s. A few of the idiosyncratic taxi stands still survive, but airbrush tattoo parlors now outnumber the real ones. The Ziggy Peelgood's truck still plies its nutritionally incorrect trade on Water Street, though it now has its own city-designated permanent parking spot, as if St. John's has given official recognition to its eccentricity.

This time of year the harbor looks emptier than ever. Fewer and fewer international commercial vessels arrive and depart from its piers. Instead, during the summer, they have been replaced by large cruise vessels arriving nearly every week from Montreal, Boston, and New York. Soviet fishing vessels, of course, no longer tie up in the harbor; instead, the *Academik Mtislav Keldysh*, a huge red and white Russian seamen's training vessel, has docked here the last several summers. It is lit up brilliantly at night, and guided tours are offered to the public. The Russian sailors, however, still walk up and down Water and Duckworth Streets, purchasing jeans and T-shirts, and hang out on the rails and gangplanks of their ship with the same, old, immemorial look of Slavic resignation.

Marlene lives on Bond Street, one of the handsomest residential streets in the city. Lining it is a colorful parade of two- and three-story, mansard-roofed, clapboarded, wooden row houses, painted in striking combinations of turquoise with Chinese red trim, brown with shiny black trim, sky blue with white trim, etc. Marlene's house is a three-story forest green and white structure with white clover in its outdoor flower box and white geraniums in the window. Along one side of her house is a narrow paved street known as Feaver's Lane, an old passageway that runs at a diagonal angle to Gower Street.

"The lane is a public way," says Marlene, "so the houses had to adapt to it. There's not a right angle in mine."

Her house looks out across the street to "Family Grocery," closed now a couple of years, but with its rusty 7-Up sign still over the front windows. Marlene says it was one of the last shops in town where the store owners lived over the store, once a common practice. The owners still live on the second floor, but Marlene doesn't see them much anymore:

"They used to be the source of all the news on the street. They told me who my neighbors were. Bill was always standing at the door, part of his head visible above the sign in the door window, looking out. They used to open the store precisely at eight in the morning and close at eleven at night. You could set your watch by it. He once told me 'If it's ten after eight and the blind isn't up, you know something is serious wrong over here.' They used to close only two days a year, Christmas and New Year's. One New Year's Day about two o'clock I noticed that the blinds were up and the lights on and Bill was standing by the door. I went over and said, 'What's up?' and he replied, 'Oh, after dinner, I couldn't think what to do, so I thought, might as well open the store.'"

Now Marlene sits and looks out. She has become the keeper of the street. The building adjoining the store, she tells me, was empty for a few years, but has now been turned into apartments. "Look, there's three little girls. They're waiting for the bus to come and take them to Sunday school. They stand out there and freeze—no coats—in those frilly little Sunday school dresses. Oh, look at her, I just love her!"

Over the past year Marlene has been videotaping details of the various landscapes of Signal Hill, the rocky, treeless promontory that guards the north side of the Narrows at the entrance to St. John's Harbour. She is able to see the craggy form of the hill—which she calls "my favorite fractal"—from her bedroom and studio windows. She calls her project "The Colour of My Voice, the Colour of the Land," which she describes as "an exploration of the relationship between language and landscape." As she tapes a segment on grass, rocks, berries, bushes, or some other feature of the hill, she repeats, as a kind of mantra, the words "The colour of my voice, the colour of the land," over and over. She says that each time the quality of her voice is different, as is the land's. Later she inserts certain printed words—carefully chosen, emotionally laden, active verbs, such as *remember* or *find*—into the tape. The verbs, she says, "constitute my diary of the year." The intent is that viewers, reading these words, will "hear" them in their own voices and thus participate in the experience. She says she sometimes spends two or three hours finding the right verbs to describe what she has done in recent days, and never repeats any. There are 738 different verbs in the final tape.

This Sunday morning she plans to do some more taping, and I offer to go along and help carry her equipment. As we drive up the road to the top of Signal Hill, the wind picks up and snow from the west begins to fly and thicken the air. When we arrive at the top, the parking lot is empty. The snow has become a blinding squall and Marlene says, "That's it, I can't shoot in this."

But we decide to wait to see if it will clear. We sit in the car and spend the time talking of aesthetics versus culture in outport folk art. She tells me how Newfoundlanders used to burn their old furniture for firewood:

"They wanted store-bought furniture because the handmade pieces represented poverty. They couldn't think the old stuff had any value, so they might as well burn it. There's a woman up in Renews who used to give me some old pieces. One day she said to me, 'It took fools like you coming here for us to appreciate what we've got!'"

In ten minutes or so the squall blows out to sea and the sky breaks apart like fresh-baked bread into islands of blue and white. We get out of the car, and down below the harbor is spread out in brilliant splendor against the snow. It looks like a white-line print, the snow graining the rock and the houses lining the Narrows on the ledges so that they stand out and shine like a mythic town.

We start down the back side of the hill, carrying tripod and camera bag, picking our way along the ledges. I wear a thick parka, and Marlene is wrapped in a black down jacket with a long red scarf. Hooded and bundled, with our wooden walking sticks, black bag, and tripod, we might be taken for a pair of eccentric nineteenth-century Oxford professors on an alpine hike, here in this frozen wilderness on the edge of the last city in North America.

The squall is far out to sea, like some great, gray, whirling phantasmagoria, but to the west we can see the next advancing storm. Several hundred feet below us there is a large terrace with what look like ditches or trails running at right angles to one another. Marlene says these were fields and pastures where eighteenth- and nineteenth-century British regiments stationed in the stone fort raised their food and kept sheep. Later on, the signal keeper lived up here alone with his family.

The trail slowly swings north, and along the steep eastern slope I notice a stone wall some two feet thick, perhaps twenty-five feet long and eight to ten feet high. It stands out, unexpectedly, in that wild flank of rock, surrounded and chinked with bleached and blackened grass. The sandstone outcrops are the same color, a kind of stained green and gray, so that the wall's artificiality is more subtle and therefore more impressive when finally recognized. It also seems much more ancient than it can be, like part of a pueblo dwelling. Above the cliff wall, a level, bare terrace has been cut into the slope. This, Marlene tells me, was the site of a tuberculosis and diphtheria sanatorium. "They were taken up here, poor souls. The treatment at the time was fresh air and the wind blew through the open windows. They must have been freezing."

As we walk down a zigzagging series of recently built, wooden steps, Marlene says that for years the trail was marked "Closed" at both ends, because the steps were made of logs and in disrepair and the government didn't want to be sued. "Of course the tourists wouldn't go past the signs. You could walk out here in summer for days on end and never meet anyone. Now in July it's like the Japanese going up Fuji."

The great flanks of land, covered in white, slide out to sea. Some ten miles to the south the little pyramid of the Cape Spear lighthouse stands out square and clear. To the north Marlene points out the sloping red cliff of Cuckold's Head and beyond it, invisible to us, the entrance to Quidi Vidi Harbour.

As each succeeding squall covers us, a foghorn begins to sound from somewhere: long, separated blasts that resound off the rock walls of the Narrows and carry out to sea. It has the sound and tone of a titanic French horn, one that might open a Bruckner symphony. Marlene says it used to be a two-note horn, dropping, she thinks, a minor third, which she liked better: "It fit the feel of the place more." But to me this kind of open-ended summons, announcing rather than warning, seems more fitting to the lofty setting that the hill presents this day.

She wanted to go to a blueberry patch today, but the one she has in mind is farther down, open to the wind, and already the air and snow are beginning to thicken and fly again. Instead, she comes upon a patch of wild rosebushes—leafless, with wizened red hips, but protected from the wind—and decides to tape them against the snow. She sets up her tripod and video camera, focuses on the bushes, and, instantly oblivious of me, begins to intone slowly, softly, and deliberately, "The colour of my voice, the colour of the land . . . "

I leave her and pick my way further down the cliffs. Here the slopes to the sea are more gradual. Were they sheer, the wind might very well buffet me over the edge. It is a fantastic scene, like some dream set of Arctic mountains with scaffolding, what I imagine the Torgnats of northern Labrador must look like: great looming snowcapped cliffs, the wind-whipped bleached grass running along the slopes and crevices like pale wildfire, and, far, far below, the sea, strangely calm, with small circles of tiny kittiwakes resting on its molten surface.

Aside from the wooden steps and the ancient fields and walls, the only sign of humanity I can see are the deserted World War II gun bunkers and the unmanned lighthouse at Fort Amherst on the south side of the Narrows. They present themselves as shifting glimpses of different time periods, appearing almost as memory presents itself in the mind's eye. The weather continues to come from the southwest in a series of sudden snow squalls alternating with interludes of clearing and calm, completely revealing, then totally obscuring the Narrows and headlands. When a storm passes off the Narrows it looks as if a great gray curtain were being pulled aside. *Here*, it seems to say, *are the colors of your history. Here is where you once lived, sufficient to your own time, before you entered history and so lost it.*

I turn and see, far above me, the tall, thin black figure of Marlene, her red scarf whipping in the wind. Her back to me, she is focused on the winter rose hips, repeating her quiet mantra, over and over, a small but still somehow significant figure against the vast gray and white slope that contains her: a spot of color offering a voice to this bleak and muted landscape.

The First Five Hundred

I have been perusing tonight an old and rather fragile volume entitled *The First Five Hundred*, being "a historical sketch of the military operations of the Royal Newfoundland Regiment in Gallipoli and on the Western Front during the Great War (1914–1918)." The book is bound in embossed green leather with gold lettering and gold page edging and has the look of a commemorative edition, designed to be treasured, whose possession in itself would serve as an expression of homage to an almost mythic episode in Newfoundland history. Curiously for its subject, it was published, not in Newfoundland, or Canada, or even Great Britain, but in Albany, New York.

It might seem an odd volume to find in the guest bedroom of a contemporary ranch-style house on a suburban street in Gander, where I am spending the night at the home of my friend Cyril Oldford. But earlier in the evening I noticed on his living room wall a large, glassed, oval-framed black-and-white photograph of a young soldier dressed in the wool cap and jacket uniform of World War I. This, Cyril told me, was his grandfather, killed in France in 1916. He was twenty-three. His wife had died in childbirth four years earlier, leaving Cyril's father an orphan.

By the summer of 1916 the war was already almost two years old, and Newfoundlanders had been involved from the very beginning, Despite having been granted responsible government—essentially, political independence—by Great Britain in 1855, Newfoundland remained the Empire's most loyal ex-colony. When war with Germany was declared in August 1914, young men from St. John's and the outlying outports rushed to sign up and be part of the "first five hundred," or the initial contingent of what became the Royal Newfoundland Regiment.

Hastily trained in Scotland and nicknamed the Blue Puttees (no regulation woolen khaki was available for their lower leg coverings, so the soldiers were issued navy blue puttees), the regiment's first baptism by fire was in the last stages of the disastrous Turkish battle of Gallipoli in September 1915. Though their casualties were small in comparison to those suffered by the Australians and New Zealanders, the regiment lost several dozen men, mostly to dysentery and typhoid fever.

From the Dardanelles the regiment was shipped to northern France to participate in the "Summer Drive," the massive Allied push along the Somme River. They were greeted and addressed by Lieutenant-General Beauvoir de Lisle, the British commander of the 29th Division who, from his horse, assured them of the overwhelming superiority of the Allied numbers, artillery, strategy, and mettle over those of the Germans.

On the morning of July 1, 1916, a date as familiar to Newfoundlanders as December 7, 1941, used to be to Americans, eight hundred members of the Royal Newfoundland Regiment went over the top of the trenches near the small village of Beaumont Hamel. It was a hopeless and doomed effort from the start. Entrenched German gun emplacements mowed down the advancing ranks with withering machine-gun fire. The bodies fell and hung on their own uncut barbed wire, many of them near the blackened dead trunk of what became known as the Danger Tree. Two of the regiment managed to reach the German lines, though it is not reported what they did there.

When roll call was taken the next morning, only sixty-eight of the eight hundred Newfoundlanders answered. According to *The First Five Hundred*, 80 members of the regiment were killed at Beaumont Hamel, 90 were listed as killed in other action, and 131 were declared "medically unfit," a category that included the maimed, the gassed, and the psychologically traumatized. Later accounts say over 270 were killed in the July 1 drive, and over 300 more were wounded. By any account, it was the most deadly day in Newfoundland history, and one that had a profound effect on the economy of the country and the psyche of its people. Although its effects would not fully be felt for decades, the unquestioning loyalty of Newfoundlanders to the Mother Country and the age-old deference paid to the merchant families of Water Street had received a seismic shock.

One of the most telling documents in *The First Five Hundred* is a letter written by Lieutenant-General de Lisle to Newfoundland's prime minister, Sir E. P. Morris. Here is a portion of it:

That battalion covered itself with glory on July 1 by the magnificent way in which it carried out the attack entrusted to it. It went forward to the attack when two other attacks on that same part of the line had failed, and by its behavior on that occasion it showed itself worthy of the highest traditions of the British race, and proved itself to be a fit representative of the population of the oldest British colony. When the order to attack was given, every man moved forward to his appointed objective in his appointed place as if on parade. There were no waverers, no stragglers, and not a man looked back. It was a magnificent display of trained and disciplined valour, and its assault only failed of success because dead men can advance no farther. They were shot down by machine guns brought up by a very gallant foe under our intense artillery fire. Against any foe less well-entrenched, less well-organized, and above all, less gallant, their attack must have succeeded. As it was the action of the Newfoundland Battalion and the other units of the British left contributed largely to the victory achieved by the British and French farther south by pinning to their ground the best of the German troops and by occupying the best of their artillery, both heavy and field. The gallantry and devotion of this battalion, therefore, was not in vain, and the credit of victory belongs to them as much as to those troops father south, who actually succeeded in breaking the German line. An attacking army is like a football team: there is but one who kicks the goal, yet the credit of success belongs not alone to that individual but to the whole team, whose concerted action led to the desired result.

What strikes me most about this passage is not its lack of any sense of responsibility for the carnage, nor its fustian and self-aggrandizing rhetoric (the same rhetoric that led Hemingway to say that the war had made "abstract words such as glory, honor, courage, or hallow . . . obscene"), but that its words and images reveal so vividly the engines of futility that drove this most disastrous of European wars to such prolonged and impoverishing lengths. They lend an insight, a disturbing corollary, into the Duke of Wellington's famous remark that "the battle of Waterloo was won on the playing fields of Eton." They suggest, and indeed make manifest, that for the upper-class English officers who directed the war and sent hundreds of thousands of men to their deaths for no discernible gain, the battles *were* sporting events, and the soldiers merely expendable players whose performance was judged not by concrete results so much as by how they represented and exhibited training, organization, discipline, valor, loyalty, and—that most cherished of aristocratic values in military lost causes—gallantry.

At the end of the war, one-fourth of the nearly twelve thousand Newfoundlanders who served overseas had died, far more proportionally than from any other English-speaking country except Great Britain itself. It is said that after the war there was almost no one in Newfoundland, then a country of only a quarter million people, who did not know of a family who had lost someone in the war.

Now, more than eight decades after Beaumont Hamel, I still occasionally encountered stories of the Great War, stories that seemed to be more present in the minds of contemporary Newfoundlanders than those from World War II (an event that actually transformed the nature and culture of the country far more profoundly). One woman from the Eastport Peninsula told me that her father, who was born in Newcastle, England, had served in the Great War:

"He was a Woodrich, and in 1914 he was serving on a ship in Gibraltar that was blown up when its magazine was hit. There were ninety-nine men on board and he was the only survivor. He came up next to a lifeboat and hauled himself aboard. There was a cadet—he was fond of the young ones—that he saw in the water. He hauled him up out of the water and blacked out. Later he found out the boy'd died. Both of his legs were off. He didn't know if they'd been blown away, or if the boy had hung in the water after Dad had blacked out and the sharks had eaten them off. It was a terrible thing to think. After the war he came over to Fogo Island, where I was born. When he first came ashore he said he thought he'd died and gone to heaven. Later he came to live with us here on the mainland. He lived with us for sixteen years. He liked all the trees here."

Cyril himself told me that he grew up knowing several of the veterans of the "First War":

"There was John Brown, and Brock Bradley's dad—those were the two I knew. They never talked of the war, except when they was by themselves. And then they didn't have much good to say about their leaders. They used to talk around me. I guess they thought I was too little to listen.

"And there was Tom King. He was what you would call shell-shocked. He used to walk around at night with a flashlight, and you could see the light going all herky-jerky. Sometimes he'd be singing, in this high singsong voice, things like, 'The warr, the warr, she's stole all my dancers.' I don't know if it was from a song or where. You always knew it was he, but you weren't allowed to make fun of him. He used to go out drinking with Jack Ralph on Saturday nights. They'd sit in the car drinking beer and toss the bottles up over the car into the woods. One night Jack had just got himself a brand-new 1964 Chevrolet coupe, and Tom tossed his bottle up and down it came right on the windshield and smashed it, but Jack never ragged him about it."

Even the young people seem to carry an almost racial memory of the war, preserved in historical amber. Earlier this evening I took Cyril's son, Josh, and his friend Simon to see *Courage under Fire* at the Gander Mall cinema. They seemed to enjoy the show, though they didn't say much. Then, on the way back to the house, Josh said, "Dad's pop [grandfather] died in the war." He meant World War I. Then Simon spoke up: "My dad's pop was killed on the last day of the war. They had signed the peace agreement and everything and he died that day anyway." Neither of them knew where their great-grandfathers were buried.

Earlier this fall, Walter Tobin, the last surviving veteran of Beaumont Hamel, died at the age of ninety-seven. Tobin, a native of St. John's, was given a high mass in the Basilica of St. John's, the Catholic church that dominates the skyline of the city. During the mass, several of the eulogies and encomiums given in praise of his fallen comrades at the time were repeated by the priest and current politicians, including De Lisle's fatuous observation that the assault at Beaumont Hamel "only failed of success because dead men can advance no farther," and the comment, made in 1924 by British General Sir Aylmer Hunter Weston at the dedication of the impressive bronze War Memorial in St. John's, that Tobin and his fellow Blue Puttees were "better than the best."

Portions of the mass were broadcast that evening on the CBC, followed by excerpts from a radio interview with Mr. Tobin last July, in which he responded as follows to Weston's remarks:

"'Better than the best'? Well, if getting mowed down by machine-gun fire is being 'better than the best,' then I'm a dumbbell. . . . We was fools to go over. Damn fools. Oh, it's nice to go down in history, to be sure, but it was a bunch of crap, it was."

Scenes from a Hunt

First Day: Going In

At 8:30 on the morning of November 2 I left Gander with Wade Kean, his brother Bill, and his uncle Ralph Melendy for a hunting cabin on the Southwest Gander River. Wade is a surgeon at the hospital in Clarenville; Bill works for the Department of Revenue in St. John's; and Ralph is a retired mechanic, also from St. John's. The three had driven in from Clarenville that morning and picked me up at Cyril Oldford's house. The four of us squeezed into Wade's Bronco, which pulled a homemade wooden trailer carrying our gear and the ubiquitous four-wheel off-road motor bike known as a quad. Just past the Glenwood turnoff on the Trans-Canada, we turned left onto a lumber road and headed south. A little way in we passed a massive wall of pulp logs at least twenty feet high, thirty feet deep, and about six hundred feet long.

The hunting cabin was about thirty-six miles in from the turnoff. As we left the highway it began to flurry, and by the time we crossed Little Careless Brook it was snowing moderately, with big, heavy flakes that fell like soggy cornflakes. It snowed continuously all the way in to the cabin, covering the ground and the trees with several inches of wet snow. On the way in I saw three spruce grouse eating buds in a grove of alders just off the road. They looked up as we passed and seemed quite unconcerned.

About twelve miles in, the good road stopped, and we crossed a steel bridge over the Northwest Gander River. From here on the road is not used by the logging trucks and is not maintained. In places there were potholes, craters really, three or four feet wide and sometimes as deep, marked only with small spruce saplings that someone had thrown into the holes and that were difficult to see through the wet snowflakes. Among the ranks of dark spruce and fir, the larches, or "junipers," had all turned the color of burnt orange, like Christmas trees left outside for a month. The small ones had dropped their needles, which gathered at their bases like small aprons of tawny gold or floated in the black streams. We kept on another hour or so, sliding over narrow culverts in the wet snow, dodging the potholes, and eventually coming up onto a ridge between the two rivers where the country became more open.

The snowflakes grew smaller and wetter as we went. I saw only a handful of cabins on the way out, until we began to approach the Southwest River. There were handmade signs every so often, marking individual encampments. One, "Igloo Inlet," prompted Wade to remark that Sandra Kelley, the Newfoundland Minister of Tourism, had recently quipped to a Toronto reporter that she "lives in an igloo" and had gotten into much hot water because of it.

"Christ, talk about not being clear on the concept. She's supposed to be in charge of the Cabot celebration next year and what does she do? Gives the contract for thirty thousand Newfoundland flags to a company in the States! Christ!"

On the left we passed "Reedville," a collection of a half dozen or so cottages owned by various Reeds from Chapel Arm. At the end of the road there were five cabins spaced along the river, ours the next to last. It was a small frame structure, perhaps ten by sixteen feet, clapboarded and painted white, with dark green trim and a rusty stovepipe sticking up through the roof.

"You see that cabin, my son?" said Wade. "Well, it doesn't exist."

I asked him what he meant, but he just gave that ambiguous Newfoundland shrug of the head, which can mean anything from "Ain't life a bitch?" to "How're you doing?" A large padlock had been placed on the door, along with two federal orders to remove the cabin, the more recent one dated last summer. Wade picked the lock to get us in. We unpacked the gear, and Wade strung wires from his Bronco battery into the cabin and hooked up two 60-watt lightbulbs for use in the evening.

His uncle Ralph doesn't hunt anymore, but serves as the official cook. He fried up some thick slabs of baloney ("Newfoundland steak, b'y") and scrambled eggs for dinner, wearing the plastic orange webbing of an onion bag as a hairnet. By then it was sleeting fairly hard. It being Sunday, a "dead" day when no hunting is allowed, we spent the rest of the afternoon visiting and drinking rum at Wally and Linda Reed's place just up the road past a yellow school bus with a cabin attached to it. Wade told me there used to be thirty or forty school buses spread out over the country here, but the RCMP had been rounding them up and concentrating them in a restricted area that Wade described as "visually challenged." Wally and Linda both had licenses, but neither planned to do any shooting this year.

The Politics of Caribou

When we got back to the cabin Ralph cooked up a supper of rainbow trout, chutney, and blue potatoes, with apple pie for dessert. The conversation revolved around stories of previous hunts, but even more around the politics of hunting and licenses, a subject of endless fascination to Newfoundlanders. In fact, the intricacies of the politics often seemed to hold as much interest as the hunting itself.

"There are some thirty thousand big game licenses issued in Newfoundland each year," said Wade, "and maybe another twenty thousand in Labrador. So figure fifty thousand licenses. That's a tenth of our whole population, two-fifths of Labrador's. How many people in B.C. have access to this kind of hunting? Yet buddy thinks that if he can work twenty weeks a year and the missus works another twenty, he's entitled to have the government pay to keep him living well the rest of the year. Oh, Newfoundlanders live pretty high, b'y! How many people in the States live as well as Newfoundlanders do, over all? Not many, I tells you. And who pays for it? The farmer in Alberta or the banker in B.C. No wonder they's pissed at us. No, b'y, I don't see much of a future for this country."

Whenever Wade got on his political high horse, Ralph would usually tell a story to bring his nephew down a bit. Ralph followed Wade's outburst with a long story about the time that he, Wade, shot three moose on one license, each time thinking he was shooting at the same moose.

Then Ralph told about a moose trip he had taken with three friends years ago. They tented out in the country north of Hare Bay for a week. It poured the first day, but on the second day he pulled down a large cow on a bog with one shot.

"It didn't even move," Ralph said. "Its knees just buckled and it fell."

They cut it up and skinned three of its quarters, but the last quarter proved bad. There was a bullet hole in the shoulder and the meat was all "pussie." They located a game warden, who said, "Throw 'em in the truck, b'ys," and wrote Ralph out a new license on the spot. The next day he saw another cow, on the bog, "at a long distance" and was taking aim when a big bull stepped out much closer, and he brought him down. The cow began to charge, which, he said, is quite unusual for a cow. Ralph had one shot left, and waited. The cow came within twenty feet of him and then swerved aside at the last second.

"If I'd had to shoot it," he said, "I'd have just left it. They just might not believe me."

I said that that cow must have been some fond of that bull. Ralph nodded solemnly and said, "I guess so. I guess she must have been at that."

Woodland caribou are native to Newfoundland, but moose were first introduced on the island a little over a century ago, about the time that the classic Newfoundland outport culture was taking shape. Moose used to be an important part of the subsistence food of outports in the winter, but the imperative now is largely cultural, although not entirely. The night before, Cyril Oldford had told me that he hunted caribou, but not often. "I likes to get my meat cheap, and mile for mile and dollar for dollar, caribou ain't it. You figure sixty pounds of dressed meat from a caribou against four hundred or more for a moose. You do the math." He also wouldn't go out as early as we had. "If I was one of these fellows coming up from St. John's, some three hundred miles, I wouldn't even go out in the woods until mid-November, after the rut is over. That's when the bulls goes off by themselves. You can find ten or fifteen yarded up together then." When he was a boy, before they had refrigerators, they liked to go out around Christmastime because the moose would keep better then. Also you could track the moose easier in the snow. Now the season starts earlier, in September, "to accommodate the hunters who come from away."

Moose and caribou licenses are allotted through a complex revolving lottery based on a tier system of five pools. If you fail to get a license one year, you move up a pool the next year. If you do get one, you fall back to the fourth or fifth pool, depending in part on whether you go in with a partner or for a "single."

"Outside" or nonresident licenses cost $400–$500. Residents pay $37.50. Moose like to eat young tree saplings, which worries the pulp paper companies, so the government sometimes concentrates licenses in areas of new plantings. One year, Ralph said, they had sixteen hundred licenses in an area of a few square miles near Terra Nova. Most licenses were "doubles," or two hunters permitted for one animal, and some were hunters out in groups of three or four. He figured there were at least four thousand moose hunters in the area, an urban density. "One day," he said, "I came up on a rise and looked down on a bog. There was as many red caps as you see on a pitcher plant bog!"

The whole system seems to be widely regarded as something to manipulate or evade. Many women, for instance, are "silent partners" on their spouses' or boyfriends' licenses. Wade said he has seen a few women in the woods, "but none with a gun. You don't even have to pass a firearms test anymore to get a moose license. There's a blind man in St. John's has been suing the province because they wouldn't issue him a license. Says he's being discriminated against."

Even though there are plenty of moose and almost everybody who goes out gets one, there is still a lot of poaching. Poaching seems to have become culturally ingrained to some degree after Confederation, perhaps regarded by some as a form of protest against Newfoundland's "absorption" by Canada.

More than outright poaching, however, Newfoundlanders seem to practice a sophisticated form of hunting-license roulette. Cyril, for instance, had told me that he belongs to a pool of four men who put in for a moose license each year, though only two of them go out each year. They share the meat, which averages one hundred pounds per quarter. They take the meat to a man in St. John's, where it is dressed, flash-frozen, and wrapped for them. "Often that moose'll be in my

freezer five hours after it was taken out of the woods." He doesn't believe in "hanging the meat—you know, in the shed till it turns green—
that's just crap!"

One can see that for Wade, hunting is as much a family affair as anything. Though he is a practicing surgeon, he is a very athletic, out-
doors person and gets plenty of exercise. He and his wife, Danielle,
bought an old thirty-acre farm on Deep Cove, where he built their
house out of spruce logs, grows good-sized plots of turnips, potatoes,
and carrots, and raises goats and turkeys. For his brother Bill, however,
the hunt is an annual weeklong escape from his government desk job
in St. John's, the kind of position held by more and more professional
Newfoundlanders.

I asked Wade why his Uncle Ralph didn't go shooting anymore, since
he seemed physically able enough.

"Oh y's, my son, he could still get his moose if he wants to. And he
likes to be out in the woods and go with us when we hunts. But he just
doesn't need to shoot anymore, you see? He's done with it. Now Ben,
my nephew, he's in his twenties and hot for it. Come fall and his blood
just starts to b'il. He'd rather shoot than anything. I know how he feels;
I used to be that way at his age. But now, I'd almost as soon go out and
take pictures as shoot them. In a few more years I'll probably stop, but
I'll always want to go out in the woods."

Around midnight, Ralph made a feeble attempt to get up a card
game, but Wade was already asleep and Bill said, "No patience, b'y—I
don't wants to play patience." We all turned in then, and for a while I
lay there listening to low Newfie patter between the two men still
awake: "Y's b'y." "Egg-zactly." "You got that right, my son." "Y's b'y." "I
guarantee ya."

I felt a deep and undeserved sense of well-being, with my belly full of
eggs, baloney, trout, potatoes, apple pie, rum, beer, tea, and bread and
butter, and soon fell asleep. I woke fitfully through the night to sounds
of loud snoring and a clearing wind whipping at the windows of the
shack; but the Coleman oil stove kept us warm and cozy. (Wade told me
that once, in the middle of the night, they woke to find a quarter inch
of oil all over the floor of the cabin and carried the stove, still lit, outside, while the chimney fell down inside.) The flutter of the oil flame in

the belly of the stove cast a soft, round, flickering shadow of light on the white pasteboard ceiling, like a pale rose window of stained glass.

Second Day: The Hunt

We woke at six to the sound of Wade, already up and dressed, singing loudly, "This-is-the-*dawn*ing of the A-a-ge of A-qua-ri-us . . . " A quick cup of tea, and we were out the door by 6:20. Wade, Bill, and I, in that order, got on the quad seat, leaving Ralph at the cabin. Then we forded the river, low this season, on an established underwater road of rocks, up into barrens country on the other side. Some years, Wade said, the water is too high to ford and they have to stay on the cabin side, where the hunting is not nearly as good.

We were back at the cabin by 10:45, having found eleven caribou: eight cows, one calf, and two stags. Wade bagged both stags, using six shots from a "small but fast" high-powered sniper rifle with a seven-shot magazine and 7.62-mm shells.

It was more like hunting cattle than wild animals. All but two of the caribou we encountered were standing right out on the lumber roads. We spotted the first animal, a doe, within a few minutes, at a distance of perhaps two hundred yards. She stood by the side of the road, browsing on the lichen growing on the shoulders. She had already changed into her whitish winter coat with a light brown saddle across the back. As we approached her, she didn't move off, but stood staring at us with that blank, passive curiosity of cows in a field. I thought that the racket made by the quad would scare anything away, but Wade said, "You'd be surprised. They don't mind the noise, only changes in the sound. That's why I try to leave the quad running when I takes a shot."

She stuck her left rear leg straight out behind her, and after a minute or two turned and began loping down the road with a curious side-to-side waddle of her haunches and legs, as if her hindquarters were a pendulum swinging back and forth.

"They'll go on that way forever," said Wade, "and scare everything ahead of it. Whereas a moose'll go right off the road." Just like flushing shorebirds ahead of you on the beach, I thought. They think they're the universal objects of desire.

When the cow broke into a gallop, her body movement straightened out and she proceeded ahead of us at a very fast clip. After about half a mile, she took off left on a side road, but stopped fifty yards or so in, looking back at us as we passed in the quad, as if to say, "Aren't you going to follow me?"

The first shot Wade took was at a stag standing with a doe by the edge of the road about 150 yards ahead of us. He missed, but to my surprise the animals didn't bolt, but only started slightly at the sound. Then they moved farther out into the *middle* of the road. The stag even turned broadside, facing left, as if to say, "Here, is this a better shot?" His torso looked like a rough map of the United States.

Wade's second shot hit the stag, which lurched backward, as if he had been punched in the jaw, then loped a hundred feet or so into the cutover brush, followed by the doe. We got back on the quad and drove up opposite the wounded caribou. Wade got off and went into the brush after it. The animal stood there, shaking his large head back and forth, as if trying to shake off flies. Bill said, "He's got a vicious headache, b'y." Wade finished him off with a third shot.

It was a young stag, its brow tines still unformed. "Maybe two years," Wade thought. "They look deceptively large at a distance. If I'd known I might not have shot it, but then, y'know, you might not see another one for three days and you'll kick yourself for not having taken the shot. "

Unlike moose and deer, female caribou can have antlers and appear very much like young stags, so that only the characteristic dark area on their rear end, the "vulva patch," distinguishes them. In this case, though, Wade said it was the situation that convinced him it was a stag: the fact that he was accompanied by a doe, and that if it had been an antlered doe, she would most likely have been with a mature stag. But he admitted he couldn't be 100 percent sure.

The animal was small, perhaps 120–130 pounds, and when Wade lifted its head by its antlers to cut its throat so as to bleed it, the dark red blood gushed from its nostrils and mouth. It still moved, convulsively, and when he cut through the jugular vein, blood spurted in two jets in a rhythmic, pumping pulse from its great, hidden heart.

We left the carcass in the brush and continued up the road. At one point four spruce partridge stood in the road before us like chickens.

Their breasts were flecked with white, as if they had been spattered with a whitewash brush. We practically had to shoo them out of the way with our quad.

Less than a half hour later, we encountered the second group of caribou: a large stag with three does, across a shallow gulch maybe 130 yards away. Wade motioned to Bill to give him the gun, then slipped off the quad in one smooth motion, silently abandoning the vehicle to me. He knelt down, bracing his arm on a stump, leveled the rifle, and squeezed the trigger. The stag seemed to crumple, then falter, but did not fall. The does did not bolt, but only moved off a few yards. Later Wade said that he knew he had killed it with the first shot. But the stag didn't know he was dead. He began to move off slowly to the right and back toward the woods. Wade was completely locked onto his quarry, oblivious of everything else. His eyes were like laser beams trained on the stag's lurching form. In his Day-Glo orange fur-lined overalls he raced down the gully and up the other side. Bill followed casually behind him on foot. I took the quad and followed the road in a wide curve around the gully to join them.

The caribou, it turned out, had been standing in the middle of the road's continuation, though we couldn't see that when Wade took his shot. There were large pools of blood on the crushed stone of the roadbed. Wade came up out of the gully, dropped on one knee, aimed, and fired. This time the big stag went down. The does trotted off, unhurriedly, with backward glances, as if expecting the stag to follow, We found it lying on its right side, on a piece of sloping, moss-covered ground, its head facing uphill. Its great tongue was lolling out of its mouth, its body was convulsing, and its legs were horizontally pawing the ground, as if still trying to run.

Wade was breathing heavily, and not just with exertion. "Jesus," he said, "Jesus. All right, I'm going to finish him off. Do you want to take a picture first?"

"No," I replied. "It's all right."

He locked in another shell, took aim, hesitated for a long moment while life struggled on the ground—and fired. At the moment of impact the stag exhaled a great, white plume of vapor—like a whale spouting—into the cold, clear air, and then, mercifully, lay still.

"Jesus," said Wade.

It had a beautiful rack, gracefully asymmetrical, with a "double shovel," or brow tine. There were lighter lines running along the surface of each antler branch, like delicately carved decorative patterns. They reminded me of a story I had read about the Inuits of Labrador, descendants of the ancient Dorset Eskimos, who carved totemic designs into the antlers of Antelope Spirit, representing a kind of "written pact" between them, which the antelope have carried to this day.

The end of the stag's penis projected slightly from its sheath. Wade pointed to a drop of semen at its tip. "I guess it had a bit of something before breakfast," he said.

"I bet those does are some disappointed," said Bill.

Bill and I helped Wade turn the stag on its back, and we each held one of its forelegs splayed as he carefully split the skin from throat to penis, and then cut through the peritoneum. (How quickly the excitement and nobility of the death is turned into the mundane meniality and disgrace of the dressing.) Then, using a stick to hit the back of his knife blade, he split the breastbone from bottom to top and opened the chest cavity. Wade was right. The stag's windpipe, the size and texture of an Electrolux hose, had been severed by the first shot. It had run fifty yards or more with a severed larynx, not knowing it was already dead.

Bill straddled the body and grabbed the white, ribbed windpipe with both hands as Wade carefully cut the organs away from the surrounding membrane. The whole multicolored sack of guts slowly unrolled into the morning sun: red, blood-rich lungs; dark maroon, marbled heart; gray-blue slabs of liver; and gun-blue messes of intestines. Wade cut out the heart and liver and placed them in a plastic bag, handing it to me to carry back to the quad. He then cut the carcass in half, commenting that he was "leaving two ribs on each hindquarter," as if he were giving a dissection lecture to first-year medical students. He pointed out the caribou's saphenous leg vein, "the same one they use for coronary bypasses."

We dragged the two halves of the carcass up behind a stump and covered them with spruce boughs to hide them from bear, jays, eagles, ravens, and whatever else might claim them. Wade guessed the weight at forty to forty-five pounds per quarter, the standard method of sizing animals. "With the head," he says, "it may have been a two-hundred-pound animal. A noble animal. Not huge, mind you, but noble." (*Noble:* of a size or appearance commanding respect. Also, an inert element.)

By 10:45 we were back in camp, where Ralph had a breakfast of turkey soup, leftover trout and potatoes, and more fried turkey waiting for us. I carried in the plastic bag containing the liver, which looked like a large piece of soft, wet slate, and the heart, the size of an alarm clock. For dinner Ralph cooked the heart in an iron frying pan, saying it was something of a tradition to eat that organ first after a kill, though he didn't attach any symbolic import to it.

At noon, Wade and Ralph set back out across the river in the quad, with Bill in tow in the wooden trailer, to carry out the larger stag and to gut the first one, which they would leave in the brush. In the river the wheels of both the quad and the trailer were completely submerged so that it looked as if Wade and Ralph were riding on a Jet Ski pulling Bill in a small wooden skiff.

Neither animal had been tagged yesterday, as regulations require them to be. Once again the reason was not simple lawlessness but the result of the complex ramifications of license roulette. The story was this: The boys have only two licenses among the three of them. Although he doesn't hunt anymore, Ralph has one for a male caribou, and Bill has an either-sex license. Wade's other brother, Paul, had gotten a moose license, but he couldn't come this year. They hadn't tagged the second, larger stag because Ralph, who wasn't with us when it was shot, had the stag only license, and they couldn't be found with two dead stags and only one license. They couldn't even carry out the head of the larger stag (whose rack is to be a trophy for Ralph's shed on Mundy Pond Road in St. John's) because if they had stopped on the way back to clean the first stag and a wildlife officer had stopped by, they'd have two heads but only one license between the two of them. Now they'll go out and tag the larger stag with Ralph's tag and bring it in, but only gut the smaller one, since if they use up both tags they won't be able to go out and look for the cow moose that Wally Reed has a license for, or the bull moose that his wife has one for. *Got that, b'y?*

This complicated shell game stems from the fact that hunting regulations, as Wade said, seem loosely observed but strictly enforced. The bottom ethical line seems to be able to say, "We never took an animal out of here there wasn't a license for," though *whose* license it is seems entirely negotiable. As Ralph put it, "I don't mind bending the regulations now and then. I just don't like breaking them outright."

Still, Wade cautioned us to tell "the other boys" that we got only one animal. "You never knows how much you tells your friends'll leak out, eh?"

The three men returned to the cabin about 1 P.M. They were all on the quad, with the carcass of the second stag cut in half and loaded on the trailer. Plastic tags were looped through the tendons of each leg, identifying their license. We strung the two halves upside down by their legs on a spruce pole trestle. The front half, with its tapered red cave of curved white ribs, looked like the frame of a schooner hull. The head, with its magnificent sculptured rack, had already been removed and lay on the ground. Its dark red tongue lolled out to one side and its eyes were open partway, giving it a drunken or debauched appearance.

Wade then took out his hunting knife and proceeded to skin the two halves, and then cut each into quarters. Some hunters use chainsaws to cut up moose and caribou carcasses, using vegetable oil instead of bar oil, but Wade is proud of the sharpness of his knives and of his surgical ability. We wrapped each quarter in large swaths of cheesecloth to discourage scrub jays, crows, and ravens and left them all hanging from the trestle like the embalmed and webbed prey of some gigantic spider.

THE CABIN THAT DOESN'T EXIST

In the evening Wally Reed dropped by and, over glasses of rum all around, I finally heard from him and Wade the story of the cabin. It had originally been a federal Fisheries observation cabin near Botwood, some seventy miles from here. About ten years ago it was abandoned and scheduled to be burned. But the Fisheries employees who were contracted to destroy it set the outhouse ablaze instead, took photos of that to show their superiors, and then moved the cabin here, thus in a sense having their cabin and eating it. The cabin, therefore, officially no longer existed. Over the years several parties, including Wade, Bill,

Ralph, a Fisheries biologist named Edgar, two men named Ned and Frank, and Reg and Dave—a father and son team—have used it.

The government, however, will not recognize a cabin on Crown Land without a permit. A second sixty-day eviction notice from the Department of Natural Resources has expired, and a court order gives the government the right to remove or destroy the nonexisting structure and to subject the owner (who also does not exist) to a fine of twenty-five dollars a day. Wade and the others have talked about moving it across the road to a piece of land that Bill has leased, but there are several interlocking questions: Could they move it without the permission of Crown Lands? If they move it, and thereby claim possession, are they liable for the accumulated fines? Has it in fact become Crown property (as, in fact, it already is—or rather was, since it doesn't exist) under the court order? Wade and Wally spent well over an hour vigorously debating and chewing over these issues.

An even thornier question, though, was whether they could lay claim to the cabin without creating more bad blood between Dave and his father, Reg. Apparently at some point Dave claimed ownership of the cabin and told his father that he could use it when Dave and his wife were not there. In response to this filial presumption Reg said, "Fuck you," and the two haven't spoken since. Bill believes the feud is over Dave's wife, Megan, or rather, over the whole question of women at the cabin, which Reg adamantly opposes. Bill said, "Megan can be pretty quick herself. I heard her say to Dave, 'If that old fucker comes down here you won't see me in that cabin anymore.'"

So, in order to save the cabin, which doesn't exist, they would have to navigate a regulatory and family labyrinth studded with potential land mines.

As it turned out, they talked for nothing. About 11 P.M. Wade went out to call Danielle on his cellular phone. He had to drive to the top of the ridge to get a sufficient signal, and during this time the wires from his Bronco battery, which powered the two lightbulbs in the cabin, were disconnected, and we were plunged into lantern dimness. When he came back he told us that Frank and Dave had paid the government $750 for the cabin and were coming up this week to move it down to

Larson's Falls. Wade seemed mostly relieved at not having to step into
a tangle of government bureaucracy and domestic squabbling.

THIRD DAY: A Morning with Ralph

A cold, clear, frosty morning. Wade and Bill went back across the river
to bring back the other (the first), smaller stag across the river. Having
learned of the imminent fate of the cabin, they decided to forgo bag-
ging a possible moose with the Reeds' licenses and to spend the rest of
the time here clearing Bill's lot across the road. Ralph offered to teach
me to play cribbage while they were gone. He was born in Wesleyville,
a small outport on the north shore of Bonavista Bay, in 1926. Ralph is
one of nine children, including two who "died young." When he was a
small child his father left home and went to New York City to find
work. So many Newfoundlanders immigrated to New York at that time
that it was called Little Newfoundland. He landed a job as a steel
welder and worked on the Empire State Building.

Referring to his family's status during the Depression, Ralph said,
"We thought we was pretty well off. We could put milk in our tea." A
common Newfoundland exchange from the time, which still persists
today, is:

"How's yer meat, b'y—tough?"

"Tougher where there's none."

He told stories about his Aunt Maud, who married his Uncle Tom.
She was from St. John's, and when she arrived by boat near Cape Freels,
a place where, Ralph said, "bloomers made from flour sacks hung on
the line," she exclaimed, "My God, I am in the arsehole of the world."
Some time after they were married, they took a trip to Lamerline, on
the Burin Peninsula, to visit some relatives. When they landed, she
looked around and said, "No, by God, I was wrong!"

One time Ralph was driving Aunt Maud and two other middle-aged
women from Wesleyville to Gambo, when they came upon two horses
in the road. One was a large draft mare, and the other was a diminutive
male Newfoundland pony. The pony was obviously trying to mount the
mare, but he was too short to reach her. She was standing right in the
middle of the road, looking back every now and then, impatiently, while

the bantam male, its stiff pecker barely reaching above the mare's rear knees, pumped away in futile effort. This went on for several minutes, with Ralph and the ladies sitting in the car in enormous silence, until finally he heard his aunt whisper fiercely, "'Quat a little! 'Quat a little!"

Ralph moved from Wesleyville to St. John's in the 1950s and had a number of stories about Joey Smallwood, the flamboyant first premier of the new province of Newfoundland.

One day Joey thought he smelled something and turned to his aide: "Ross, did you break wind?"

"No, Sir," Ross replied. "Do you want me to?"

Another time Joey was speaking to a crowd from his office window in the new Confederation Building just outside St. John's. An aide said to him, "Oh, Mr. Smallwood, why don't you throw something out the window that will do the poor little children some good?"

At which a reporter in the room was heard to comment, "Why don't you throw yourself out, Joey, and do everybody some good!"

I mentioned to Ralph how quiet and diffident Bill seemed to be compared to Wade. "Oh, Bill *appears* to be the worrier and naysayer, and Wade all confident and enthusiastic, but it's Bill who's really the ca'm one. If a warden showed up, say, and they had an animal without a license, Bill would be some ca'm, and Wade would be nervous as a flea."

Moreover, he said, although Bill is the quiet one, he is also mischievous and loves to "set up" people: "Like the time when Wade had just installed skylights in Danielle's art studio. It started to rain and Bill squirted water on the inside sills of the skylights just to see Wade dance. Ah, Bill's a trickster and Wade's stubborn and doesn't know when to stop, but they're both good as gold."

When the two brothers returned with the other stag, having left its head for scavengers, we quartered, skinned, wrapped, and hung it with the first one. Now we had eight caribou quarters hanging by their hooves, encased in a gauzy bubble of cloth—sides of meat that yesterday were moving on those hooves through the barrens, grazing on lichen from the rocks, copulating with females. I did not know whether or not I would ever be able to pull the trigger on an animal in my sights, but I realized I felt undeniable, if vicarious, satisfaction at having witnessed life taken so directly and at such close range.

Fourth Day: Clearing

Wednesday was overcast but the rain held off. We had pears and pancakes for breakfast, and then Wade, Bill, and I spent the day clearing the half-acre lot across the road that Bill has leased for a cabin site. It is a piece of moderately sloping land composed of shale ledges and littered with glacial boulders. We trimmed the live trees, cut brush and standing trunks, hauled fallen logs, and dug out stumps. We burned everything along with our garbage and the caribou skins in a bonfire in the gully in the center of the lot.

We moved stones downhill to form a wall at the front of the lot in order, as Wade said, "to put our mark on it." Some boulders weighed well over a ton, and these we leveraged out of the hillside with twenty-foot green spruce "sticks." Wade, mostly by himself, built nearly sixty feet of stone wall. At mid morning, Ralph, still wearing his onion bag hairnet, brought us out tea, crackers, and cheese in a bucket. For dinner we had more beans and baloney. There were a couple of beer breaks, and then, for supper, Ralph cooked a Jiggs dinner with caribou liver sautéed in onions.

In the evening Wade heard some noise in the boggy woods behind the cabin, a kind of steady, deliberate cracking of twigs, as if something heavy were moving slowly through the woods. He got his 12-gauge with slugs, and we walked down into the woods, but the noise had ceased. After it got dark, Frank, the man who would be moving the cabin tomorrow, stopped in. He said he had seen a bear in the area last week, so we threw all of the caribou quarters and the trophy head into the Bronco for the night.

Fifth Day: Moving Out

In the morning we cleared our stuff out of the cabin and into the Bronco, moving the caribou quarters into the trailer. It was beautiful and clear all day. We spent several hours hauling lumber from the old cabin site across to Bill's lot. Wade had brought the lumber up from various places over several years. There were sixteen long, curved gray floor joists, rounded on the sides like railroad ties, from an old house that had "sat for years" in Gambo; dozens of short railroad ties, about four feet long, gathered from the abandoned narrow-gauge tracks that carried the famed "Newfie Bullet" until it ceased operation in 1972; matched boards, assorted wide boards, short chunks of larger, creosoted ties, plywood concrete forms, and a large pile of half-inch boards of varying lengths. All of these were hauled on the trailer with the quad, with me standing on the tongue of the hitch to provide traction, as Wade churned his way up the bare slope of the new cabin lot.

The lumber was piled neatly halfway up the slope with the best wood at the bottom, and held down with a hundred-gallon oil tank we hauled out of the brush. I asked if the wind really got that strong here, but Wade said it was to discourage "borrowers." The oil tank will eventually be used as a septic tank for the new cabin. Ralph discoursed on the absurdity of the septic system rules relating to cabins. He said you are allowed to get by with only a traditional outhouse, but if you have an indoor toilet you have to have a septic system that meets residential house codes. Once more, regulations seemed to represent a challenge for evasion. What happens, Ralph said, is that many people build the outhouse, and once they move in, put a toilet inside.

"So, you have your outhouse, then you put your toilet inside and squat, and the shit goes down a pipe into the outhouse and you don't freeze your arse."

At about eleven o'clock Frank, Dave, and Ned showed up with a front-end loader. They placed skids under the cabin, wrapped a long chain around it, and chainsawed off the posts. Then they dragged it off to their lot, about a half mile away, where the cabin that officially does not exist would begin its third life in a new place.

Sojourns in
Squid Tickle

The Last Fish in
Bonavista Bay

My first visit to Squid Tickle, a small outport at the bottom of Bonavista Bay on the island's Northeast Coast, occurred in the fall of 1989, three years before the Canadian government imposed a moratorium on the catch of all Newfoundland groundfish, including cod. I stopped there to visit my friends Mark and Fraser Carpenter, who had emigrated from the States to Newfoundland the year before and had built a small Cape Cod-style house at the edge of the slate landwash. They had just completed their first summer running a tour boat business out of Terra Nova National Park, and they offered to take me out in their new boat, the *Northern Fulmar*, to some of the reaches and sounds around Squid Tickle. Joining us was their neighbor, Bert Burden, an eighty-year-old lifelong resident of the town, who in his time had been the cook on a fishing schooner that went down to the Labrador each spring. He had also pursued the local inshore fishery and had built several boats and skiffs by hand, the last one when he was sixty-seven.

As we chugged out into the bay, Mark turned the helm over to Bert and asked him to take us out to a stretch of fifteen-fathom shoal bottom several miles out, one that Bert had not been to in twenty years. Although Mark had the latest navigational equipment on board—radar, loran, depth finder—Bert used none of it. His memory of the sounds and the bays and the bights and the reefs and everything else remained remarkably intact, so that he instinctively took us within a few meters of the shoal, confirmed by the depth finder. Mark said that Bert carried "an underwater memory map of the bay in his head."

"Now," said Mark, "I'll show you what's wrong with this place. Look at this," and he pointed to a color monitor in the cockpit. "That's our new electronic fish finder. We use it to find fish on our natural history cruises in the park. It can scan to all depths, at different magnifications. It can show different schools of fish, different sizes, even what species an individual fish is."

He turned the fish finder on and the screen lit up, showing a depth graph, a crooked layer of brown zigzag lines indicating the shoal bottom, and a number of small fish-shaped forms in pink and yellow. "Now those," he said, pointing to several dozen small, concentrated shapes in the middle of the water column, "are bait fish, herring and mackerel. But look down here"—and now he indicated a single, much larger yellow fish at the bottom of the middle of the screen, directly beneath the boat—"that's what we're looking for. Now watch." He went out on deck, picked up a lead cod jigger, threw it over the rail, and within a few seconds hauled up a codfish weighing a good eight to ten pounds.

"There you are, b'y," said Mark, unhooking the fish and tossing it back in the water. "The last fish in Bonavista Bay. They han't got a chance."

Six years later, I was given the opportunity to spend the summer months in Mark and Fraser's house. The winter before, they had finished building a steel-hulled sloop in their driveway, in which they planned to sail around the world. They were now testing it out in Arctic waters and had generously offered me the use of their house while they were away. They had shut off the water and electricity before they left, but I hauled in water from a dug well in the front yard, brought blocks of ice down from the village store to put in the refrigerator (which served as an icebox), cooked on a small gas camp stove, and had several lanterns for light in the evening, though the long northern light remained in the sky until ten o'clock and after.

My plan was to use their house as a base from which to explore parts of the island and Labrador I had not yet seen, but as the first few weeks there ended, I found myself more and more drawn to the village and its people. I made up my mind to travel widely in Squid Tickle that summer and rarely left, and then only briefly.

Barren Waters

Summer 1995. There are no children here, and the waters are barren. The silence of the early morning is peaceful but appalling. When I walk out on one of the old wharves, the waters seem so empty, not only of fish, but of the darting minnows, scuttling crabs, crawling periwinkles, and stationary clams and mussels that one sees almost anywhere back home in the shallow salt waters of Cape Cod. Even the terns and seabirds are scarce by comparison here. These wooden stages and wharves are mostly empty, too, as though both men and ocean life have both absconded from this place. Oddly, there is something about the light here that suggests Ohio, 1942. All the young men are away at war, but where are the mothers and the young children?

The Northeast Coast of Newfoundland is one of the oldest and most densely settled parts of the province and, traditionally, one of its richest fishing grounds. Since the moratorium on cod and other groundfish was imposed three years ago, fishing has struggled to survive as a vocation on the island. Many local fishermen blame federal and provincial politicians for the collapse of the cod fishery. They point out that after the Department of Fisheries and Oceans (DFO) banned the huge foreign factory ships from Canadian waters in 1976, presumably to protect fish stocks, the government continued to subsidize and encourage the large offshore Canadian trawler fleets that dredged and decimated the cod's spawning grounds. Even more Newfoundlanders doubt that the cod will ever come back, in which case Squid Tickle, as well as most of the hundreds of other small outports that still dot this rocky coast, may dry up and blow away in not too many years. This is the thought that seems to be on everyone's mind here, though it is not spoken of much, as there seems to be nothing to do but wait and see if the fish come back.

The children are another story. Squid Tickle, like many of the smaller outports, is already mostly a geriatric community. There is only one family with school-age children left, and they are building a new house in Eastport, where the regional school is. Almost all of the local young people have moved away—to Gander, St. John's, Halifax, Toronto, Calgary, Fort McMurray, or Vancouver—in search of work. Con Oldford's daughter, Linda, and her husband, Cyril, live in the city of Gander, about an hour away, though they often come down and stay at Cyril's family's house here. One of Fred Oldford's daughters is a nurse in Halifax and visits a couple of times a year. Jim Moss's daughter, Audrey, lives in Fort McMurray, Alberta, where the extensive oil sands have made it the new employment mecca for Newfoundlanders and to which a sizable community of Newfoundlanders have already emigrated. Howard and Christine Moss's two boys, Michael and Christopher, recently moved to Calgary. Essie Chayter's only child, Frank, also lives in Calgary; she hasn't seen him in eight years.

In one sense, this has always been a pattern in Newfoundland, which has suffered from chronic poverty through most of its history. In times of no fish or poor markets, the men would "go away," to mainland Canada or to the States, to find work and send money or other goods home, much as immigrants from Mexico and other Central American countries do today.

In the past these periods of being "away" could last for years. Although some stayed, most of the men would return to their families and to fishing when they could. And always they would return when they could no longer work, to be cared for by their families and to die in Newfoundland.

But this is changing. For one thing, a revived fishery is likely to be much more streamlined, high-tech, and government-regulated. More important, it seems certain that it will no longer be family-based. Whereas in the past everyone could get a license and fishing was traditionally intergenerational, with sons going out with their fathers, and grandfathers continuing to assist their sons where they could, licenses will be much fewer and will not be allowed to be handed down to the next generation.

Moreover, the ancient ties themselves seem to be weakening. Last summer I spoke to a young man who had been born and grown up in Squid Tickle, had fished with his father in the summer, and wanted nothing more than to stay and raise a family and continue to fish. Two years ago he and his wife, a young woman from the neighboring community, went out to Calgary, where he found a job as a sales representative for oil-drilling equipment. They have a young child now, and he had returned for a visit to show off the boy to his grandparents. It was a warm and raucous reunion, as Newfoundland reunions usually are, and one could see that the ties of affection and family remained as strong as ever. But when I asked him if he would ever come back to Newfoundland to live, he gave a thoughtful look and said, "No, I don't think so. It's not likely the fishing will return, and even if it did, well, we like it out there, we have friends, you know, and there's opportunities for our children when they grow up, so they don't have to leave home like we did."

On the other hand, for those who have stayed, it is more than just nostalgia for a vanished past that has caused such a profound reaction to the crash of the fish stocks and the prohibition on traditional cod fishing. In outports where the moratorium directly affected the majority of the working inhabitants, it has increased the common effects of widespread unemployment: stress, domestic abuse, alcoholism, depression, and divorce. But even where the direct effects were minimal, there have been significant psychological and cultural consequences. From the beginning, the *identity* of Newfoundlanders has been that of fishermen, and even when the majority of the population no longer made their living directly from the sea, it has been the ongoing connection with it, the seasonal rituals of going out for herring, lobster, caplin, salmon, mackerel, flounder, haddock, halibut, and, always and most important, cod—that has kept the fibers of community life and the connections between generations together.

On a local level, even though only two or three men in Squid Tickle still actively fish now, one can see how the psychology of fish continues to pervade the lives of the community. The other day, having gone up to the store to get some ice, I was talking to Bert Burden when another man came in carrying a headless salt cod that he was going to roast for lunch. He hailed us with "There's a couple of dandies!" and walked toward us with a fisherman's lurch.

"Bert, b'y," he said, "I was getting the bilge out of my boat this morning when Cal showed up and I says, 'Fine morning for fish, eh?' Now Bert, you knows if we was down the Labrador and a northeast blow kicked up like this, there'd be plenty of fish when it cleared out." Bert allowed that there would.

One morning in early July I walked down to the wharf, where the ferry to St. Brendan's had been docked for several days awaiting some engine repair parts. One of the crewmen was straddling the railing, painting one of the wooden pilings a federal red. The captain, a St. Brendan's man, leaned out the window of the ferry, talking and joking with an elderly man on the dock. There was a distinctly Irish lilt to his voice and he seemed in good spirits, despite his lay-by.

"Lovely morning to go fishing," he said as I approached, much as he might have said, "Lovely morning to have sex"—the weather calling up the memory and ghost of desire without the wherewithal.

Another morning in late August I found Cleves and Ettie Oldford picking blueberries across the road beside the cemetery. I went over to talk. The day was brilliant and sunny, with a light northwest wind. "Fine day for making fish," said Cleves, and then, as if savoring the recollection, said it again, looking out wistfully over the water. His wife, a tough cookie, said, "Well, old man, you can't fish, so get over it. It's a nice day for anything."

Often, too, I see some of the other elderly men in town cruising the roads in the evening in their cars, just going slowly about for no apparent reason. At first I thought it was just the restlessness of old men who no longer get around on their legs very well, out trolling for someone to tell their stories to. But lately I have been thinking it may be archetypal, vestigial behavior, from the days when they walked the paths or climbed up the hill to the cemetery or the church to size up the weather, the wind, and the water in the bay for the next day's fishing.

But it is not just an internalized, obsolete vocabulary or residual patterns of movement that suggest how deeply fishing remains ingrained in the local psyche. Often there is a conscious recognition of the deeper community losses that have been suffered. Late one winter's day Cleves stopped in for a visit and a cup of tea. As we sat at the kitchen table in the dying light, he pointed out the window to the western point of Squid Island:

"Fred and me, we had the finest salmon berth there out by the point. We had a net there for years and could take twenty salmon before breakfast and go in for a day of work at the sawmill, till we lost our license."

"How did you lose your license?"

"Well, b'y, cause we was part-time fishermen, and they took all that away twenty years ago. There used to be eighteen families on Squid Island, and the boys would go down and set the lobster traps before going to school. Now they've raised a generation of idle youths, nothing to do, nothing they *can* do, except collect the dole. Now you tell me, does that make sense?

"I used to jig squid with my son Terry when he was home. It was all jigger and hook. They never came in before August-month. Oh, my son, there used to be a mess of them would come in here, by the tickle. The place would stink. A man with six or seven children could keep his whole family busy jigging and splitting and drying squid. We had ten flakes on the wharf where we cleaned and split and dried them. We could make a thousand dollars a month. Now you can't split a damn fish without a license. Now tell me, does that make sense?"

I pointed out that there didn't seem to be many squid these days.

"The foreign boats got them all, outside the bay. But the fish now . . . " and with that he launched into a lengthy polemic on the vagaries and periodic disappearances of fish in the past. There were records, he said, of fish scarcities in Bonavista Bay as far back as 1835. He himself remembered the crash in the early 1930s, which made the Depression particularly hard here and sent legions of men away seeking work.

"I remember as a young man how there was no fish here. You'd jig all day and just get enough to get the pot boiling. When Henry Oldford's uncle would go down to Salvage to visit, his wife would say, 'Now ask Uncle Jack for a scrod to bring back for Sunday dinner.' That's how scarce they were. But they came back.

"And there's still millions of fish in the bays now. They comes in to get the bait, the herring. Come in for the caplin, too, but the caplin's gone now. And you know if the cod was feeding on the caplin, what *else* was feeding on them that's now got to feed on the cod? No, b'y, this time I don't think they'll come back."

Although they no longer depend on the sea for a living and are all far more comfortable on their government pensions than they ever were before or ever thought they would be, it is the older generation of Newfoundland men for whom this latest disappearance of the fish may be hardest psychologically. Cleves's brother, Fred Oldford, is a man of great vitality, who has served for decades as the lay reader at the Anglican church, delivering the Scripture readings each Sunday in his booming, gale-piercing voice and West Country accent, as if he were delivering the shipping news. Fred seems to express more visibly than most the deep sense of frustration that characterizes these outports today. Hobbled and weakened by a stroke and heart problems, he is like some great, restless steed, snorting and puffing stories and pronouncements, prowling the town all day and evening in his car, stopping for an hour to talk with the staff at the Heritage Foundation building, whose board he is chairman of, or at his own father's house near the wharf, uninhabited for years, to supervise the restoration work that his younger brother, Con, and his nephew, Paul, have been doing there, or serving on the Regional Liaison Committee for Terra Nova National Park or the Committee for the Development of Progress on the Eastport Peninsula—in other words, being everywhere except, perhaps, where he most wants to be.

The other day I was talking with Shirley Oldford, Fred's younger daughter, who grew up in Squid Tickle, earned a doctorate in mathematics, and was for twenty years a geophysicist for an oil company out in Alberta. A few years ago she returned here to live and care for her aging parents. She spoke of what the closing of the noncommercial fisheries has meant to the older members of the community:

"When a man retired here, he would continue to engage in the activities he had always engaged in: cutting wood, getting and making fish, hunting moose and caribou, trapping rabbits, picking berries, though of course on a smaller scale. People here don't retire and go to Florida. Most wouldn't want to if they could. They don't have hobbies. They have their life and their work. To tell someone my father's age to take up golfing or tennis would make you think they weren't right in the head, and they mightn't be. To be able to get up and go out in your boat for some fish was a reason to get out of bed in the morning. It was why they could spend so much time keeping up their boats, mending nets, repairing the stages. It was a way of keeping in touch with their lives, keeping it going. Anyone could, if he wanted, put out a cod trap or a salmon net. Everyone had a commercial license then, so Dad and Uncle Cleves would keep theirs, though they hadn't fished commercially in decades, not because they needed to, but because it gave them a reason to keep their boats in the water.

"I remember, as a girl, going out with them in summers before light, to tend the salmon nets. It was dark and cold and you'd be out there thinking, I could still be home in bed, and then the sun would come up in the east like a movie in Panavision and light the world and warm you. I wished I had my portable stereo in the boat so I could play a symphony or something, though everyone would have thought I was crazy.

"Last year was the last time they opened up the bay even for recreational fishing, what they call the food fishery. For four weeks you could go out two days a week and get ten fish a day. Pitiful, but it was something. Of course, everyone was out there, by Ship Island. It was in the fall, October, before the cod come into the harbor for the winter, and on that first morning it looked like the old community of skiffs and dories jigging for fish. But it was awful, because the DFO had patrol boats out and helicopters buzzing us, you know, to make sure we didn't take more than our limit. It was like some war zone, and we began to feel like the enemy, or worse, criminals. They were checking to make sure that, if you got your ten fish, and buddy had only gotten two, you didn't give him some of yours and go on fishing, which after all was the old way. If you had the luck and filled your boat, why, you'd give the next boat some and go on fishing until both boats were filled. It was all feeding the community. But this, this was some kind of travesty of fishing. It took all the neighborliness out of it, you know? Now, of course, there's not even that."

How HARD, how *obscene* it must seem to these people, in their quiet, desperate frustration, to look out daily on the waters of their youth and work and not be able to touch it, as if they had somehow become toxic to the fish and to each other, to be treated, in effect, as potential male-factors by a government that itself is seen as largely responsible for the collapse of one of the richest ground fisheries the world has ever known, one that fed a large part of the population of Europe for over four hundred years and the economy and culture of these small New-foundland outports for nearly that long. Europe no longer needs their fish, or so it thinks, and Newfoundland, it would appear, no longer needs these communities.

Tonight the wind still threshes the brown-topped grasses and the tops of the junipers in the feather bogs, rattles the leathery leaves of alders and aps, cards the stiff-spired stands of spruce and balsam fir on the beaten hillside of the bay out in the inconceivable and endless darkness that en-circles Squid Tickle's small soft circle of light. I know that compared to whatever Belgian Congos or Armenias or Dachaus or Hiroshimas or Viet-nams or Northern Irelands or Chiles or El Salvadors or Bosnias or Kash-mirs or Sri Lankas or Rwandas or East Timors or Afghanistans or Iraqs or Palestines or Darfurs or whatever new inhumanities to mankind fester in turn to hold the world's center stage, the sorrows, losses, and deep loves of this place and its people must appear small and uncommanding, but they are not therefore inferior or negligible.

Whatever larger global marine environmental crisis Newfoundland's depleted fishery may or may not be a bellwether of, men and women have been tested here as deeply as they have been in most places, and more than in many, and have not been found wanting. Life is still seen and felt and spoken of primarily in terms of work, home, and kin. Now the first leg of that hereditary tripod has been removed, perhaps per-manently, but those who remain continue, somehow, to perform an im-possible balancing act, believing in a future with no apparent basis for doing so—which is perhaps all any of us can do, or hope to do.

Rollin'

There were some reports last week that caplin have been seen at some of the local beaches where they come in to spawn. So far only a "scattering" of them have been sighted; or, as one local woman put it, they were "in, but not rollin'." Then on Monday morning Howard Moss told me that the caplin were beginning to come ashore in numbers at dusk at Sandy Cove on the other side of the peninsula, about eight miles by road from Squid Tickle. The next day, out for a walk, I encountered Fred Old-ford and his grandson David driving by. They had just come back from Sandy Cove and had a bucket of caplin. Fred said that the fish were at the far end of the beach, at Caplin Gulch, between the rock outcrops.

Caplin, or *capelin*, as the word is usually spelled outside of Newfoundland, have been an integral part of the island's economy for centuries. Because they are so abundant and feed primarily on zooplankton, they serve as an essential link in the marine food chain. Caplin provide the primary food source for a host of marine species, including whales, seals, squid, gannets, alcids, and many commercially valuable fish, most importantly cod. In fact, the entire traditional inshore cod fishery of Newfoundland has been dependent on caplin. Following their offshore spawning in June and July, cod follow the caplin into shallow coastal waters to feed, where they can be taken with trawl lines or jiggers. (The traditional cod jigger, now illegal, was a lead weight with two or three hooks that was formed from melted lead poured into a soapstone mold carved in the likeness of a caplin.)

Caplin have thus always been important baitfish, but they have had other uses as well. Outport residents still dry or smoke caplin, or sauté them up whole, ungutted, for breakfast or dinner. Likewise they have long been used as a cheap source of fertilizer for local gardens. As the Newfoundland writer Ray Guy vividly phrased it, "The caplin pit, moving with little white maggots, or the fishes guts pit in a like condition, was a useful source of nutrients for the potatoes."

The following evening I decided to head over to Caplin Gulch for a look, and asked Jim and Jesse Moss, a local couple in their seventies, if they'd like to come along. Jim is from Flat Island, and he and Jesse lived there in the first years of their marriage, but they moved to Squid Tickle in 1958 as part of Joey Smallwood's policy of "resettlement" for Newfoundland's smaller, remote outports. When we arrived at the gulch, we found that the wooden steps down to the beach had been washed out over the winter, so we drove back to the parking lot at the other end of the beach, about a half mile away. There were already some twenty trucks and cars parked there. Jim, always uncomfortable among crowds, muttered, "Best be heading back, b'y." But we got out of the car and headed off to the cove on the fine, flat, hard, gray sand beach. The tide was flooding but still several hours from high. The moon, two days shy of full, began to shine over the water, as deep-red, purple-fringed clouds from a fiery, hidden sunset floated up above the sandy cliffs to the west.

Sandy Cove is one of the longest stretches of sand beach in Newfoundland and the only part of its coast that has ever reminded me of home. Its half mile of continuous hundred-foot-high cliffs of sand and gravel bear a striking resemblance to the glacial bluffs on the Outer Beach of Cape Cod, and it is this abundance of unconsolidated material that provides ideal spawning beaches for the caplin. As we walked, Jim acted as if I had taken him to a foreign country. He kept saying that he didn't know any of the people we encountered, though he has lived in Squid Tickle for almost forty years.

"I knows more about you than I does them," he said.

"You mean you've never been to this beach?" I asked, somewhat surprised, since he had lived most of his life less than ten miles from it.

"Oh, yaas. 'Course Jesse and I have been *off* the beach many a time— in a boat, you know—but not to go ashore. No reason to, my son."

As we made our way to the spawning beach between the granite outcrops at the far end of the beach, we passed several people walking back to the parking lot carrying bright yellow "Naval Beef" buckets full of caplin. I stopped one man, a gap-toothed elderly fellow with a distorted, Quasimodo-like face and a shock of straw-colored hair, and asked to look at his fish. The caplin lay coiled in the bucket on their slippery, fusiform sides—dark backs and silver-white undersides with faint, pink iridescent colorings and large, staring, yellow eyes.

Jim picked up a fish, calling it a "good-sized 'un," about six or seven inches long. He showed me how a caplin, unlike the similar whitefish, has a ridge on its back. Almost all the fish were males, or "cocks," which he said come in first. They were a dark emerald green color on top, darker than the females, which he called "hens," and their skin was covered with a gridded pattern of tiny scales. Jim pointed out the distinct black lateral ridges running the length of their sides, which the females lack. These ridges appear during the spawning season, formed from elongated scales that are soft, or hairy, to the touch. (The caplin's scientific specific name, *villosus*, means "hairy," as does the Norwegian word for the caplin, *lodde.)* In addition to these ridges, males possess a prominent ventral posterior fin, which the females also lack.

I reached down into the man's bucket to pick up a handful. They slipped through my fingers like silken ropes of water. He grinned grotesquely and said, "It's good to see them here again, you know."

With the decline of the cod stocks, the caplin commercial fishery has grown in importance. Though they were once used primarily for fish meal and oil, a lucrative niche market for caplin roe, or "capelin caviar," has developed in recent years, most of it going to Japan. Caplin are short-lived fish, usually living only three or four years; their numbers can fluctuate wildly. Many fishermen and scientists have expressed concern about the increased taking of caplin. They are worried that the caplin, like cod and other groundfish, may be being overfished. Also, because caplin are the primary food source for cod, they argue that overfishing the caplin may slow the recovery of the cod stocks. During the past several years in the waters around Squid Tickle, caplin have been scarce.

When we reached the rocks, I beheld a scene that, except for the bright neon colors of nylon windbreakers and jackets and the plastic buckets, might have taken place here a hundred years ago. Forty to fifty men, women, and children were spilled out on the rocks and the moonlit beach. Most were on the sand or at the edge of the tide, wading in with boots and long-handled nets and netting the fish with short, expert swipes. On the other side of the rocks, a father and two young boys were standing farther out in the water than the others; he was instructing them, telling them to stand still, don't move, let the fish move in around them to the beach. Another tiny boy, no more than two, wearing a corduroy cap, a red-and-blue knitted body sweater, and bright yellow boots, wandered among a forest of tall legs inspecting the buckets.

Leaving Jim and Jesse on the beach, I climbed up onto a ledge of tortured, quartz-grained igneous rock that ran out into the water for several rods, and there, for the first time, I saw them: like a roiling black cloud, the caplin hovered some twenty feet from shore in water only a few feet deep, thousands upon tens of thousands of them, a solid mass of fish that stretched twenty yards or more along the shore in a twisting band eight to ten feet wide. They looked like black tangles of seaweed flecked with innumerable white barnacle spat. Like some sprawling nest of short dark snakes, they swarmed over and around themselves, a vast fishy Medusa. They moved as one giant organism, like a sentient storm cloud shot with millions of bright eyes.

The man with two boys had moved further out, the water now above their boots, only a few yards from the oscillating, leading edge of the fish. One could sense an odd, mutual mental awareness going on: the father, admonishing his impatient boys to "Hold still! Don't move! Don't make a sound!" and the fish, seemingly conflicted between the ancient imperative to come ashore and spawn and the hesitating awareness of the obstacles and threats in the water between them and the beach. Then the cloud of fish began, cautiously, to send out probes, like dark, soft pseudopodia, toward the shore, as if it were indeed some kind of mass intelligence that moved them.

The sight reminded me of a story I had heard on the CBC the other day discussing the latest frontiers in robotics, something called "polygonal interconnected metamorphic robots." These robots use separate but electronically connected computers imbedded in small polygonal units, so that masses of them are able to move together and conform to any shape. As I watched the shifting assembly of fish roll in, I thought, once again, how nature anticipates technology.

The father, now standing waist-deep in the water, seemed somewhat indecisive, despite his authoritarian manner. Come-from-away, I thought, or perhaps a self-exiled native, come back to reclaim his roots. At one point, he reached out with his hand into the water, as if to wave the fish ashore. As if touched, the dark mass instantly withdrew offshore for several minutes; but at last the fish's primal urge got the better of them and they began to move landward, like a mud cloud stirred up and moving through clear water. As they wound around the legs of the man and the two boys, the father shouted, "Now!"

They plunged their nets into the dark, moving mass. The older boy snagged several heavy netsful, dumped them into plastic grocery bags, and carried the fish to shore, where they lay on the beach, the bags jerking with their movements like very large Mexican jumping beans. The father, with the largest net, swept the water energetically, but seemed to get only a few. Then, with a lurch, he inexplicably threw his net up onto the edge of the beach, where most of the caplin fell out and were washed back into the water. The younger boy was not quick enough to get any fish, and as the black cloud withdrew offshore again in the wake of the commotion, he stood, frustrated, at the edge of the tide, shouting, "C'mon, suckers! C'mon, you suckers!"

But the fish had been spooked, and probably would not come in again until we all left. Jim, Jesse, and I started back toward the car with the dispersing crowd, amid the lilting buzz of Newfoundland English. The men, wearing feed caps and green rubber boots, lurched along the beach with their yellow plastic buckets in each hand, buckets filled with the slick, coiled, eel-like bodies of caplin, to be salted, dried, smoked, frozen, broiled, or fried in pork fat. Beside them walked their wives and girlfriends with their children, all smiling. The caplin had returned.

Youth

Now it is time to write of Darren Lane of St. Chad's.

Early yesterday morning there was a beat-up gray Honda Civic with a rock station sticker on the rear window parked in the driveway of my neighbor, Bert Burden. Later I saw Bert with a tall, lanky fellow out on his wharf. This was Darren Lane, the "helper" Bert had told me he was going to call to assist him in rebuilding his wharf. Bert has a typical Newfoundland fisherman's "stage," consisting of a large wooden shed, or store, built on the edge of the shore, containing his workshop, tools, fishing gear, and other equipment. The store opens out onto the wharf, which is a wooden dock built on pilings and planked with "longers," or thin barked logs. The dock ends in an expanded platform set on a square wooden cage built of "bedding sticks" (thick, unbarked spruce trunks) that are laid in alternating layers like Lincoln logs and then filled with rocks for ballast. The wharf platform has a chain hoist on one side, fish-cutting tables, and a heavy, homemade wooden skiff tied up on the other side.

Earlier in the week Bert and I had talked about the repairs he wanted to make. Most of the planking and several of the bedding sticks were rotten, and some of the latter below the low-water line had come loose, spilling out much of the rock ballast. When I walked over there about 9 A.M., Bert and Darren had already taken up all the planks on the west side of the wharf and put several of the new bedding sticks in place.

Darren is a tall young man of twenty, lean and muscular, weighing (he told me) 230 pounds, with light, short-cropped hair, a pleasant

smile, an engaging manner, and intelligent eyes. He is a veritable dy-
namo of energy, of focused, youthful exuberance and strength. He ex-
ults in his skill, strength, and energy, all of which are prodigious. In
another era he would be the pattern for folktales, a Paul Bunyan figure,
though without the verbal bragging. Instead, his body brags for him,
leaping from one wet bedding stick to another; single-handedly carrying a twenty-two-foot spruce trunk eight inches thick at the base and
tossing it, casually, into place, then manhandling it around and into
position, wrestling it like a crocodile; cutting shims from old two-by-
fours with an ax by scoring them with a few chops on each side, and
then breaking them over his knee, or else, if the top stick is too thick,
chopping out a notch with a few deft strokes; grabbing foot-long
eighty-penny spikes and pounding them down with a maul through
one pole into the one below it as if they were finishing nails, never
missing, giving each one a last superfluous stroke as if to disabuse it of
any ideas it might still harbor of raising its head. Once, when he had
"tacked" a bedding stick at each end to within two inches of each nail
head, he told Bert he thought it should be reversed, as one might suggest ripping off a shingle, and proceeded to pry out the spikes with
Bert's six-foot iron bar.

He did all this with great bursts and leaps of energy, but no wasted
motion: flying through the air, seeming to be in three or four places on
the wharf at once, pounding a spike, reaching for an ax, fashioning a
jury-rigged come-along from a piece of rope to pull the end of a log
into alignment (before I even had time to offer to hold it in place for
him), leaping across the open framework of the wharf with his chainsaw
in one hand, still idling, to cut off a series of planks, while the rough
chop of the waters below him rarely wet his soles.

"Helps to have long legs," he said several times. "Especially since I
can't swim."

Grin. Big grin. (He was not exaggerating. Most outport fishermen do
not know how to swim. The usual explanation is "Why would you want
to learn?" Out on waters whose maximum temperatures reach only the
low fifties in summer, swimming in most cases, so the common thinking goes, would only prolong the agony.) On the other hand, he said

that he doesn't use his legs to lift, as they are too long—meaning, I assumed, that it takes him too long to bend down with them.

Mostly, Bert and I just stood around watching him—me in awe at this natural force in action, Bert with obvious pleasure, not only at getting his money's worth by having such a good worker (he told me that Darren and his father, Dara Lane, painted Bert's entire house a few years ago in fourteen hours: "Now that's scraping and painting"), but also, I suspect, because he sees in Darren the Bert of his own youth, boundless in energy and taking an almost sensual pleasure in the intensity and ferocity of work.

I have rarely seen such a self-possessed twenty-year-old. He quickly got used not only to my camera, but to me as well. He showed no particular deference to my age, but quickly treated me like the novice I was in this kind of work. When I offered to help, he said I could tap old nails out of the used planks that he had ripped up, which he could reuse. After a few minutes, during which I broke off several nails trying to get them out, he turned to me and said, in a spirit of pure helpfulness, "The secret to getting out rusty nails is to hit them lightly."

He seemed not only to be doing many things at once, but to have his attention in several places as well: on what he was doing, on what Bert and I were doing, and on what he was going to do next. Though he was obviously self-sufficient, he made a point of pausing between tasks to ask Bert if a particular stick were level enough, or where Bert wanted him to start the planking. He had a knack for giving Bert the sense that it was still *Bert's* project, needing *Bert's* judgment, agreement, and experience. It came not out of patronization, but out of a genuine respect for Bert's knowledge. It was a fiction that both readily assented to.

These fifteen- to twenty-minute bursts of frenzied energy were punctuated by pauses to light up a cigarette and assess the previous and next steps in the process. He was not resting, for he showed no signs of being even slightly out of breath. He would stand calm, mentally resting, while a kind of restless energy continued to flow disengaged within him, like a powerful engine idling. I thought of Thoreau's French-Canadian woodchopper, Therien, in *Walden*, another man totally absorbed in his work. But Darren is a far more gregarious, loquacious, and sociable figure than that Concord Canuck. He enjoyed, I think, not only working, but also being watched as he worked, as a high-wire artist or a professional athlete or a lion tamer does. It was like watching some natural force or phenomenon—a waterfall, a herd of migrating buffalo, or, more accurately, the Boston Celtics in the heyday of Bird, Parish, and McHale: that superabundance, or superfluity, of youthful strength and energy filtered through a fine intelligence that is wonderful to watch, not only for itself, but because it gives you the sense of the earth's inexhaustible ability to renew itself and its unshakable faith in its own vitality. Along with Bert, I, too, felt renewed, younger, just by watching Darren, the way grandparents light up at the sight of their young grandchildren: Here is the light of our race rekindled, the spark our own youth and energy, refelt and relayed into the future.

He was not, of course, omnipotent or invulnerable. When I first arrived, he had already placed a half dozen or so large "bedding rocks" down below the waterline. By noontime the new cage was finished and spiked down. When I came back after dinner, he had planks back on one half of the wharf, and we began carrying to the end of the wharf the smaller pieces of shale that Bert had levered out of the bank of the landwash. Since Bert had lost several of the bedding sticks below the low-water line, we could not put these rocks down in the cage, for they would just spill out again. Instead, we placed them in a cairn-like pile at the end of the wharf, where they would stay, acting as vertical ballast, which, according to Darren, was all that was needed, as it is the rising and the falling of the ice, not its sideways movement, that does the damage.

Still, there were a couple of larger pieces of shale that even Darren could not carry by himself, and these he rolled out to the end. He cut his hands several times on the sharp edges of the shale, and immediately jumped down the side of the wharf, holding onto Bert's chain hoist with one hand and pulling up with the other a swag of rockweed to use as an antiseptic rag to clean his wounds.

Darren, with his father, Dara, builds houses and garages, and runs a small sawmill in St. Chad's, hauling and selling wood in the winter, and doing "anything else that'll make a dollar." But he likes nothing better than wharf building. It was he who had delivered the pile of new bedding sticks to Bert last winter. He had cut and hauled them out of a steep ravine where no one else had ever tried to cut. To pull them out he had hooked up two Skidoos in tandem, then had dragged them several miles on the ice, over the "ballicatters," or the berms of shore ice that build up in winter, and onto Bert's wharf.

The whole structure in its repair was a wonderful illustration of the old Newfoundland tradition, which still persists, of making do with what you have and improvising as you go. Portions of the old poles were bolted onto others to extend them; old nails were rescued and bent spikes straightened; the ends and middles of sticks were shored up with shims cut from old planks, or lowered by notching out by ax or chainsaw. (Darren used the chainsaw like a Swiss army knife, casually, deftly, and multipurposefully. I think he could have performed brain surgery with it if necessary, or even if only convenient.) Blocks and shims were sometimes set atop older blocks and shims, or cantilevered out several inches. If a bedding stick, being set into place, started to turn its flat edge over, Darren would wedge the ax beneath it and drive in a spike to hold it level. To every problem there was an instant answer in his mind, without his having to think of it. And all of this was done with the simplest of tools—ax, crowbar, pry bar, and maul—plus the chainsaw. "The man who came up with the chainsaw," he liked to say, "did something."

There was no measuring, only eyeing, unerringly, the sticks into position and the cutting of planks to length. When we had finished nailing the planks on the other half of the wharf, there were not enough rocks left to hold it down, so we began piling on an increasingly eclectic assortment of old fluke anchors, grapnels, camshafts, old "one lunger" engines, an enormous "devil's claw" ice anchor about four feet long, spring coils, old iron machine wheels with reversed-S spokes, rusty levers, etc.—so that eventually the pile looked like some untidy specimen box in a giant's collection of rocks and early twentieth-century machinery.

When finished, the whole edifice had the kind of rickety, patched-together, jerry-built appearance of Al Capp's Dogpatch or Snuffy Smith's shacks, but the roughness and haphazardness were in appearance only. There was a fineness and intensity of intelligence in the work that held it firmly in place, as if it were wrapped in steel bands. Each spike Darren drove home seemed like an unassailable thought, an un-movable conclusion. Each shim, block, and timber was placed with a precision and rightness that belied not only the roughness and flimsi-ness of much of the material, but also Darren Lane's scant years, which seem to harbor generations of experience.

In retrospect now, I have an image, or rather a series of overlapping, multiple images, of him, as if he were a whole crew of workers, doing in one day what it would take five ordinary men to do, with chips con-stantly flying, ends of planks buzzed off and falling like leaves into the dark blue water, whole tree trunks being tossed and bounced, landing precisely in place, as if they were wild animals trained by him. As the af-ternoon wore on, he came to trust me more and would toss up several planks at a time for me to denail; and if I have a crick in my hip this morning from that, it is a pain I bear gladly, even proudly, to have been privileged to watch, and even to marginally participate in, such a pure spectacle of youthful confidence, strength, and ability. When we fin-ished for the day, about 4:30, he lit up a final cigarette, looked around, and without false modesty said, "Not too bad a day's work, eh?"—to which Bert replied, "I dare say." Then Darren excused himself, saying, "Now I've got to go home and start building for myself."

Later that evening, I found Cleves and Fred Oldford, both now in their eighties, with Ron Crocker in his store. I told them about watch-ing Darren on the wharf and what a fine worker he was.

"Wash your mouth out, son, wash your mouth out," said Ron, in hu-morous acknowledgment of the young man's prodigious capacity for work. But then, with that criticism of overweening pride, or rather of overdoing anything, that seems such a strong part of the Newfoundland character, he dourly predicted that "in five or six years it'll begin to show on him."

Both of the older men also granted Darren's prowess, calling him "the last of his breed," and then reflected on the folly of their own sim-ilar feats of youthful prowess. Fred told how once, when Cleves had gone off somewhere and a new two-inch-thick, twenty-foot-long, rolled steel shaft for their sawmill came in by boat, Fred had hoisted it to his shoulders and single-handedly carried it up to the mill from the ferry wharf. "I still feels that on me shoulder, b'y, cutting into it."

Cleves, who has back problems, said Darren was "making the same mistake we all did when we was young. We didn't hold nothing back, and nobody told us to lift with our legs." Darren's father, he said, used to be as strong as his son is now, but he "wrecked his back and now he wears a body cast. Darren will come to that in time, b'y," he predicted dourly.

Perhaps so, I thought. But meanwhile, Darren Lane, like a racehorse or an athlete or a stunningly beautiful woman in her prime, is creating a local legend that will not dim with the years, but will, if anything, burn more brightly as the physical frame itself is consumed by time.

The Oldest Man in
Newfoundland

One day Jim Moss asked me if I'd like to meet "the oldest man in Newfoundland." My first reaction was that the phrase was a good mnemonic device for remembering the correct local pronunciation of the island's name: Newfound-*land*. Jim had first mentioned John Chayter to me months before, pointing out his house as we passed it, a small dwelling on the water at the entrance to the fishing port of Salvage.

"I stops in and sees him every now and then. He's hard to talk to, though—he's deaf."

"Do you think he might talk to me?"

"Oh, I don't knows, b'y, I couldn't say."

John Chayter, aged 106, is now officially the oldest *person* in Newfoundland, ever since a 107-year-old woman on the Avalon Peninsula died last spring. He was born on Flat Island in 1889, but now lives in Salvage with his 77-year-old daughter, Liz, in a small house on the water at the entrance to the town. Next door is the house he lived in for over thirty years with his son, Harry, and his daughter-in-law. The house was floated over from Flat Island when he left there in 1957. Harry died two years ago, and Liz says her father misses him very much. Liz took her father in, though she is not well herself, having had ovarian cancer sixteen years ago, "when they took me bowels out," and breast cancer five years ago. But she is a cheerful, pleasant woman, and says her father is "no trouble at all," the way she might speak about a pet, or a sick child.

He is, in fact, a sweet little man, probably no more than four and a half feet high, though I never saw him standing. When Jim and I come into the living room, we find him leaning back on a chesterfield, neatly dressed in a mauve shirt, a black wool cardigan, and soft flannel pants. He sits up to greet us, though he is nearly stone deaf and no longer sees well.

"Me eyes was good till I were a hundred," he says in a small, soft voice, devoid of gender, "then they give out. Me ears was good till I were ninety-seven. Reverend Butt, he says to me, 'John, you ought to get a hearing aid,' but I says, 'Father, it wouldn't be worth it. I won't be here that much longer.' That were ten years ago."

Llewellyn John Chayter. An owlish little man, with a thin fuzz of gray hair on his head and remarkably clear skin. A pleasant, peaceful smile sits on his face, though he has had "hard times" since he left the island, having lost both sons. He turns to Jim, himself seventy-three, and says, "Don't wish to be old."

John Chayter first went to the Labrador in 1901, at the age of twelve, where he fished for forty-eight summers. He went to the ice seven times when he was in his twenties, and had a berth on one of the sealers in 1914, the winter of the great *Newfoundland* disaster, when sixty-seven men from that ship froze to death on the ice. He seems isolated, though not agitated, in his deafness and dimmed sight. Jim (who seems positively adolescent in contrast) shouts each question several times into his ear, and then acts as translator for me. John Chayter's voice is that unconsonanted Flat Island growl exaggerated many times, so that Jim seems to be translating from the rhythms and tones of his sentences, rather than his actual words.

His surname is a common one in the area, though most of the other families spell it *Cheater*. Apparently one of his ancestors in the previous century went to the States, and there found the original spelling of his name somewhat disadvantageous, especially in business dealings. So he began to sign his name "Chayter," which is, in fact, the way it is pronounced.

One of the few clear memories that we manage to elicit comes when we ask him what year the church on Flat Island was built. He says he doesn't know, but he does remember when the ship *Passover* brought the bell for the church, and rang it (here he pulls with both hands on an imaginary rope) from the deck as it was coming in for all to hear. That was in 1903, ninety-three years ago, when he was fourteen.

Another is an incident that occurred on a trip to the Labrador, when an Irish bayman named Paddy Powers claimed their fishing berth and threatened to come aboard their schooner and drown the captain. "I says to him, 'You come up, Paddy Powers, and I'll knock you on the noggin and throw you overboard!' Nor ever he did, b'y." He likes the story so much he tells it again, a moment of self-assertion apparently so rare in this peaceful man that it still rings bright across the decades.

Still, I feel frustrated, though not by his deafness, nor by his inability, reluctance, or simple disinclination to relate stories from the old days. I realize that I want to think of him as *old*, to put a frame around him, with a rhyming caption beneath: "The Oldest Man in Newfoundland." But he is not *old*, despite his having been born in 1889. Conrad Aiken was born in 1889, T. S. Eliot in 1888, D. H. Lawrence in 1885, and they were not old. They were modernists. My grandfather was that old, but he was not *old*.

When I was a young boy in New Jersey, *old* was one of those handful of surviving Civil War Union veterans trotted out in wheelchairs every Memorial Day (though they themselves predated that holiday), some of whom claimed to have met or caught a glimpse of the Great Emancipator himself. Old was the ancient, wizened man found living in Trenton who appeared on a local television show in the early 1950s, claiming to be 104 years of age and, far more astonishingly, to be the real Jesse James. He asserted that he had faked his own death to escape would-be assassins and the law, thus anticipating Elvis's tabloid afterlife by nearly a century.

Old was an Indian Head penny found in one's change. Old was the ragman with his horse and wagon clomping along our paved urban streets, chanting "Any ra-a-a-ags?" Old was Ty Cobb, the greatest baseball player in history, still alive, still bitter and unrepentant in his last years, living across the Passaic River from our house, where, with my dime-store telescope, I scanned the buildings across the water, thinking it possible I might spot him, still famously filing his famous cleats into sharp points.

John Chayter is not old. John Chayter could not have known Abraham Lincoln; John Chayter is the same age as President Eisenhower.

John Chayter is younger than Pablo Picasso, Bela Bartok, and Arnold Schoenberg, and only a few years older than F. Scott Fitzgerald. John Chayter is not old; he is simply the Oldest Man in Newfoundland.

Still, he grew up in a world that was undeniably old, older than any world I had knowledge of, direct or indirect. It was a world without electricity, telephones, or telegraphs; without motorboats, trains, automobiles, or even roads; without horses, without running water or indoor plumbing, without newspapers or operas or doctors; a place where, for a good part of the year, access to the outside world was difficult, sometimes impossible; where the inhabitants made nearly everything for themselves except guns, stoves, compasses, steel traps, eyeglasses, and timepieces; where survival was not a chosen adventure but an everyday necessity, a world where "men must die so men may live."

John Chayter never drove a car, read a book, watched a movie, or encountered a black man. It is unlikely he ever tasted a fruit other than berries and apples, or vegetables other than potatoes, carrots, turnips, parsnips, and peas, until he was a grown man. He learned his culture's history from songs and oral tales, went to sea when he was still a boy, saw mountain-like icebergs and polar bears on ice pans passing by. He crushed the skulls of baby harp seals with spiked clubs, shot murres and moose with flintlock rifles, and made his own shoes. Perhaps he slept with Inuit women.

But to none of that does he seem to bear witness now. He sits, propped up like a doll, partly supported by the larger bulk of his daughter sitting next to him on the comfortable contemporary sofa in a warm, well-lit, electrically heated house. He is still largely cut off from the outside world, though now it is by his deafness and failing vision. With his small, shrinking frame, his somewhat loose clothes, and perpetual, almost beatific smile, he seems more a child than an ancient man. Age has removed him from his own history.

I realize that, after all, I don't want to make him old, don't want to turn him into some specimen or living fossil of a vanished age, a life-tenant of biblical longevity. I want to leave him just where and who and how he is: John Chayter of Flat Island, now living in Salvage with his daughter, a pleasant, quiet man, no trouble at all.

Transparent Beauty

Over the past several days there has been unexpected life in the waters here. Waves of jellyfish—lion's manes and moon jellies—have moved into the inner harbor. I saw the first one on Monday morning, down off the Oldfords' wharf: a lion's mane with a reddish-brown umbrella perhaps six inches across, trailing a thick ring of long, pale, angel-hair tentacles. It pulsed like a dark heart in the water, moving slowly but with seeming purpose among splintered piers, jagged shale ledges, frayed ropes, and protruding spikes. How does such exposed fragility remain intact in such a ragged world?

It moved beneath the wharf and emerged on the other side, where it pulsed, suspended, in one position just below the water's surface, its bell breaking water now and then like a whale's back, as if for air, its muted colors suddenly reflecting in bright gashes of color the newly painted red store and the bright green hull of a schooner onshore. From time to time it would stop pulsing, spread out like a deflated parachute, and slowly sink toward the bottom, where it would lie, throbbing darkly, hypnotizingly, in the depths for a minute or two, like a heart giving out. Then, slowly rising again, it began to pulse forward at an angle, so that it seemed now like a soft, undulating, full skirt, tipping slightly and parting its stringy petticoats to reveal the thick ganglia of hairy black and salmon underparts. This mixture of gonads and thick feeding-tube lips excited, momentarily, a flicker of the fascinated horror John Ruskin reported experiencing on his honeymoon when he first discovered the primal mess between his beloved's legs. The bell itself, with several dimples in it, resembled a face that seemed to look at me and ask, "So what did you expect?" Then it moved off with a more than deliberate slowness through the clear waters, an expanding and contracting galaxy, a pulsing loop of plasmatoid fission, the swelling and shrinking foot of a moon snail without a shell, and on and on, into a deepening sea of simile.

The lion's mane is not only the largest of all jellyfish, but also the world's largest invertebrate. Individuals of over eight feet in diameter have been reported in the Gulf of Maine (though specimens over three feet across are rare). Tentacles on a creature that size are estimated to be two hundred feet in length. Lion's manes are found along the entire North Atlantic coast, growing darker and larger as they move north. They are pinkish and five inches across or less south of Cape Hatteras; yellow to orange brown and up to eight inches between Cape Hatteras and Cape Cod; and dark brownish-red and eighteen inches and larger north of Cape Cod.

Yesterday afternoon I saw several more, this time off Gus Oldford's wharf. The bells are a bruised purple, with softly lobed edges, like a mushroom, which they resemble when they relax between each contraction. When they pulse forward, it is like a fist or a face softly pushing against a silken shroud. One large one I saw had been ripped on one side almost to the middle of the bell, and the ribbony red-orange guts slipped in and out with each pulse, like a repeated disembowelment.

While watching their slow, but coordinated and balletic movements, it is hard not to think of them as individuals, but biologists are ambivalent on this point. For instance, the well-known Portuguese man-of-war, a hydrozoan jellyfish, is sometimes regarded as a single organism, sometimes as a "colony" of thousands of separate, tiny animals, with no central nervous system. These individual animals are, in fact, known as *persons*. These persons have, through a process one textbook calls "devious," become highly specialized, functioning as parts of the tentacular, propulsive, digestive, or sexual systems. Some scientists see jellyfish and their relatives as living remnants of early stages in our own evolution, when independent microorganisms gradually joined together to form single cells, then more complex and specialized bodily systems.

But if a jellyfish has no "brain," no central nervous system at all as we understand it, then what is it that creates its graceful and unified patterns of movement? Whatever turns it first one way, then another, whatever makes it first slowly sink, then rise to the surface, whatever pushes it out across that dark, quilted water, has that old element of decisiveness in it. But what could possibly *decide* anything in such a decentralized and tentative amalgam of life? Imagine the U.S. Congress actually agreeing on a national policy and you see the problem.

I find myself oddly touched by these silent and ethereal creatures moving through the cold, clear waters of the bay. They move with the transparency of ghosts, though they do not seem the visible forms of souls, but rather the opposite: disanimated bodies, bodies that have left their souls somewhere behind, or whose souls have not yet caught up with them. They move with a transparent lack of will, like the fragile, distilled beauty of the earth itself, moving deliberately yet purposelessly through a sharded and empty sea.

Flat Time

The Newfoundlander's concept of time, at least as I experienced it in Squid Tickle, is a peculiarly flattened one. I first became aware of this while listening to many of the local stories that had a historical basis: the fatal "Magic Arm Disaster"; the notorious "Cornwall Incident" on Flat Island, when a British warship was sent to quash the local moonshine industry; the "Great Fire" that destroyed Squid Tickle early in the last century; the settling of the town itself. Whenever I asked in what particular year an event had taken place, I would usually get a puzzled, even slightly irritated response: "Oh, I couldn't tell you that, b'y"; "Some time ago, my son"; or a curt, "Don't know." Once, when I asked Fred Oldford about this reluctance to assign dates to events, he replied, sphinx-like, "All bedtime stories begin with 'Once upon a time.'"

At first I attributed this inability or unwillingness to pin down dates to a general lack of written records in most rural Newfoundland communities, but the capacious and accurate memory that so many of the older inhabitants exhibited for details, relationships, locations, and events in the distant past suggested it was something else. It seemed that it was *because* the culture had been oral for so long, and for so long rooted in a landscape of known places, that linear or sequential historic time, demarcated by specific dates, was, if not irrelevant, then trivial. If everything happened in the same place, under essentially the same conditions, then why should it matter exactly *when* something occurred? The Magic Arm Disaster, for instance, in which five men from Flat Island drowned in a boating accident in a cove above Squid Tickle, had occurred within living memory. Some of the survivors were still alive, and many of the men I spoke to not only could describe the exact place where the boat had sunk and the specific conditions under which the tragedy had taken place, but would also tell it as if it had happened last year. Yet I could determine the actual year it occurred—1933—only when I came across a written history of Flat Island in one of the summer people's houses.

As in many long-settled oral cultures, events, and even utterances, in Squid Tickle are tied to people and places rather than time. For instance, I heard many times the story of Damnable Bay, the old name of the nearby outport, which has a very narrow entrance into its harbor. The name, I was told, originated "in the old days" when a pirate ship hid in that secluded harbor from a pursuing British man-o'-war, but the inadvertent ringing of the ship's bell gave away its position, causing the pirate captain to utter the eponymous oath, "Damn the bell!" Probably the most resonant place-name in the area is Bloody Bay Hills, referring to a six-hundred-foot-high ridge of worn mountains across the bay, which supposedly commemorates a massacre of the native Beothuks by early settlers (or vice versa, depending on the teller) at some unspecified time in the past. At the other end of historical import, but no less significant to the speaker, Fred Oldford once pointed out to me a rock in the bay where he had cut a pine tree ("Oh, some years ago, now") from which he fashioned the table that sits in his living room.

Often people themselves live on in the names of places. Cleves Oldford once showed me a small rock in the bay called Jimmy Deal Island, which he said his father had named after a local preacher because "he didn't like him and the island is so ugly." Another time, when I was out in the bay with Cyril Oldford, he gestured to a rocky point on Tumbler's Island known as the Devil's Lookout, and told this story:

"In the old days when there were plenty of Beothuks around, two men were out fishing and they left their lunch onshore. Now the Beothuks, they didn't just steal things, they left things in return, so when the two fellows got back, they found the grub gone, but somebody had shit in their lunch pots. And buddy says, 'That's the devil's lookout—we shouldn't have left it there!'"

What is common to all these stories, ancient or recent, is a lack of specification of time. The rich memory bank of the people of Squid

Tickle seems to exist in a single, fluid layer called the Past, out of which stories and events can be withdrawn at will, in great detail, and with a freshness that makes a conflagration that occurred almost ninety years ago seem as recent as last year's fishing season. Part of the immediacy of the local past stems, as it does in other oral cultures, from the fact that important or memorable events were almost always fashioned into poems, songs, or ballads. Most common were the numerous ballads recounting some disaster at sea or other loss of life. The effect of such ballads was not only to preserve these events in the communal memory, but also to mythologize them, the way docudramas and films "based on a true story" do in our electronic media culture, and thus to place them outside the mundane rubric of real, linear time.

Events commemorated in verse or song were not always historic or tragic. Most communities had a "singer" or versifier to celebrate more personal events, and these were often used as an opportunity to set down some local history and memories. Here, for instance, is Fred Oldford's rendering of a poem he wrote for the fiftieth anniversary of Char and Mary Oldford, with some interpretive gloss he threw in for my benefit:

> It's nice to reminisce a bit as along life's path we go,
> So I was thinking about Char, took his bride just fifty years ago.
> Those that weren't born are sure to ask, "What was the difference then?"
> But to us older folks we say, "Does you remember when?"
>
> There were no telephones nor motor cars in our neck of the woods;
> You either went by motorboat or got there the best way you could.
> In wintertime we used our dogs, we traveled here and there.
> But when we went a courtin', 'twas usually on shank's mare.
> ("That's by foot, you know.")
>
> What would I give to walk the Old Line Road to all the favorite spots,
> The water cross the old footbridge, or sit down on Sweet Rocks.
> ("There was a rock we called Sweet Rock, probably ten people could sit down on it.")
> But life goes on its merry way, we accept whatever comes,

B'y, there are so many times when I could taste those chocolate plums.
("You probably calls them choke cherries.")

We all walked that narrow road in sleet and mud and snow,
But Charlie made more trips than us just fifty years ago.
("He married a girl from Sandy Cove, see, and he used to walk
over on Sundays to see her, in his God stompers.")*

Unlike true indigenous cultures, however, Newfoundland seems to
have little or no genuine mythology; that is, there is a lack of creation
myths or legends about truly fabulous or heroic beings, far fewer, in
fact, than are to be found in American folklore. The closest thing to a
creation myth I ever heard was from Jim Moss, who one day pointed
out to me a series of small islands stretching out in the bay between
Squid Tickle and Flat Island: "You know, when the Man Upstairs was
making Newfoundland, his ladle leaked there, dribbled those islands,
you see"—but even then he had a smile on his face and a tongue-in-
cheek tone in his voice when he told it. And despite its heroic and often
tragic history with the sea, Newfoundland has produced no comparable
Paul Bunyan or John Henry figures. In fact, feats of individual accom-
plishment are rare in Newfoundland folklore, which tends to concen-
trate on communal events.

On the other hand, the storytelling *manner* is old and often reminiscent
of ancient forms. One day at Fred's house he turned to me without preface
and said, "I've got a riddle for you. Goes like this: 'I washed in a water
never rained nor flowed, dried my face in a napkin never spun nor sewed.'"
It gave me satisfaction to guess the answer (dew and grass), but I was more
impressed by the very old Anglo-Saxon form in which the riddle had survived here. Riddles themselves, in fact, are an ancient form of verbal com-
petition, and I answered him with one or two I remembered from readings
in early English literature—"I Gave My Love a Cherry without a Stone"
and "I Have a Gentle Cock"—which he seemed to appreciate.

Often, when telling stories, the teller will proceed partway in the
narrative, then seem to stop and start again, or go partway back, giving

---

*"God stompers" were shoes worn on Sundays to church.

the tale a slightly different turn, and proceed in this manner throughout the story. At first, it gave a fractured, overlapping effect to my ears,
and I thought that the teller's memory was failing. Then, one night,
while reading in *Mimesis*, Eric Auerbach's magisterial survey of modes
of representation and narrative in Western literature, I came upon a description of Merovingian and *chanson de geste* histories and epics of the
early Middle Ages, which have a similarly loose and overlapping narrative structure. Auerbach describes it as "not evenly progressive, but
spastic, now gaining, now losing ground, like generation or birth."
Such a style, still alive in obscure places like Squid Tickle, may have
represented, or mimicked, more "realistically," the raw processes of
memory and interior narrative centuries before James Joyce and Virginia Woolf.

   The nature of the seasons, and of the sky itself, works to usurp the
sense of an ordered and sequential, if cyclical, progress here. The Newfoundland growing season in particular is so short and compressed that,
to one used to more expansive summers, normal subdivisions of time
seem hopelessly confused. Strawberries, for instance, can sometimes
still be harvested in early September, along with the first partridgeber-
ries, and apple trees on some of the outer islands bloom in late July, just
as the first blueberries are ripening. In contrast, the sky here is so wide
that the day itself seems broader, holding multiple times in a single moment. At dusk the eye, looking westward, still holds onto the dying day,
its draining light and color, when eastward, the soft cowl of night has
already settled on the land and its scattered inhabitants.

   In Squid Tickle, even the local geography seems to foster a sense of
flattened, or nonlinear, time. The "tickle" of Squid Tickle, is a narrow
tidal channel that separates the mainland part of the community from
Squid Island. It was formerly a communal gathering place when the squid
came in and were harvested there in August. It is still a central experience
for the remaining residents, since most of them have to cross the bridge
over the tickle at least twice each day to pick up their mail from Christine
Moss at the small shed next to her house that serves as the post office. As
it is a tidal channel, one might expect the flow through the tickle to follow the normal diurnal tidal patterns, that is, to change direction roughly
four times a day at regular intervals. But because of a complex fractaliza-

tion of the currents as they approach the tickle, the water running under the bridge actually changes direction at irregular intervals, sometimes as frequently as every twenty minutes, and in no predictable pattern. Thus even the tides beg the question "When?"

The educational history of the island, I think, has also contributed to the preservation of a fluid, mythic view of the Newfoundland past. Before Confederation with Canada, and for some years after, the history books used in most outports, and in St. John's as well, were usually histories of England, or mainland Canada, or even the United States. As one older resident explained, "That was all the books we could get." Schoolchildren thus grew up with a more-or-less ordered idea of the sequence of British monarchs or the course of the American Revolution, while their own history survived in a dreamtime of stories, verses, ballads, jokes, and a dialect that shared more with nineteenth-century Devon than with twentieth-century Toronto.

Among many older Newfoundlanders there is still a widespread skepticism about, and even resistance to, the idea of a deep and ordered history developed by modern archaeology and geology. For instance, at the top of the Bloody Bay Hills there is a major archaeological site known as the Quarries. The site is an ancient rhyolite mine, a mineral used for making arrowheads, knives, and other implements. Laurie McLean, the archaeologist in charge of the local Heritage Foundation, believes it was worked by three different indigenous cultures over a period of six thousand years. This chipping away over several millennia has left an enormous cut in the side of the ridge and over a half acre of rock flakes lying about. The foundation is currently building a wharf at the base of the quarry in order to be able to take tourists to the site by boat.

One evening I was chatting with Bert Burden and I mentioned that I had been out to the Quarries.

"That's all nonsense, you know," said Bert.

"I beg your pardon?"

"Building the wharf and all that over there." He gestured contemptuously out to the hills across the bay. "A damn waste of money, that is. It cost thirty thousand for that museum and everything so far and it ain't worth a pot to piss in. It was a *thunderbolt* blew that mountain apart. I used to go up there once or twice a week with Father to cut wood. I remember when that was solid rock all the way across. Y's, b'y, I were about ten year old when we had a big storm in the bay, and the next time we went out, it were all blown apart. I talked to Brock Bradley about it the other day, but he don't remember it no more."

Oh, well, I thought, there's nothing for it but to break the bad news to Laurie and tell him to pack up and go back to St. John's. Or, conversely, I could imagine Bert, standing at the end of his wharf, as boatloads of tourists went by to visit the Quarries, raising his fist and shouting, "You durn fools, go on home—it's all nonsense!"

Others are not so autocratically dismissive of archaeological and geological theory as Bert, but remain skeptical, or at least ambivalent. Cleves, for instance, was cagily noncommittal when I referred to a large boulder in the middle of his field as a glacial erratic.

"I don't know about that, b'y. Now, Father, he said that stone was brought here by a big piece of ice—but he didn't say how or when." In this way he does not necessarily reject science's view of the past, but he also stands by his father's stories of indeterminate, or flat, time.

Such views of the past are changing, of course. As a younger generation, even in the more remote outports, is being exposed to the more standard views of geology, prehistory, and history, Newfoundlanders' idea of themselves and their island is expanding and ordering itself into the accepted corridors of historical time. And with this change will come—is coming—a greater self-consciousness of their history, both how it stands in relation to that of the rest of the world, and also how their generation and its history differ from those of their fathers and of their fathers' fathers. For history in Newfoundland is, as in the rest of the world, becoming more and more linear, and thus more alienated from the past, even as it becomes more aware of its potential value as a "commodity."

But it seems to me there is something lost in exchange for this greater "accuracy" and increasingly linear concept of time. The old notion of flat time is rooted in a felt connection with place, the sense that one can draw on the features, stories, and figures of an amorphous, but still living, past, in which all narratives are equally available and relevant. For the older people of Squid Tickle, at least, the past is Everywhere, more so here than in many older and more densely settled areas of the continent. It has not yet been routed by the omnipresent, has not yet undergone a sea change into history, into that which we are done with and which is done with us.

Such a rooted intimacy with the past and with a generous, undemarcated sense of time still manifests itself in the casual, diurnal rhythms of life in Squid Tickle. I have noticed, for instance, that when I am visiting someone and get up to go, no matter whether I have been there five minutes or two hours, I am sure to be met with what seems a universal mantra of all visiting here: "Plenty o' time, b'y, plenty o' time."

Of course there is, literally, plenty of time for most of Squid Tickle's residents, nearly all of whom are either retired or unemployed for most of the year. But the phrase, it seems to me, predates current conditions, goes back to a time when everyone worked constantly. One likes to think its persistence is a sign that human intercourse—chewing the fat, sharing stories, discussing prospects, neighbors, and fish—has always had a certain precedence for these people—and that, like the dream of every Orthodox Jewish man to be in a position to spend all his time studying the Torah and *discussing* it with others in the temple, the dream of Newfoundlanders is to have time to talk and visit to their heart's content, a dream that this aging generation seems, to its own surprise, to have found itself living.

It is a contagious dream. One afternoon, I was walking back from visiting with a summer resident, an octogenarian from St. John's who was the scion of one of the old Water Street merchant families. I was coming around the curve at the high part of the tickle road, watching the banks of fair-weather clouds ranked in the west with the sun slipping down between them, and I realized that my days here, though not yet very long or numerous, had already begun to meld and blend together into Squid Tickle Time. I had already begun to lose track of dates or days of the week or even how long I had been here, a few days or a few years. I seemed to be experiencing, for the first time, just how time compresses here, how events and people and generations meld seamlessly together with the rest, and how, though there is no apparent timeline to hang them on, they can be picked out of the plastic time stream with remarkable clarity and detail, like a trout plucked out of the depths of a clear, flowing stream. Like the tickle itself, time here is not linear but diastolic, pulled by centripetal and centrifugal currents. Like the year, all things here go out from and return to this one place.

The patterns are subtle, but deep, and at times one can, almost without knowing it, slip out of the present into something older, wider, and unbounded. Last night, after supper at the Mosses, we all sat in their living room: Jim and Jesse; Jim's daughter, Julia, and her husband, Jerry; Jack Casey from St. Brendan's; Jack's girlfriend, Ruth, and her mother, Bea, from down at the ferry wharf; and myself. The talk flowed softly as the men sipped rum and ginger ale and the women smoked and knitted. As the outside light began to go, the figures inside became dim outlines, so that, no longer able to see who was talking, I tried to pick out individual voices; but instead it seemed that what I heard was a confused overlapping of voices, especially among the women—counterpoints, descants, obbligatos of sound. It was as if they were disappearing into their own past when, on summer evenings, there was no reason to turn on the lamps and burn oil—there was nothing to read and no one to read it. They stayed in touch through the sound of their own familiar voices, telling stories, singing songs, commenting on the world and its familiar doings. The women probably knitted in the dark, as the voices wove together the familiar repetitions of kinship, boats, health, generations, and weather. As a child, forced to listen to my parents and their friends converse in this desultory fashion, I had been bored to tears, feeling that I was being involuntarily withheld from my own life. Now, I found myself strangely content to sit there, bathed in the susurrus of disembodied voices that seemed to move like fish between past and present. Sometime after ten o'clock, when it had grown completely dark both inside and out, someone switched on a lamp, and, like that, we were all back in the defined present, familiar to one another again. Then Jack Casey took out his button accordion and began to play some old tunes, beating time in his cotton socks.

The Future

Howard Moss swings by after sunset to tell me that the crab strike has been settled and that they put their pots out today, so that I can go out with them tomorrow if I like. He will call me in the morning.

A couple of weeks ago I asked Howard if there was any chance I might go out snow-crabbing with him, and he said, with derisive curtness, "I doubt it—I doubt it, my son." He explained that the DFO requires the captain of any boat to get a permit for anyone he takes out with him, a permit specific to that boat. Technically, if Howard's eighty-year-old father helps him load lobster pots from his skiff at the wharf, he could be fined. In fact, some older men were cited for just that this spring in Salvage, and were told that next time they would receive $150 fines. Howard shook his head and said, "Foolishness"—but I could see it was much worse than that. He regards it as the deliberate, if ignorant, tearing apart of the very fabric of cooperation, community, and family that has been the core of the bay-outport culture for hundreds of years. The government, having screwed up royally, is now in fear of itself, bludgeoning these small fishing villages with blunt, blind regulation. Nonetheless, Howard said he would see what they could do.

It is still pitch black outside when the phone rings at 4:45 A.M. I tell Howard I will meet him at the tickle bridge in half an hour. I layer myself in long underwear and a sweater, grab a cup of tea and a banana, and set off. The morning is calm and mild, the sky completely dark and clear as I get in Howard's pickup and we set off for Salvage. Fast-step country music plays on the radio, "I Know This Town" and "You Can Call on Me."

By the time we're on the highway out of Eastport there is faint light in the east, outlining the humped hills and headlands of the islands and the ridges of the inner bay. On the outskirts of Salvage we stop to pick up the crew. The skipper, Calvin Brown, is a round-faced boyish-looking man of forty-nine. His crew consists of his younger brother, Bob; Bill Brown (no relation), also from Salvage, with a grizzled beard, a wife, and a five-year-old son; and Howard. They have been crabbing together since 1989 on the standard shares system,* and seem to have a loose confederation at other times. During the lobster season, for instance, the four of them go out in three different skiffs, but "all work together," sharing the catch. Their friendly, joking demeanor puts me immediately at ease, making me feel not at all like the intrusion into their community and routine that I am.

Since the cod moratorium took effect in 1992, snow crabs have become the mainstay for most Newfoundland fishermen. The area crabbers have been on strike the past two weeks trying to get the Salvage plant to honor their previous contract to buy crabs at $2.50 a pound. The plant in turn offered $1.60. They tried negotiating with the plant at Valleyfield, but in the end settled for $1.75 a pound, a fifteen-cent gain.

We park on the west side of the harbor near Cal's wharf and in the dark make our way along a path beside a house down to the stage. The shed is a large new building, painted red in the old fashion, with a two-foot gap between the shed door and the wharf where harbor ice moved the wharf out last winter. The shed is a typical mixture of old and new materials: pressboard on the inside walls with freshly debarked spruce-trunk joists and rough plank floors.

Six or seven other boats are at their own wharves with their cabin lights on. In the darkness and silence they look like a scattered community of shore houses. One by one, they emit the sound of an engine and begin to move out toward the harbor entrance, calling to mind the dwellings of abandoned outports that were floated on barges to other communities such as Salvage a generation ago.

---

*A time-honored system in which the owner of the boat (usually the captain) would receive half the profits of a voyage and the other half would be divided among the crew—hence the name "sharemen" for such a crew.

Salvage is one of the earliest, if not the oldest, settlements in Bonavista Bay. At the entrance to the town there is one of those "portrait-of-the-view" signs, an illustration of the town one is about to see, and the legend "Welcome to Salvage—One of the Oldest Continuously Settled Communities in Bonavista Bay." True enough, but not as old as the sign might imply. Official records do show as many as five to seven families living in Salvage in 1675, but these are described as "migratory fishing families," which could merely mean Englishmen from those families who were here in the summers, rather than permanent families with women and children. The first recorded marriages and baptisms in Salvage do not appear until the 1820s, which may mean that there were true families here by about 1800.

Nonetheless, Salvage possesses a sweet little harbor, remarkably protected on all sides by high, rocky hills, with good, deep mooring inside. The harbor entrance, however, is winding and narrow, with only a ten-to twelve-foot draft, and can be tricky to get in or out of in a sea. Bill tells me that when the old coastal freighter came in, it had to do a full 360-degree loop to follow the channel into the harbor. In addition to enjoying one of the most beautiful natural settings of any outport in the province, Salvage has also retained, more by chance than design, an increasingly rare architectural purity of old houses and buildings.

The five of us climb aboard Cal Brown's boat, *The Future,* a thirty-five-foot, fourteen-year-old wooden long-liner, and motor out of the harbor a little after six, as the sun rises in blue and gold splendor across the bow over a gently rocking horizon of deep, light-filled swells. On the way out I stay with Cal in his new cabin, which is furnished with quilted maroon Naugahyde fabric on the console. He proudly shows me his electronic navigation equipment and rings off the names of the islands as we pass them: Shag, Ship, Puffin, Little Denier. The crew is already busy baiting long metal skewers called "skiffers" —a half mackerel and six whole squid to each skewer, like some marine sushi shishkabob. I feel chilled, even inside the cabin with oilskins over my other clothes, but I know the sun will soon warm us as it climbs.

Cal tells me that for the fall season they have per boat quotas of ten thousand pounds "inside" (Bonavista Bay) and eight thousand pounds "outside." We are staying inside today, and Cal thinks we will probably get the bulk of our limit on this trip. Most of the crab is processed and sent to Japan and to the States. At this point it's not clear whether there would be a bigger market for crabs if the government allowed the taking of more. Like the cod of only a few years ago, the previously unexploited crab stocks seem inexhaustible, but everyone is more wary now. Cal says they will likely spend a total of four to five days crabbing this fall, grossing some $31,500. He uses about twenty gallons of fuel on the bay run, at about $1.50 a gallon.

As we head out I become aware of a strong, stomach-churning smell rising from the galley well. Bob, the ship's cook, is making Jigg's dinner—a stew of salt beef, potatoes, carrots, turnips, parsnips, cabbage, and pease pudding. It will simmer the entire trip, effectively barring me from going down below.

They put out the crab pots the day before, in gale-force northwest winds. "No need to wash down the decks yesterday," says Bob. They have three "fleets" of fifty pots each in two hundred fathoms. Each pot is in the shape of a truncated metal-mesh cone about four feet across at the bottom, with a white plastic collar at the top to which the bait is attached (double-baited on the first tow) and down which the crabs slide into the pot. The pots are put out in the manner of a fish trawl, attached to a main line about a mile long with floats at each end. Each pot is on twelve to fifteen feet of line attached to its top, which lets it sink down bottom-first. The pots are generally laid out in the bay in a northeast-southwest direction, following the lines of the underwater ridges on the bottom and thus minimizing the likelihood of fouling on the submerged "cliffs."

We motor out to the furthest fleet of pots, as it was the first one set the day before. Cal runs the winch, hauling each pot up out of the water on its line; then Bill swings it on a crane over the hold deck. The remaining bait, if any, is flung overboard off the skewers to a gradually accumulating cloud of gulls behind us. Then Bob releases the net knot on the bottom of the pot, spilling the catch out onto the deck on the starboard side of the hold well where Howard will sort them.

The snow crab, *Chionectes opilio*, is a species of spider crab found in deep, cold waters from Greenland to the Gulf of Maine. In body outline the snow crab, also called the queen crab, is a smaller version of the Alaskan king crab, with a carapace five or six inches across, and legs up to a foot long. As with Alaskan king crabs, the meat is in the legs. The shells are light brown on the dorsal side, darker when the shell is harder, and pinkish on recently molted crabs. As they spill out on the deck they seem like throngs of shanghaied violin sections, hauled up from some underwater orchestra and dumped out in a clacking confusion of intertangled bows, bridges, keys, and necks. Though fairly lively when they first pour out, they lack the mobility, the aggressive strength, and the fierce resistance of the blue crabs I catch in the tidal creeks back home.

The crew sorts them by size first, using a four-inch plastic spacer with one end put in the eye socket and the other at the rear tip of the shell. Keepers are tossed into the hold, which is filled with shaved ice, while softshells are discarded with the undersized crabs, since they haven't yet filled with meat. Among the snow crabs are a few toad crabs, smaller crabs with darker, purplish, gnarly shells. One has a bright yellow fig sponge attached to the top of its shell that looks like some monstrous brain tumor. There is also a scattering of small, stubby, yellowish starfish that look exactly like the stars in a children's book. All the snow crabs are males, for the females are much smaller and go out through the net mesh, a serendipitous design that, according to Cal, "makes it hard to destroy this fishery."

The whole operation seems well designed for a four-man crew: Cal hauls the pots, Bill swings them over onto the deck, Bill and Bob fling the bait and toss the skewers into a pan, Bob pulls the net knot, Bob and Howard shake the net empty, Bob stacks the pots in the stern in two piles of twenty-five each, and Howard and Bob sort the crabs as Cal and Bill haul in a new pot. These men have been fishing together for years and work smoothly, with the same instinctive awareness of each other's position and movements as one sees on a well-matched basketball team.

After the first fleet is hauled and sorted, the pots are rebaited and reset. As we steam to the next fleet, Bob and Bill go below for dinner, but Howard stays on deck to keep me company, pulling a liter of Coke and a thick baloney sandwich out of a plastic pail.

When we start hauling the second fleet, the winch begins to stall and struggle. "Fuck it," says Cal, and the unusual expletive from this mild-mannered man lets me know it is something serious. It turns out that we have fouled on another line that was laid across ours ("There's always some nonconformist," quips Bill.) The winch motor strains and strains, the gears clacking louder and more slowly, as the green polypropylene line twangs and shivers off minuscule droplets of seawater in the morning sun, until finally the crossed line is lifted on ours near the port rail. Bill severs it in an instant with heavy wire cutters, and the two ends relax and sink swiftly beneath the waves. There was nothing else to do, he says, and besides, whoever laid it will be able to pick up both ends from the attached floats.

As the second haul of pots begins to spill onto the deck, Bob dons a yellow plastic hard hat and climbs down into the hold, where he begins stacking the crabs with their claws facing inward, against the curving wooden sides of the hold. He works as fast as he can, with crabs literally raining down on him like corn into a grain elevator. But this is unshucked, unshelled corn, brown living ears of corn, clicking articulated corn, the long triple-bent legs hanging like husk blades from the crabs' bodies. It reminds me of watching Howard stacking stove wood under his house. The crabs, too, are a kind of marine wood that will later burn in our bodies, turning, in John Updike's phrase, "against their furious wills into us."

During the first haul I simply watched, but now the crabs are coming in so thick that Howard can't keep up sorting them, so he asks me to help. My shellfishing experience at home helps me to get the knack of sizing the crabs rather quickly, and after a few minutes I can sort the crabs mostly by sight, measuring only the close ones.

As we continue to toss crabs down into the hold, Bob works with ever greater urgency, as crabs and old crab jokes are rained down upon him like frogs upon Pharaoh: "I got my first crabs aboard a boat!" "After all day in the hold, I scratched all night!" He layers them tier upon tier onto the crushed ice up against the slanting sides of the hull, and as they mount higher and higher around him, there rises from the darkness of the hold an eery, staticky sound of thousands upon thousands of pincers and arms, clicking and waving—almost as if they are applauding his performance in stacking them. One could say it was a miniature Newfoundland version of La Scala, packed to the rafters with a crabby, cool, somewhat subdued, but still appreciative audience, a full house of thousands of carapaced opera lovers, stacked up to the seventeenth balcony and higher. Bob himself appears as some Brobdingnagian Rigoletto or Otello, beset on all sides by those who plot against him. Or perhaps, given his somewhat Elizabethan accent, he is more like a giant mechanic in a Globe production of one of Shakespeare's comedies, the pigmy audience rude and impatient, some of them passed out on their backs, or fallen into the pit, some openly embracing or at least holding hands, some even attempting to grab Bob as he performs in that dark, icy-breathed "little O."

By the time the third and final fleet is hauled, Bob has been forced up out of the hold, as the level of crabs continues to climb with each pot, rising steadily, incrementally, like a brown, articulated tide, until it boils over the rim of the well and spills into a half dozen or so large, gray plastic fish pans. Finally, the last pot is pulled, sorted, and stacked, and we begin to head for home a little after 1 P.M., seven hours after leaving the harbor.

By midday the high clouds have cleared and it is a mild, warm, autumn day on the ocean. The boat rocks in gentle swells, a few gannets dive a way off, scattered sea pigeons (guillemots) and sea parrots (puffins) with their brightly painted faces flutter over the water's surface, several dolphins chase a school of baitfish, and dozens of tickle-aces (kittiwakes) sit calmly on the water behind us outside the circles of opportunistic gulls. The scene is suddenly intensely bucolic, lending substance to the phrase "farming the sea," though I know a day like this is rare in these men's lives. But on such days, heading out before first light in skiff or schooner or long-liner for the inshore fishing grounds or the offshore banks, spending the long morning hours hauling in cod the size of small children, reaping God's plenty, it must have seemed more than enough and this place a glory on earth. All one would need is a few such days in one's seed time to sink a place and a pattern for living into one's bones, into the heart, and to hold all the outnumbering gray, hungry, bone-chilling, and dog-weary days as of no account—or so it seems on a day like this.

Gradually we work our way back toward the great, beetling brow of Cow's Head guarding the entrance to Salvage harbor, its ancient sedimentary seams cracked and cloven into great blocks of rock silhouetted against the southwestern sky. Now it is one of those brilliant September afternoons of light, sky, and shadow, with the houses and rocky foreshores lit up in intense sunshine and color, sharply etched and set off by dark backdrops.

When we pull into the harbor, we find we are the first boat at the wharf. Instantly a half dozen men come down to greet us, though only the forklift driver and another man loading the pallets are authorized to work. The rest stand about at the edge of the dock or sit on the pilings offering advice or general commentary on the proceedings as a kind of articulate displacement of their frustrations at not being able to exercise their intuitive, cultural impulse to join in and help.

We begin unloading the catch, at first all four of us pulling crabs out of the hold into fish pans, then heaving the pans up onto the wharf. When we can no longer reach them easily from the deck, Howard and Bill climb down into the hold, filling pans and handing them up to Bob and me for us to heave ashore.

It occurs to me that, in spite of all the sophisticated electronic navigational equipment aboard and the pneumatic winches and mechanized cranes for hauling in the pots, the work itself remains strikingly manual in nature. Each crab is handled individually at least twice, and usually three times—once when it is sorted and thrown down into the hold, once when it is stacked in the hold, and again when it is placed in a fish pan to be hauled out onto the wharf. The pots are baited by hand, emptied by hand, and stacked on deck by hand. The crab pans are manually lifted out of the hold, heaved onto the wharf, and placed on the pallets for the forklift by seven different pairs of hands.

After lifting the first few dozen pans of crab, I say to Howard, "There must be a better way of doing this."

"There is," he replies, "for a bigger boat—a sixty-five-footer." On larger boats, he explains, you have room to take along enough pans to stack the crabs in in the first place, and even to put nets in the hold to haul them out with, as they do with cod.

Soon a second boat pulls alongside the wharf, and the crew, in their olive green oilskin pants, saunter over to chat and joke until they, too, are ready to unload. Cal's mother and daughter appear as well, the latter a young woman in her early twenties, slightly hefty, with a full bosom, wearing a red sweatshirt and tight black leotards that plainly outline her mons veneris. She banters with the men in that easy, straightforward, slightly bawdy manner so many outport women have. Though she is just this side of pretty, she gives off waves of healthy sexuality, so that I find it hard to keep my eyes off her. At one point a tourist couple comes down to the wharf and snaps photos of us. Howard gives his head a shake and says that this past summer there were whole busloads of them getting off with cameras and videos. I feel absurdly pleased to have been mistaken for—and likely to be shown to their friends as—an example of a "real Newfie fisherman."

After about a third of the catch has been unloaded, Howard asks to be spelled, so Bob and I go down into the hold, grateful for its icy, shaded coolness, and continue loading and handing up pans of crabs. By now the ones that were stacked first, deep in the sides of the hold, are mostly lifeless, and the melted ice at the bottom is swimming with detached legs and pincers. By 4:15 we have unloaded 148 pans of crabs, nearly ten forklifts full, totaling 8,096 pounds of crabs, giving Cal a gross profit of $14,168 Canadian. Eleven hours, dock to dock. "Not bad, b'y," says Bill.

When I finally climb up out of the empty hold there are two sets of boats, three deep, tied up beside us, waiting to unload. A kind of party atmosphere prevails, with beer drinking, kids running aboard the boats, women talking with their men, the older fishermen telling stories . . . and I think, *This is how it was here, this is how it has been, with only minor changes, for centuries: men coming in with the catch, families coming down to greet them from nearby harbors. Here it was the boys imbibed the lore and irresistible longing for the sea, had planted in their minds and hearts what it means to be a man, an idea that would take root and prove invulnerable to the lures of education or any land work—except of course when fish or markets failed and they were forced to leave home to find work, only to return at the first sign that they might make a living fishing again.*

And how can it be otherwise, seeing these ships come in from over the horizon, their holds full, the old men and the women of the tribe come down to welcome the hunters, the stories and the drinking and the electric flow of sexuality and good spirits? Here is the Center of Things still, proving that if you are only resourceful and brave enough and the government will allow it, the sea—as all outward signs attest this day—remains inexhaustible.

Then the local DFO inspector appears, a comfortably plump, middle-aged woman with a meringue pile of hair who climbs aboard the boat with her notebook. It is clear that she is a local, and that none of the fishermen's deep resentment of government bureaucracy and regulation attaches to her. She goes through a pantomime of inspecting the empty hold for untallied crabs and smuggled contraband—liquor or drugs—to much good-natured kidding from the men: "Don't slip on the slime down there, my dear." "They already got the dope off, my love."

When she finishes, we slip the mooring hawsers and head back across the harbor to Cal's wharf as the next boat takes our place. The men ask me to stay and have Jigg's dinner on board with them, but I decline and accept a bag of crabs instead. Cal says, "Well, b'y, come back and take another trip with us next year." I shake hands all around and say good-bye to the crew of *The Future*.

ACKNOWLEDGMENTS

This book has had a long history, and without the generous assistance, encouragement, suggestions, and participation of many individuals, it would have been even longer. In its genealogy of editors, I owe thanks to Deanne Urmy, Chris Carduff, and Chris Greenberg. My agent, Ike Williams, and his staff found it a good home at Counterpoint. Laura Geiges deciphered many of my notes and typed them into readable form. My copy editor, Margaret Ritchie, brushed my prose with a fine editorial comb, and my Wellfleet neighbor, Gloria Nardin Watts, gave the manuscript a final proofreading. David Godine first suggested the use of Newfoundland's wonderful stamps as section heads, and Brian Hennessey graciously made available his philatelic scans for this purpose.

Earlier versions of several chapters appeared in the following publications: *The American Scholar, The Georgia Review, River Styx, Ecotone, Wabash Magazine, Sail Magazine,* and *The Boston Globe.* For much information in these chapters and for their patience in correcting many of the errors that might have otherwise made it into print, I am greatly indebted to Penny Hansen, Marlene Creates, Ken Roberts, Peter Gard, and Shirley Oldford. Debbie Andrews, staff librarian at the Centre for Newfoundland Studies in St. John's, also provided valuable assistance.

Several friends generously provided their houses as writing retreats. They include Mark and Fraser Carpenter, David and Ann Brown, Pat de Gogorza, and Alice Gorman.

Canada also treats its visiting writers well, and I am indebted to the Canadian Tourism Commission, as well as to many tourism officials in Newfoundland and Labrador, Nova Scotia, and New Brunswick, and to

Marine Atlantic, for their generous assistance in my travels in Atlantic Canada.

To all of the people of Newfoundland and Labrador who opened up their houses and hospitality to me, I sincerely hope this book reflects something of the deep gratitude I feel.

Finally, a special thanks to Kathy Shorr my chum and mechaieh, plucky sidekick, first and last reader, invisible but everywhere present.